THE CHILDRENS HOMES V

My Very Best Wishes

Jill Crumley

This book is dedicated to my husband ROY for his patience and understanding and to my late father whose memory I cherish.

THE CHILDRENS HOMES VILLAGE

One Hundred Years of Memories of
The Shenley Fields Cottage Homes.

by Jill Plumley

BREWIN BOOKS

First published
by Brewin Books, Studley, Warwickshire, B80 7LG
in November 1992

ISBN 1 85858 003 X

British Library Cataloguing in Publication Data.
A Catalogue record for this book is available from the British Library

Typeset in Plantin by Avon Dataset, Bidford on Avon, Warwickshire, B50 4JH
and made and printed by Alden Press, Osney Meade, Oxford OX2 0EF

Contents

PREFACE

This is a book of memories about life "In Care" at SHENLEY FIELDS COTTAGE HOMES. The homes were built in 1887 and the last children left the 'Drive' as it was called then in 1987.

Many people including myself and family were very sad to see those lovely old houses being pulled down. Many memories were stirred, some happy and some sad. I felt a great sadness that they were all disappearing and nothing had been written down about the caring work that had been done over the century.

I wrote to the local papers about this and my letter was printed. Many people wrote to me about their own personal memories and experiences. I decided to put them together and write this book. Some people have very long clear memories and can write long accounts of their many years in Shenley Homes. Others only spent a brief period there but long enough to make an impression on their young lives. I have printed many of the letters. Not all may be entirely accurate but they are their personal memories as they remember Shenley and who am I to take or change that memory for them.

This has given me a great deal of pleasure as many friends and families have been re-united through the book. I have made over 200 friends who like me have shared a little bit of history that was once

SHENLEY FIELDS COTTAGE HOMES.

FOREWORD

When I heard the last children were to be moved out of Shenley Fields Childrens Homes I was horrified. I had worked and lived there for many years and had grown both very fond and possessive about the lovely old buildings.

Several people had said over the years "We could write a book about this place and all the tears and laughter we've shared". But it never did get written. So I decided to collect as many stories as possible from my friends and colleagues of some of the good and not so good times of Shenley Homes.

An article in our local paper about what I was doing brought a tremendous response from people who had lived at the homes from as long ago as 1907. They all wanted to share their memories with me. With their permission I have put their stories together to form this book.

I must admit I was very surprised to find the homes were opened in 1887, so this is 100 years of memories.

I would not have been able to take this on board if it had not been for the endless support of my very long suffering family. My daughter Helen has spent many hours helping with organising reunions and delivering letters, making phone calls, listening to me read out loud some of the hundreds of letters that have had me laughing and crying and generally being there to do a lot of shopping and running about for me. Luckily Helen was brought up from the age of 3 to 14 in the Shenley Fields Homes while we were residential houseparents, and she understood and shared my feelings about the homes. My son Steven was also brought up 'in care' at Shenley but he took a different view of life in the homes. He looked on his life there as something he tolerated so he could be with his parents. He enjoyed getting away from the drive. He feels I have 'lost my marbles' wanting to remember living there. As far as he is concerned the past is past so let it rest. My husband Roy has a very different attitude however. He shared my life as a houseparent in Elmdene and loved almost every minute of being there. Like me he was devastated when we had to move out of the home we had shared with so many boys for over 11 years. He has put up with make-do meals when I have got so engrossed in writing and not noticed the time. He has put up with the constant chatter about the latest letter I have received and missed his favourite programmes on the television while I have spent hours talking to people who have phoned me up. Like my son he thinks I am completely mad but he can understand why I have felt this need to write down all the memories before they are lost for ever in time. I have had enormous support from my colleagues at Northfield Social Services. They have spurred me on when I felt like giving it all up and even arranged my work schedule to accommodate my writing. This book would not have been written at all if so many people had not bothered to write down their memories of life in a childrens home. For some it has been very painful remembering. For others it has helped them put together their childhood memories and given them something they could talk to their families about. I am happy to say that many friends and even families have reunited through this book. To me that makes all the hard work of the last four years worth while. I must add however that everything written in this book is not necessarily correct. They are written how people have remembered them and over the years memories play tricks on us. So please be tolerant of any little mistakes, after all who is to say who is right and who is wrong. At the end of the day it's 'Our Memories of Shenley Fields Childrens Homes'.

A Brief History of Shenley Fields

Cottage Homes

Shenley Cottage Homes were opened on 31st August 1887, on which day the First Annual Report tells us "eighty children were removed from the workhouse, and were placed in the cottages under the foster fathers and mothers who had been for some time preparing for the reception of the children".

At the time the building of cottage homes at Shenley and Erdington was a major step forward in child care practice. After the passing of the Poor Law Amendment Act 1834 all those in care for one reason or another were placed in the workhouse. The object of the workhouse system was clear, to be a terror to the poor. All classes of people, be they orphans, mentally disordered, geriatric or homeless vagrants, were placed in the same aweful environment purposely created to be worse than the living conditions of the poorest labourer. Obviously such a system couldn't work. There were reports of widespread riots against it throughout England.

Even those operating the system could see how detrimental it was in the lives of the people who had no other possible alternative. The cottage homes were one such alternative and the First Annual Report states that they were erected for "the purpose of furthering the desire to separate the children whose unfortunate circumstances placed them in care, from contact with adult paupers in the workhouse".

Many Boards of Guardians built separate homes for children in their care, and in particular, the Kings Norton Board formulated plans to move their children from the workhouse in Selly Oak. They began a search for a suitable site where the children might have substantial benefits of pure country air, bright cheerful and elevating surroundings and be free from the interference of undesirable relatives and friends. This they found in the wooded glades near Weoley Castle. They built eight houses on this site and these were opened in 1887. Four more houses were added between 1887 and 1910 and a further house in 1936.

In 1932 the Poor Law system was broken up and the function of the Boards of Guardians transferred to County Councils and the County Borough Councils. The Childrens Act of 1948 (which was passed as result of the report of the Royal Commission headed by Dame Myra Curtiss) redefined the responsibility of local authorities so far as children were concerned and required them to approach their responsibilities in an entirely new way. It further required each local authority to set up a special committee, the Childrens Committee, to carry out this new work and Shenley Fields Homes passed to the control of the City's new Childrens Committee.

From the time that the homes were built until 1932 great emphasis was placed on segregating the children from the community as a whole. A special school was built for them on the premises. Their freedom was rigidly restricted and on leaving school they were trained in a trade and were then found work, preferably residential work, by the superintendent. In 1932 this policy altered and particularly since 1948, it has been recognised that the children's best interests are served by intergrating them into the community. For this reason all but nursery age children attended school outside the grounds. As many different schools as possible were used. Shenley School passed under the complete control of the Education Committee in 1952 and was then used as an ordinary nursery school. It had about 60 places and on average about 55 children from the local housing estate used it.

The children were encouraged to mix as freely as possible with outside society and no efforts were spared to see that they joined youth clubs and similar organisations. There was an Aunt and Uncle scheme in existence which linked individual children with private families and another scheme which encouraged organisations to take an interest in a home as a whole. These organisations included The Birmingham Junior Chamber of Commerce, a Round Table, clubs attached to works (some set up solely for this purpose) and local public houses. They sent birthday and Christmas cards and presents to the youngsters in their houses, took them to Christmas parties and pantomimes and on day trips to the sea-side. They helped out with extra pocket money when they went for their sea-side holiday. All the children participated in school outings and camps and were encouraged to join outings and camps run by Youth Clubs such as The Square Club and Stonehouse Gang. All long stay children had two weeks holiday at the seaside every year.

Over the years the concept of child care changed and grouping children together in one place was not considered the best place for them. Scattered homes were built in the neighbourhood and a Child Fostering Scheme was developed.

In the early 1980's Shenley Fields Homes began to close down. The first homes to go were the baby homes. These homes were for children and babies under the age of 5 years. Every year another home closed, some closed altogether and some moved to new locations. The last home to close was Pinewood. They moved out in 1987, just 100 years since the start of Shenley Fields Cottage Homes.

The Estate Under Its Late Owners

The two families of Jervoise and Ledsam brought Weoley and Northfield as an investment. After the appropriation by Richard Jervoise, more tenants became 'Free' and held their farms by payments of an annual rent. The number of farms and smallholdings carved out of the estate increased: the Feudal Lord had given place to the modern landlord. But the change in the situation became more rapid and complete with the Ledsams.

Daniel Ledsam took over in 1809 and the first large sale of properties took place eleven years later. A bill of sale detailed properties to be auctioned on Monday, Tuesday and Wednesday, 18–20th September 1820: "A very extensive and desirable estate comprising The Manor of Northfield and Weoley, the advowson of the very valuable Rectory of Northfield and Cofton Hacket, together with diverse farms and land containing together upwards of two thousand and forty acres of land, in 94 lots.

Of these lots, most were certain fields on various farms, but the sale began with the seven large farms complete with farmhouse and outbuildings including in most cases barns and stable, cowshed and foldyard. The seven were Selly, New House, Lodge, Whitehill, Shendley Fields, Shendley Court and Weoley Castle Farms. In the case of Newhouse Farm, the residence was described as a mansion and there was also a coach-house. The total area of arable meadow and pasture is given in each case, together with the annual rental paid by the tenants. Lodge Farm supported an acreage of 215½ of farmland consisting of 32 'inclosures' and was occupied by Charles Cooper by virtue of a lease dated 30th August 1805 for a term of 21 years at the yearly rent of £189. The fields all have their individual names, such as Gosty Leasow, Tree Leasow and Brickiln Piece. Selly Farm, tenanted by John Lees, covered an area of 197½ acres, part under a lease expiring at Lady Day 1823 and the residue at tenant at will £235 – 15s. White Hill was farmed by William Willett and Shendley Court by Thomas Green paying £107 annually. Shendley Fields, where no mention is made of the house, was occupied by James Whitehouse, holding 119½ acres for an annual payment £117. Weoley Castle Farm, tenanted by William Green, covered no less than 248 acres and commanded an annual rental of £179. This farm included Quarry Wood and the Quarry itself, the advertisement stating that "The quarry is within a short distance of the Dudley Canal, to which a road is formed for the purpose of conveying the stone". Charles Norton leased the quarry for a rental of £20.

A group of fields forming part of Stonehouse, Nonsuch, Ley Hill, Northfield, Mill and Bell farms was scheduled for sale and, in addition, the pool, house and buildings of the Water Corn Mill, operated by James Bissell. Each field was named on the schedule, Great Park, Pear Tree, Broad Leasow, Barn Close, Castle Meadow, Further Oak, Peas Croft, Coneygree and Big Five Pound being examples.

At this time there were some fine country houses in the district: Selly Oak House of John Downing, iron master; Bournbrook of William Waterhouse, land proprietor; Selly Wood of John Worthington, wool merchant; The Davids of George Jones, iron founder; Staple Hall of Thomas Cooper; Griffins Hill of Sheriff Officer Thomas Hancox; Edward Hobson's Pigeon House; and Aglett Kell's New House which in 1894 George Cadbury purchased and renamed Northfield Manor.

Though no more bills are available, we can assume that more farms were sold by the Ledsams, for the Tithe Apportionments made in 1838 present new owners such as

Robert Dolphin of Selly Hall (236 acres). George Attwood of Middleton Hall (182 acres), James Nock of Broad Higley (150 acres), Isaac Flavell of Stonehouse Farm (143 acres) and Isaac Whitehouse of Moat Farm (105 acres). Besides, there were other speculators who had invested in Northfield farms which they leased to tenants, e.g., Richard Brown, Samuel Ryland, Challenor Blake Ogle, and the Rev. William Ledsam, not all of whom were local people. Later in the 19th century the Cadbury family became interested in parts of the Northfield parish. In 1879, the 'Factory in a Garden' was opened by the two Cadbury brothers, 120 acres having been acquired for the site of the factory and for 20 houses for the principal work people. Two years later, George Cadbury purchased Woodbrooke House which later became a college of adult education for members of the Society of Friends. At which time he and his family moved to the manor, which today is the centre of an extensive development of student accommodation for Birmingham University. Weoley Hill Limited and other Public Utility Societies which merged into Bournville Village Trust, invested in more and more land, resulting in the growth of the 'model village'.

Finally on the death of James Goddington Ledsam in 1929, his executors sold what was left of the estate to the City of Birmingham and the rural scene was very soon transformed into Weoley Castle Housing Estate, a thriving new suburb.

The old landmarks have in many cases disappeared, but some may be traced on old documents. The Brick and Tile Works do appear in the recent edition of Birmingham and West Midlands street maps. But to discover the whereabouts of the old quarry and many of the 'lost' farms the 1st and 2nd editions of the ordnance survey 6 inch maps are required. The source of material for building the Castle is still known to children as the old quarry and the early tenants of Quarry Road collected the raw material for providing a rockery in the back garden. Aged inhabitants claim that the rifle range in the quarry was used by the Bartley Green Militia in the late nineties, by private shooting clubs and by the Home Defence during the 1914–1918 war.

Farms of which there is no trace on the ground include Weoley Park Farm (rear of Selly Oak Park), Middle Park Farm (behind Bournville Technical College), Shendley Court Farm (opposite the Shenley Court Comprehensive School), Shendley Fields and Yew Tree Farm on either side of the dual carriageway by Shenley Green. On the other hand, Selly Park (not in Selly Park) is now the detached house 98 Weoley Park Road and Old Park stands at the corner of Whitehill Lane, a house without land. Street Farm made way for the Y.M.C.A. Hostel, Weoley Castle Farm for the Curators House, Bell Farm for the Autistic and other special schools on Bell Hill and Tinkers Farm gave place to Northfield Secondary School. The last farm to be demolished was Ley Hill Farm, halfway down the Holloway, opposite the doctors surgery. It was rendered obsolete when the land was given by the Kunzle family of Ley Hill House to be converted by the City Authority into Leyhill Recreation Ground. One former centre of production, Scotland Farm on Frankley Lane, formerly belonged to the Palethorpe and then the Kunzle family, still continues as a pig farm under the management of Mr L'Anson. One other landmark remains as it was, the Fish Pond at the western end of Witherford Way.

From: Mrs EDWINA CURRIE MP

HOUSE OF COMMONS
LONDON, SW1A 0AA

Secretary 071-219 6635
071-219 3611
Fax: 071-219 6835
Swadlincote 0283 224969

8 February 1991

Mrs J Plumley
128 Shenley Lane
Weoley Castle
Birmingham
B29 4HA.

Dear Mrs Plumley

How very nice to hear from you.

You ask for my memories of the Shenley Fields Cottage Homes. I was a manager there in the 1970's and 80's (1975-1982 from memory) appointed by Birmingham City Council. At that time I had two babies of my own, born 1974 and 1977, and would frequently attend meetings with a sleeping infant in a carrycot, or leave an active toddler playing with the resident children, while I got on with my statutory business!

The concept of an orphanage, a home from home, was vanishing by then. Nearly all the children had at least one parent ; NCH increasingly was working with families rather than replacing them.

I have special memories of all the staff I met over the years, many of them shining lights of compassion and competence. I learned a lot from them.

I hope this is helpful.

With best wishes
Yours sincerely

Edwina Currie

The Kings Visit To Birmingham
8th July 1909

On the 7th July 1909 King Edward 7th and Queen Alexandra were to visit Birmingham. The children of Shenley Fields Cottage Homes were to be treated to a special day out to see their King arrive.

Bag waggons were hired from Dickens Bros. They had rails fitted around the sides of the waggons to prevent the children falling off. The children had to be over 10 years of age. Each child had a brown paper bag to sit on and the wagons were covered with straw for added comfort. Each child carried a balloon.

The menu for the day included bread and butter, one egg and a cup of tea for breakfast. Stewed rabbit and bacon with pudding and sweets to follow for lunch. Bread and butter, strawberries and two fancy cakes and a cup of tea for their tea. This was not the usual menu and had probably been put on for show as the children were to be seen by the public.

The children were seated on the pavement outside the university gates at Bournbrook to watch the procession go past. It was a very exciting day.

During the evening some 214 children were taken on wagons around the town to see the illuminations and all the officers accompanied them. They took plenty of blankets and the wagons were covered with straw. The children had supper on route.

The children rode around the streets admiring the lovely decorations, flags, buntings, streamers, banners and the various trades' arches built across the main streets. The arches were the main attractions erected by the many trades and services. The Water Department arch was in Broad Street, The Fireman's in Temple Row, The Bedstead Trade arch on the corner of Temple Row and Colmore Row. The Cycle Trade's arch was best but all were splendid examples of decorative art and admired by everyone.

It was a very exciting day that must have remained in their memories for years after.

1. The entrance to Shenley Fields Cottage Homes photographed around 1940. Photograph loaned by Miss Longman.

2. The entrance to Shenley Fields Cottage Homes on Shenley Fields Drive, photographed by Jill Plumley in 1989 after the homes had closed down.

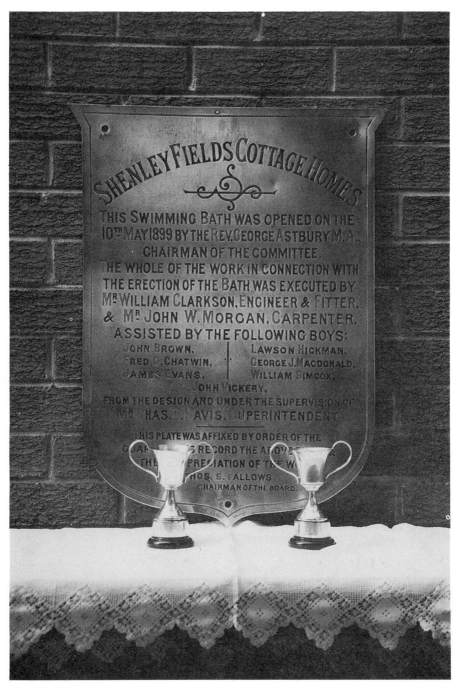

3a. The brass plaque that was once on the wall of the swimming baths. It was found buried in the orchard. The two cups are Table Tennis Trophies from the Elmdene Home. Photographed by Mrs Jean Coulter.

SHENLEY FIELDS COTTAGE HOMES

This swimming bath was opened on the
10th May 1899 by the Rev George Astbury M.A.
Chairman of the Committee.
The whole of the work in connection with
the erection of the Bath was executed by
Mr William Clarkson. Engineer & Fitter,
& Mr John. W. Morgan. Carpenter.
assisted by the following boys
John Brown   Lawson Hickman
Fred G. Chatwin   George J. McDonald.
James Evans   William Simcox
John Vickery.
from the design and under the supervision of
Mr Chas. T. Davis. Superintendent.

This plate was affixed by order of the
Guardians to record the above facts and
their appreciation of the work.

Thos. S. Fallows

Chairman of the Board

The above inscription is engraved on a heavy brass shield found buried in the earth on Shenley Fields Drive and is believed to have originally hung in the wall of the swimming bath. The swimming bath was later closed when new water purification regulations came into force which proved to costly to enforce. Many children remember learning to swim by being pulled across the bath supported in a harness round their waist attached to an overhead pulley.

—

3. A photograph of some of the Shenley staff loaned by Christine Bateman.

4. Sports Day at Shenley. The pavillion in the background was burned down in the 1970's. Photo loaned by Christine Bateman.

5. Children from several Birmingham Homes took part in the races on sports day. Photographed on Shenley sports fields. Photo loaned by Chris Bateman.

6. The children with their sports trophies including the Shaftmoor Cup. Photo loaned by Christine Bateman.

7. One of the winning exhibits in the Morney Contest with the Morney Cup. Photo loaned by Christine Bateman.

8. Some of the children on holiday in Gosport after enjoying a bedpush. Photo loaned by Christine Bateman.

9. Mr Collins the gardener photographed by Ryedale, Home 10 (on right of picture). Photo loaned by Christine Bateman.

10 and 11. The lovely gardens that were looked after by Mr Collins until he retired. Photo's loaned by Christine Bateman.

Mrs Christine Bateman nee Cloudsley
1955 – 1962.
Child of Officer in Charge
The Trees

Like Lesley (my sister) I remember coming to Shenley in the winter of 1955, and sharing our lives with twenty-four boys. This was not entirely alien to me because we had had a boys home in Bristol prior to this.

We lived as one big family, sharing both leisure time and meal times together. Friday nights during the winter months, were film nights. Gordon Knight a voluntary worker would show a film in the Assembly Hall. Every child went to these evenings unless very young or on punishment for whatever reason. The older boys and girls would use the opportunity for "courting", whilst the younger ones enjoyed being together on mass.

Miss Stallards dance class was held on Thursday evenings. All the girls attended and learned the rudiments of basic dance steps including ballroom dancing and ballet. Miss Stallard also ran a girls netball team, but I remember very little of this.

Each home showed great competitiveness when time drew near for the annual exhibition for the "Mornay Cup". We all spent many evenings persuing various handicrafts in preparation for this. Mornay Moseley, whom the cup was named after, became I believe a physiotherepist at the Queen Elizabeth Hospital.

Summer evenings were spent practising the high jump and sprint, in preparation for the annual sports day. This was another opportunity for everyone to get together. I think, because we lived in a home with just boys, I particularly enjoyed the opportunity at weekends and during the evening, to mix with the girls either on the sports field or Friday film nights.

Janet Russell (now Jones) was my best friend. She lived in Merriland with her two sisters and brother. She eventually went home to live with her family and we lost contact for several years. We are now in fairly regular contact by phone.

We always had a houseful of animals, both domesticated and wild, ranging from birds to hedgehogs. My mother had a real love of both children and animals and strays of both species found their way to our door. One ex member of Shenley, who had joined the Navy, was found sleeping rough in our wash house. He had no family and nowhere to go when on leave. From then on he spent his leaves living with us.

Other memories that really stay in my mind are evenings spent playing "kick the can". We had so much open space in which to hide, it took hours before anyone found you. We shared a large tarmac yard with Ryedale. Roller skating was a favourite pastime of many of us.

Charlie Walton one of our boys, seemed to have a streak of architectural genius. He would build dens in the field behind the house and even installed central heating, albeit very crudely. We younger lesser mortals were not allowed in.

Mom always made toffee apples on bonfire night and one year burnt her hand very severely whilst making the toffee.

We always had cats and kittens who would spend the winter nights sleeping close to the big old coke boiler in the kitchen. The cats had always got frizzled whiskers because they used to huddle too close to the boiler.

These are my very special memories of Shenley, of no particular significance but they helped to form my personality and shape me into the person I am today, and I will remember them always with great fondness. Sadly our parents Francis and Nellie Cloudsley have now both passed away. They also loved Shenley and devoted so much of their time to the children.

Mrs Joan Blackwell nee Price
HOME 1 1925 – 40.

I was brought up in Home 1 by Miss Saunders. She was a wonderful person who replaced my real mother all through my childhood. I only saw my real mother once while I was in care. She brought me a doll but I wouldn't speak to her.

Home 1 was the first home on the drive past the lodge and office. There were many of us children there. Miss Saunders was very kind and caring. Every night she would come into every child and check they were alright before going to bed herself. Every-one had frilly night caps and long nighties and had to say prayers and sing 'Now the day is over, Night is drawing nigh'. We all had a tooth brush with our name on it in the bathroom and tins of Gibbs solid toothpaste. Our hair was Derbacced and checked. The bathroom was down stairs. It had a red brick floor and very high bathes with curved legs. Miss Saunders was very careful how every one was dried.

I was brought up very innocently and was very naive. I was taught never to lie or hurt people but when I came out of the Homes other people hurt and lied to me. I don't think I was prepared for this and I remember feeling very hurt and humiliated.

We had benches to sit at the long tables. Every morning we had porridge or bread and dripping. The bread and dripping was prepared the previous night and kept in the pantry with damp tea towels over it. Every Sunday we had seed cake for tea. I did not like the seeds and picked them out. We also had stew in the week with pearl barley in it. I hated the barley. We had to say prayers before meals and before going to bed.

The vegetables were grown in the gardens on the drive and the milk came in big urns from the local farms. It had to be ladled into jugs. We used to go blackberry picking with Miss Saunders and she made lovely blackberry pies. She also made wonderful bread pudding and rice pudding. On our birthday she made us a birthday cake. Every Friday Miss Saunders cut a hole in a sock and taught us how to darn it.

There was a sewing room over the office where they kept rolls of material for the girls clothing. I always wanted a dress with rabbits on and one year I had one made for me. I

12. The rear view of Merriland Home 1 photographed by Jill Plumley in 1989 just before the staff moved out, to work in new premises in Northfield. The large Tarmac area was originally the playground for the children attending the little wooden built school situated behind homes 2 and 3.

will always remember that dress. All the girls had nice dresses in the summer and wore big panama straw hats when they went out. We also had to wear combinations that made us itch.

Every night I had dozens of pairs of shoes to polish before tea. They were inspected before I sat down to eat. I felt the discipline and hard work was good for me. We were never allowed off the campus only for walks with the house-mother. We had bikes and animals to play with. Miss Saunders used to walk us to Bartley Green in a long line. There was a farm on the corner of Cromwell Lane. Miss Saunders taught me every-thing I know even how to tell the time. I spent a lot of time in the infirmary. When I was born I had a problem with my bowel. When I started my periods Miss Saunders took me on her lap and explained that life was changing for me now and I must not look at men. That was the extent of my sex education. As I said I was very naive when I left care at 18.

I went to school on the drive. The headmistress from Ilmington School lived opposite the homes and gave me extra tuition. I was a slow learner because I spent so much time in the hospital. She was very good to the Homes children.

Dr Aldridge was the Homes doctor. He was very good to me. I used to stutter a lot as a child and had to go to a place in town for treatment. Miss Saunders used to make me slow down and think about every-thing before I spoke. I still stuttered when I got married. My husband cured me with a lot of patience. I was taught to swim in the Homes swimming baths by a lady called Mrs Tabbener. We had to swim with a candle on our backs.

Christmas time was lovely. We used to put our heads up the chimney to ask Father Christmas for a Christmas present. I asked for a pillow case full of toys but I didn't get it. There were lots of pantomimes to go to. We often went to concerts at Middlemore Homes.

There was a Maypole on the field at the bottom end of the drive and every year we danced round it holding ribbons. I always wanted the red one. We danced to tunes on the barrel organ. I had dancing lessons.

Every year we went to Towyn on holiday. We slept on the floor and used our pillow cases to hold our clothes and use as a pillow. We went there by Midland Red Bus. We saved our own pocket money for our holidays. During the year we had our pocket money given to us out of a big black box. I used to have 6d each week in a Donald Duck envelope. I spent all mine on gobstoppers. Miss Saunders was a lovely person but she could be strict. If we were very naughty she tapped us on the legs with a slipper.

I always remember the day a young American couple came to meet me to consider me for adoption. I ran to Miss Saunders crying "Don't let them take me I only love you". She would not force me to go against my wishes. I think she spoilt me because I was the eldest. I called her mom and still regard her as more of a mother to me than my own mother. My own mother didn't want me and Miss Saunders became my substitute mother giving me love and care.

There are a lot of little memories about Shenley Fields Homes especially Home 1. I remember the doses of Cod Liver Oil every day, being confirmed in the Homes own church, the toilets down the yard. There was no electricity only gas lights. I remember the little basket I used for cookery, one of my favourite subjects. I still enjoy cooking and regard myself as a good cook. One thing I still do now is have a bowl of hot soapy water handy while I am cooking. I am always washing my hands. Miss Saunders taught us how to be clean and tidy. I still fold my clothes up in a neat pile every night before going to bed, something we all had to do. They are all good habits. I dread to think what would have happened to me if there were no childrens homes.

Punch and Judy was a regular visitor to the homes. We all enjoyed them.

When I left the Homes I was given a huge case full of clothes and a prayer book from Miss Saunders. I will always remember her in her dark blue dress and white apron. Every morning she rang a bell at 6 a.m. She checked us all over to see we were clean and tidy. The daily job list was put up on the board. Every mother looked after her own group of children and no one mixed with children from other homes. When Miss Saunders was dying she sent for me to see her.

When I left Shenley I went to Pebble Mill House on the Bristol Road. They prepared me for work and taught me how to become a house maid. I then went to work at the Childrens Hospital and became Head Maid to the Matron. I earned £1.5s. every week.

Just before I got married I went back to my real mothers' home. I was treated like a slave. When visitors came I had to go up stairs so no one knew I existed or asked questions. I was not happy there. Since I have been married I have been extremely happy. I married a good man. He helped me overcome my stutter and looked after me when I was ill and had to go into hospital. I had many operations including a hysterectomy which meant we couldn't have children. We tried to adopt a baby but Miss Cadbury was on the Adoption Committee and turned us down because of the amount of time I had to spend in hospital.

We used to buy lots of toys for the Shenley Children every Christmas until one year there was a new House Mother. We looked through the window to see the children playing with the toys and saw her giving all the toys to her own children instead of the children in care. We never bought toys again.

I remember Shenley Fields Cottage Homes with great fondness. It was my home and taught me how to look after myself. The discipline was strict and sometimes the work was hard but I feel a better person for having been part of that place. I feel very sad now that the Homes have been pulled down.

Mr Frederick Bright. (deceased)
Home 1 and Home 9
1903 – 1918.

The following article was written by Mr Frederick Bright who was born on the 8th of July 1903. His mother being unable to keep him, he was placed in the Shenley Fields Cottage Homes in about 1904.

From the age of five until he was twelve he was constantly in and out of Selly Oak Infirmary for mastoids.

At the age of fourteen and a half he was found a job at Cannon Hill Park as a gardener and went to live in lodgings in Balsall Heath Road. In 1921 he left Birmingham and joined the Cheshire Regiment Band at Chester. Whilst there he met his wife.

He never returned to Birmingham until approximately 1974 and decided to call in and see his old home, now known as "The Trees".

'REMEMBER THE HONOUR OF SHENLEY'

This advice was given to me by Mr Cohen the Superintendent of Shenley Fields

Cottage Homes, Northfield, Birmingham, and most likely to hundreds of boys and girls going out into the world to start working for themselves. The Homes comprised of five girls and five boys homes, holding about two dozen each. The girls homes were on one side of the drive and the boys homes on the other side.

I was in Number Nine home which was the biggest, it accommodated 27 boys. Each home had a foster mother except Home 9 which had a foster mother and a foster father. The father used to be a clerk in the office.

During my time in the homes I had four foster mothers but none of them had much love for the children. Times were very hard, it's very hard to explain, it was like a little world inside a big world.

There were spiked railings all round the home about 5 feet high and the gates at The Lodge were always kept locked. If you wanted anyone you had to ring the bell and the servant would come and ask your business. She would go and tell the matron and then you were let in.

There was a school on the drive and every Sunday the school was used as a church. On a Sunday morning Mr Cohen the superintendent would take us for hymn practice. I should think we learned every hymn in the book. In the afternoon we would have a service. Every fourth week we would go to Frankley Church where I was conditionally baptised and confirmed at the same time. I was in the homes during the First World War. I remember all the boys being called outside on the playground and we saw a German Zeppelin. I think the pilot was looking for the Austin Motor Works; luckily they didn't stop anything.

One day we were taken to the Tally-ho grounds to see Captain Huce loop the loop. I think he was the very first man to do this.

Now the big boys were allocated certain work to do, but they used to make the small boys do the work. We had to get up at 6 a.m. and all the work had to be completed before breakfast. Everything had to be scrubbed white, there wasn't any lino or carpets on the floors only a coconut mat in the dining room in front of the fire place, no table cloths on the tables. If the youngsters refused to do the work the big boys thrashed them. As you came downstairs in the morning the boys would start fighting, it was nothing to see boots flying through the air.

If we were caught doing wrong we had to go before Mr Cohen at 9 a.m. He would make us touch our toes and with a cane came down on us with all his might. I have known boys to put newspaper down their trousers only for it to be taken out by Mr Cohen. The smaller boys used to be stood in the corner if they did wrong and sometimes forgotten.

When I was 12 I joined the band and during 1914 – 1918 war we used to march round Birmingham recruiting. We would finish at Curzon Hall and sit down to tea. We would fill our pockets with the Curzon Hall cake and bring it home for the boys because in the homes we only saw cakes once in a blue moon. When we had band practice the band master Mr Granger who was over six feet tall would come behind us and if we made a mistake he would come down with his hand on our head and knock us through the floor.

In the winter when it froze hard we would keep throwing buckets of water down on the playground and we had a slide lasting all winter. Each pair of homes had a large playground between them and when it snowed each home would make a snow fort and we used to have snow battles. It snowed quite a lot in those days, if it was snowing when we went to bed by the next morning one couldn't get out as the snow used to be over the top of the door.

When Christmas came Mr Newman the head gardener would cut down a large conifer tree for each home and put it in a tub in the dining room. This used to take place about 10 days before Christmas. He would also cut a lot of Laurel and Holly and we were very busy making garlands to hang up in the dining room. On Christmas day we would be given an apple, orange, sweets and a toy off the tree. Then we would play games.

Every home had a relieving Foster Mother. The one that came to number 9 was Miss Hacket. She was very small. One of our tricks was to open the back door a bit and place a clothes basket on the top of the door. We did it one day intending it for one of the boys but who should come along and open the door but Miss Hacket! These were the sort of tricks we used to get up to. Inside the homes we had swimming baths and work shops where I used to spend a lot of time seeing how things were done. Believe me it came in very handy! One day, when I was 14, Mr Cohen sent for me and asked what sort of trade I would like to learn. I said a joiner or boot maker but he advised me to go in for gardening on account of my health.

When we were weeding he would come to me and say every weed we pulled up we killed a German. One of the gardeners was Mr Brown whose job every week was to empty the dry closets, in those days there wasn't such a thing as water closets. He used to come with a big tank on wheels and when the lads saw him they would all start singing "John Browns Chariot Number 99". The closets were all outside in the yard and if I remember right there were six.

The school teachers came from Northfield and Harbourne. The head teacher was Mr Freeth. One day he came to school with a frog in his pocket intending to give a talk about frogs but this wasn't to be because before he could start the frog jumped out of his pocket and ever since he got the name "Froggy".

Now for over 50 years I always wanted to pay a visit to the homes where I used to have terrible nightmares nearly every night. I'd dream about Zulu's being under my bed sticking spears into me. Then I'd jump over the bottom of the bed and down the stairs in about two strides. I used to dread night-time coming. The mother would pick me up to the gas light, we didn't have electric in those days.

Well, two years ago I made up my mind to pay a visit to the homes. I knew I wouldn't know anyone but, oh what a welcome my wife and I were given. Tears came into my eyes. I shall never forget the very warm welcome from the Matron. If only she had been my foster mother how different my life would have been. She showed us all around the homes. The homes are not called orphanages now, they are reception homes. I expected to find the gates locked but they were wide open and anyone could come and go as they pleased. The children go to outside schools now. It's home from home for them. I still can't get over the changes. The workshops are closed; the swimming baths have gone; you can't even tell where they have been. All the nice apple and pear trees have either overgrown or disappeared. In fact everything had changed. I noticed my old home which used to be number 9 is now number 14 and called 'The Trees'. The large Eagle range which I used to black lead and clean is now replaced with a modern easy to clean grate. We had no chairs to sit on only forms which were scrubbed white as were the tables. We had no table cloths and no curtains up to the windows, only calico blinds. Outside the homes was nothing but green fields but now its all built up. I often think about some of the boys and wonder if they are still alive. The two Heyward brothers, two Hockley brothers, Archie Reece, Arthur Snow, Arthur Edwards, Billy and Frank Gabb, Ben Bird and Mr Hall of Northfield. It would be nice for us all to meet again.

The following letter was sent to Mrs Bowes (now Mrs Hornby) following a return visit by Mr Bright to his beloved Homes.

My wife and I thank you very much for the kind way you received us. We very much appreciated the refreshments and the very kind way you showed us around. The dinner was lovely, far better than I used to cook but then in my days at The Homes we couldn't get the same food and had to cook what ever was given us and then again the First World War was on. I left the homes about 6 months before the end. I must say the homes didn't look the same. I could see that when I arrived at the main gates. When I was there the gates were always kept locked and any-one calling had to ring the bell at the gate. I couldn't get over the homes being mixed and I am sure it must seem home from home for the children and they must be much happier now than when I was in the homes especially if all the mothers are like you. So considerate and understanding, far different than when I was there.

I remember one Sunday before the Sunday service a boy named Jack Mansell was caned. The boy was made to touch his toes and given six strokes with a long thin cane before all the boys and girls. A short while later the boy died. The caning was done by the superintendant Mr Cohen. I don't know what the boy had done.

I can just imagine the band marching up and down the Drive and all the boys and girls running down the drive to see and hear the band which was a treat for them. I always remember the first march that I played, it was called Peace and Plenty. I still know the tune. There was a boy named Harry Hayward in the band and at the age of 14 he was the best trombone player in the Midlands. When he left the homes he joined the Royal Marines Band at Chatham and later went through Neller Hall. This would be about 1917.

When I was at the homes the other week I noticed you had electricity. When I was there we only had gas lights. Conditions in the homes weren't very nice then.

The boys were always fighting and the big boys were allocated jobs of work to do before breakfast but they used to make the little ones do the work. I remember on one occasion two brothers came to the homes from Liverpool and they were always setting on the other boys including myself but one day they went a bit too far and I set about them. In doing so I knocked one of my knuckles out of place on my right hand. It was very painful but I daren't say anything to the mother or I might have been sent to Mr Cohen. I was in agony for a few weeks. My knuckle is still out of place. I still remember the brothers name, (Lockley).

I was born in Selly Oak Infirmary so you see I must be part and parcel of the homes. We had visiting day once a month but very seldom did my mother come and I would lean up against the wall of number 9 and have a good cry. One day Mr Cohen sent for me and gave me 4 pennies and told me to go to Harborne and get on a bus to Birmingham to go to Western Road Infirmary to see my mother as she was very ill. When I arrived there I saw my mother and she told me she was dying and that I had no one in the world. That was the last I saw of her. This would be about 1916. I was always looking forward to working for my mother when I left the homes but this was not to be. Well I left the homes about six months before the end of the First World War and was found a job at Cannon Hill Park as a gardener, also a boy from next door at home 8 came out with me. He went to Cannon Hill Park as a boat builder. We both went to the same lodgings in Balsall Heath Road with a Mrs Handwell. The other boys name was Ben Bird. It would be very nice to get in touch with him but I don't know how to go about it. It is over 50 years since I saw him. I don't suppose there is such a thing as a get together for old boys. I shall have been married 50 years next year if I am spared. I got married young because I was all alone, no brothers or sisters or aunts or uncles but I must say the girl I married turned out to be a very good wife and mother. I couldn't have done better. When I think of Harborne it reminds me of a little shop nearly at the top of Highfields Road. On Saturday morning two of us used to go for the papers for Mr Cohen and if we had a penny we used to buy a Fill Bellie which was a very thick piece of bread pudding and did we enjoy it. We used to go through the Castle fields and past California Brick Works to get there.

Well matron I could go on for ever telling you things but before I close I would like to thank you once again for the very kind way you received my wife and I. I thought it was a very kind gesture when you let us out of the front door. It really brought tears in my eyes as it was the very first time I had gone through the front door. I was in that home for 12 years and before that I was in the tiny tots home which was by the Lodge. My wife wishes to be remembered to you and thanks you very much. May I say you made the day one of the best days of my life which I shall never forget.

Frederick Bright

As you can see Mr Fred Bright really enjoyed his visit to the Shenley Fields Cottage Homes.

Another of Mr Bright's visits was featured in the Evening Mail in June 1974 with the following write up;

Together again — the Trees 'children'.

Oliver Twist has returned to Birmingham for more. This time to meet his old friends who shared the agonies of life in an institution 50 years ago. It was mentioned in an earlier "Mail" article of Mr Bright's wish to find his former childhood friends. Mr Bright has been haunted by his past. He always wondered what had happened to his friends who shared his early years at "The Tree's" Shenley Fields Cottage Homes. Now he has found out. It was tea at "The Tree's" for former children of 'The Homes'. Toast, trifle and cakes were on the menu. For the children at the home today it would be a normal tea but for the 'children in care' at the turn of the century it would have been a real treat. The dormitories and iron bedsteads are gone. Now there are small and cosy bedrooms. The caning and discipline is replaced by love and care from the Matron Mrs Bowes. Its no longer an 'institution' it's a real home. Over tea there is great chatter of the good old bad old days. Poverty and punishment . . .strories of stowaways and runaways.

A lifetime itself has separated each of them. Some have married once, twice. Some are widowed, have grandchildren and great grandchildren. but for all of them the re-union was a happy link with the past.

Mrs E M Burrows nee Norris
Assistant House Mother
Ryedale and Greenways
Jan 1953 to Nov. 1954

I am one more person who has been interested to read the article on 'The Drive' and it brought back memories of my time there. I had to think about when it was but I

13. Mr and Mrs Judson and Mrs Burrows nee Norris with the boys from Ryedale dressed up as King Richard and the Crusaders for the Coronation in 1953. Photo loaned by Mrs Burrows.

remember that I was there on Coronation Day 37 years ago. I am retired now but still quite an active person.

I think I started there in January 1953 and worked in 2 houses Ryedale and Greenways as assistant house mother.

On Coronation Day each house represented a king or queen of England. We at Ryedale (a 16 bed boys home) chose to be King Richard and the Crusaders. They were rigged up with grey jumpers and trousers and made balaclava helmets and swords.

Mr and Mrs Judson were the Houseparents and Mr and Mrs Griffin the Superintendants.

I wasn't there longer than November 1954 when I went on to do midwifery training.

It was difficult work at Shenley but there were many highlights. I wonder if anyone remembers the Temperance classes I took on Sunday afternoons. I remember going on holiday with Mr and Mrs Judson and all the boys to Bideford North Devon.

It was a fairly difficult job especially when the houseparents were off duty and I was alone. We had to be careful about punishments and the children could be really unruly. I wasn't really happy there and didn't stay for quite 2 years.

I suppose my happiest memories were of teaching the children lessons on Sunday afternoons, celebrating birthdays and the Coronation. I remember wrapping up parcels for the children and Mrs Judson saw to their birthday occasion and always made the boys a beautiful chocolate cake. Good or bad the memories of Shenley Fields Homes will always be with me.

Mrs Doris Bushell nee Oakley
1923 –
Home 5

I have wondered for years about whether Shenley Fields Homes still existed and my question has just been answered. I have just been reading your article in the newspaper about the homes. I was there in 1923 when I was 10 and my younger? was 6 years old. We were in Home 5 with a housemother named Miss Ford. Mr and Mrs Cohen were at the lodge when I was there and they really were a lovely couple. Mrs Cohen was a tall gracious lady with white hair styled in a bun at the back. Each year they took us to the seaside for a fortnights holiday, sometimes it was Llandudno and another year Wallesey.

We all had pocket money and they took us to the amusements and told the owners we were from a children's home in Birmingham and we had quite a lot of concessions because of that.

At the Homes there was a lovely church, school and swimming baths. We were all taught to swim. I did quite well at school and Mr Locke who was headmaster at the time would have liked me trained as an English Teacher. I won a certificate for swimming and I was in the Girl Guides. We went to church regularly and even now I know all the old hymns off by heart. We used to go to Lodge Hill Cemetary on Remembrance Sunday and the service was read by the Reverand Reginald Haysom who arrived in uniform on horse back. All the girls my age, I was about 12 then, had a crush on him. I was confirmed from the home at St Lawrence Church in Northfield by the Bishop of Birmingham Dr Barnes. I still have my little book The Pilgrims Path. There were lots of hard times and we all had to work hard but looking back it didn't do us any harm. I would also deny that any child of our age was better educated or better mannered whatever walk of life they came from.

I met someone about 3 years ago who was in the homes about the same time as me and it was so strange. I had just collected some photographs and was looking at them while having a cup of coffee in a cafe near my home. Someone said "Can I have a look Doris". I just looked up and said "Hello Gladys".

The years had rolled away and we knew each other instantly. Her name was Gladys Winter and mine was Doris Oakley.

When I was 13½, Mrs Cohen would fetch me to look after her little son Denys. He was lovely. I used to look forward to it as I had my tea there also. I shall never forget Mr and Mrs Cohen, indeed I never have. When I left the homes I worked at a clothing factory owned by a Mr Blumenthall and both he and Mr Goldberg were just as kind and thoughtful. I have a strong fondness for Jewish people because of these lovely people.

Mr Denys Cohen
1919 – 1932.
The Lodge.

I was born at Shenley Fields on 13th April 1919, Palm Sunday, in my parents bedroom at the Lodge which overlooked the drive and Lodge lawn. It was usual in those days for children to be born at home and my mother was attended by the family doctor, Guy Dain of Selly Oak and Nurse Rollins.

I had the great good fortune to live at Shenley for the first thirteen years of my life, and it was for me a period of immeasurable joy. My father and mother were as near perfect parents as human beings could be.

I know that my father had a quite extraordinary knowledge of the child mind, born no doubt of long training and experience. I only knew at the time that he was a kind loving father who gave generously of those qualities and of his time.

When I was very small he used to put me on his knee and let me listen to the tick of his handsome gold watch, which delighted me. I later learned that he had been presented with this watch and chain by subscription from all the Birmingham elementary school teachers, for negotiating an increase in their woefully inadequate salary scale. My father was to lead a delegation to appear before the Education Committee to present the case. When the day came the rest backed out and my father faced the committee alone and successfully. What an illustration this is of his gentleness and understanding towards children and of his steely determination and courage when confronting anything he perceived as unjust or unfair. Such was the character of the man, which he impressed on Shenley Fields for half a lifetime, high principles, penetrating intelligence directed at the problems, gentleness, understanding and justice.

My mother was just perfect, and when unusually, she was not in "the place" as they called it, I could scarcely wait for her return. The family was completed by two kind elder brothers.

Those 13 years at Shenley gave me the qualities that have stood me in good stead through all life's ups and downs, a life which at times has been quite extaordinarily stressful, including long periods in action in the Second World War pitted against the cream of the German army on grounds of their own choosing, which was some of the most difficult in Europe. Certain experiences since have been even more stressful and for the fact that at the age of 73 I have surmounted them all to come through happy and healthy I undoubtedly have my parents and Shenley Fields to thank.

Shenley Fields in the 1920s was a self contained community in which everyone knew everyone else. Each home had a name but was referred to by number. 1 to 5 for the girls homes, 6 the babies home, 7 to 10 for boys and 11 for the new arrivals until they had been what would now be termed "assessed" in the peculiar jargon of today. I reckon dad and mother would have said "until they settle down".

There were two schools, the infants and the main school with standards 1−6, headmaster Mr Locke, assistant head Mr Dunn (something of a choirmaster) and some lady teachers. I can only remember Mrs Rapp, who used to give all her class an outing to the Botanical Gardens Edgbaston in the summer and include me when I was small. Boys and girls left school at 14. The boys chose a trade at the "shops" and the girls were trained by the housemothers in domestic matters.

There was a swimming pool in a corrugated iron building situated between the school and the fields. There was a rudimentary heating system, but no method for continuously purifying the water, nor so far as I know was it ever tested for contamination. No doubt environmental health officers would have something to say about this now. It was changed when it looked dirty and no one ever caught anything. In any case the air at Shenley was quite exceptionally wholesome. The prevailing west wind came straight from the welsh hills and in those days there were no significant sources of pollution in its path. I believe that my eldest brother had a "weak chest" when they moved to Shenley from the City and the doctor predicted that the air would effect a cure, which it did.

At the far end of the grounds from the Lodge, near the "bottom gates" stood the

25

workshops. On the side facing the drive up an iron staircase on the outside of the building were the carpenters (Mr Humphries and Mr Appleby) with the tailors (Mr Brownlow) next door. Underneath on the ground floor were the bootmakers (Mr Smith) and a shop which housed the artesian well, and an ancient and unreliable gas engine for pumping the water to a large storage tank on the first floor above. Leading out of this was the main engineers shop (Mr Meredith and Mr Kettle junior). The other end of this shop communicated with a large yard laid with blue bricks on the other side of which were the paint shop (Mr Williams) and a long dark apartment on the end of the block for the "labourers" Mr Bennett, Mr Brown and Mr Cooper. Mr Kettle senior and Mr Newman (head gardener) had no house of their own I think. Only Mr Appleby and Mr Newman possessed a bicycle, the rest walked from as far as Woodgate. Mr Appleby cycled to Ladywood and Mr Newman to Bartley Green. In any case a cycle was a doubtful asset on the local lanes which were full of potholes and waterlogged in winter and dusty in summer. Unwary entry into a pothole entailed a visit to Mr Dingleys cycle shop in Harborne to have the wheel trued up.

As a child I spent an immence amount of time at the shops, particularly the carpenters always called the "carps". I used to make things, rabbit hutches, pigeon cages, kites and various articles taken from a book called "100 things a boy can do" published annually round about Christmas. I must have been a nuisance but was always made to feel welcome and helped as required. People were kind and considerate in those days. One of winter's little joys was to see Mr Appleby light his large Lucas "King of the road" acetalene lamp to light his way home on his bicycle. The water supply needed fine adjustment to drip correctly on to the calcium carbide, but when right provided a splendid light along the winter lanes. Especially delightful were the times when the lamp needed cleaning as the smell was so foul as to be particularly appealing. There was only one street lamp between Shenley and California situated on a bend of the hill near the stile leading to the castle fields. A lamplighter on a bicycle used to attend to it with a pole with a hook on the end. Later it was switched on and off by clockwork.

The centre of my world was the Lodge which I remember as happy and cosy. It was especially appealing to come in as the winter dusk was falling and to know that there would always be a welcome. The main meal was midday dinner but tea was always a substantial meal also, and I used to look forward to my mother and father's company and to my brothers coming home.

Reading was a great pastime for all the family and my mother used to read to me often when I was small, although the gaslight must have been trying on the eyes. I was allowed to use the committee room as a playroom when not used for its proper purpose which was about once a month. The members used to be brought up from town in a large Daimler Limousine driven by a surly chauffeur whose name escapes me.

My main indoor hobbies as I grew older were meccano modelling and reading. There were also cardboard models to make, given away in a paper called "The Modern Boy". My dear parents took this for me and prior to this when I was younger a childs weekly published on Thursdays called "Puck". I kept early hours and I reckon I was in bed by seven until quite a big boy. Until the late 1920's the cook was Miss Rose Sinclair who was a true mistress of her art.

Most of the supplies were from the bulk deliveries. My father either paid for them or they formed part of his remuneration package, I don't know which. His deputy Mr Wilkinson used to break down the bulk deliveries of meat, fish and groceries according to the numbers resident in each home. There was a grocery store and a butchers cellar which was cool all year round. Stores boys would take the rations round on a handcart.

I shared a bedroom with my middle brother in what was called the nursery. My eldest brother had his own bedroom as did my parents of course. The cook had her own room with that of the two lodge girls leading off it.

I first remember the office and stores connected to the lodge by a covered passage but in the mid 20's, 3 more offices were built off the passage by Mr Kettle. At the back of the Lodge yard was a tiled area covered by a glazed veranda to which the milk was delivered daily in churns and taken round in the same way as the other provisions. There was a stores boy who went round each home in the morning with a book into which went small requirements. He then cycled into Harborne, purchased them and delivered them around.

Everything had its seasons in those days and they were strictly adhered to — slides and sledges when the weather permitted, then kite flying (home made, 2 patterns, criss cross and bendy bow) whips and tops, hopscotch and London Pride and I ackee (a form of hide and seek) — of course also cricket and football (especially "shots-in") and conkers in the autumn.

In summer the countryside was a delight and none of the farmers minded the wanderings of a careful small boy who had been taught to respect animals and crops. Any such errors soon got back to my parents, although if P. C. Percival caught one on a bike without a light after dark the usual choice was "a clip or tell your father". I usually chose that brave man's mild clip. He cornered and arrested an armed man once at California brick works only armed with a shovel, and was decorated. Particularly prohibited was the Selly Oak to Halesowen canal accessed from the road bridge at California.

The summer camps at Llandudno was a wonderful time. The boys and girls went separately for 10 days. In later years there was an advanced party so that meant 3 weeks at the sea. Twice in my time the school in Trinity Street was repainted and then we went to Wallasey and Southsea.

My father personally raised the money to build a fine assembly hall. The contractors were Maddox and Walford of Tyburn Road. He worked at fundraising for years with whist drives, jumble sales, dancing classes etc. It was a splendid building with a sanctuary at one end and a stage at the other. The chairs were turned as required. I remember the Bishop of Birmingham, Bishop Barnes attended by the Vicar Mr Gillard coming to consecrate it. There were some lovely stained glass windows and excellent quality joinery in oak. It was designed and decorated by a neighbour Mr Tommy Gronow who served in the Royal Tank Regiment during the first world war. He worked at an ecclesiastical furnishers in Edmund Street. I think their name was Jones and Willis. In the winter the stage was used for sing songs conducted by my father, and which everyone attended. There were also occassional concert parties from outside and sketches played by the children. I was often allowed to manipulate the curtains.

When I was seven I went to school in Harborne, and in those leisurely days was easily able to get home for my mid day meal. This was easier still when my generous parents bought me a bicycle for my 11th birthday.

Shenley was isolated. Until a shuttle bus was started from Harborne to Bartley Green in about 1925 it was walk to Harborne for the number 4 bus to town or stay put. There was quite a large water splash to negotiate on the Northfield Road by Strawberry Cottage. It started from the area of Tom Knockers wood and joined the Bournbrook at Selly Oak. My father had a pony, Bob and a trap later replaced by a Calthorpe car which though a stylish and pretty, semi sports model was woefully unreliable. In 1928 he bought a new

27

14. The late Mr and Mrs Cohen with some of their charges outside Home 9 (The Tree's). Photograph loaned by Miss Longman.

Austin 12 tourer which was totally reliable.

All through my boyhood I was fond of animals. I made a rabbit hutch and run from scraps and also a pigeon loft which I put on top of the bicycle shed. I was offered a pigeon for half a crown from one of the local fancy in California, Mr Culwick. Not having half a crown, or anything like it (money was not required at Shenley) I applied to my father. He looked at me in his whimsical way and said "I've got a friend who will give you a pigeon". In due course one came from Mr Harris's loft in Harborne. I took his advice as to how long to confine it, adhered to it strictly and when the great day came for release it circled twice and that was the last I saw of it. No doubt it returned to its home loft as Mr Harris well knew it would. The star turn in the pigeon world in Harborne was the foreman carpenter at the Chad Valley toy works who had a magnificent loft in his garden in Serpentine Road. Mostly Homers were kept but there were some fantails and tumblers.

Our dog Bonzo was a tremendous character. In decent weather he used to trot down to California and hop up on the bus beside the driver who sat in the open and ride between Harborne and Bartley Green, especially if a member of the family was aboard. On reaching Harborne my father once asked the driver to put Bonzo off at California so that he could make his way home. The driver replied "I will if he'll let me".

On my fathers retirement in September 1932 the time came to leave Shenley. I thought it would break my heart and it very nearly did.

28

Mr Harold Cohen
Superintendant's Son
1908 – 1932.

Little Hal Cohen had 250 brothers and sisters. The family materialised overnight when his headmaster father Harry Mitchell Cohen, one of the most noted educationalists of his day decided to swop crowded Rea Street School, near Birmingham city centre, for the wide open fields of rural Selly Oak. At that time Rea Street School was the largest school in Birmingham but Hal Mitchell Cohen saw his career moving in a different direction.

The year was 1908, Harry Mitchell Cohen, son of carver and gilder who restored heavily varnished Victorian oil paintings for Birmingham's richer citizens, had already held the headmastership of "rough" schools in Staniforth Street in the city centre and Garrison Lane, Bordesley Green. He knew at first hand the hordes of ragged, shoeless and often starving children, who gathered around cafe doors in prosperous New Street and Corporation Street hoping for scraps. Before the turn of the century the alternative to starvation had been the workhouse, but rich Victorians with social consciences had decided to set up special children's homes or Cottage Homes in various outlying areas of the city. One was at Shenley Fields where Selly Oak runs into Kings Norton. Hal Mitchell Cohen applied for the job of superintendant with Mrs Cohen, who had been governess, as Matron. The couple with young Hal and baby Ronald moved into their cluster of "homes" which were actually 11 cottages each housing up to 24 children.

15. Mr Hal Cohen as a young boy. Photograph by courtesy of Birmingham Evening Mail.

The only transport was the horse bus or train at Harborne or the tram to Selly Oak.

There were no public services. They had earth closets, oil lamps and water was pumped from a well into a storage tank. The floors were flagged and the older girls were expected to help scrub them every morning. But the children, who were boys and girls of school age had bread and butter for breakfast, a midday meal with meat, vegetables and a pudding, and bread and butter with home made jam at teatime. They also had warm clothes and knitted their own stockings, the bigger girls helping small boys with awkward problems. There were warm beds, a good basic education, and training for a trade.

Mrs Cohen always found the girls positions in service with rich families in places like Edgbaston. She insisted they went to homes where there were several servants because she felt if they were on their own they would simply be treated as skivvies. The boys learned trades. The Cottage Homes had their own carpenter, tailor and boot maker. Many boys were eventually apprenticed in trades like blacksmithing where they could live in with the family.

Treats including long walks in the fields around Shenley, Christmas parties with fruit and toys as presents and annual visits to a pantomime in Birmingham and eventually summer holidays at the seaside.

Corporal punishment was almost unknown. Mr Cohen didn't think caning did any good. He introduced pocket money and went along to see people like the butcher and the grocer if he thought supplies for the children were not coming up to his standard.

Bread was baked at Selly Oak Hospital and arrived daily in a horse drawn cart.

The Board of Guardians employed washerwomen at 4½d per hour to deal with the

16. Mr Hal Cohen on his return visit to Shenley. Photographed at the rear of 'The Trees' Home 9. By courtesy of the Birmingham Evening Mail.

hundreds of sheets used on the homes 250 beds. One of the ladies walked every day from Halesowen. Religion was low key, with school assembly and a service on Sundays, although Mr Cohen liked to explain The Bible as a series of stories. Any form of class distinction was frowned upon. They played cricket with the boys of King Edwards, and Mr Cohen introduced football. The bare plaster walls were brightened up by covering them with posters from the railways and shipping companies. Mrs Cohen had curtains put up to all windows.

The children were particularly well behaved. They were so afraid they might loose a trip to the theatre or get their pocket money stopped. One boy however did merit a rare beating from Cohen. He put a live sparrow through the mangle. Mr Cohen was furious. All life to him was precious.

Mr and Mrs Cohen had a third son and all of them became dentists. They stayed at Shenley Fields Cottages Homes until Mr Cohen retired in 1932.

Mr and Mrs Cooper
Ryedale. Home 10.
1958 – 1960.

On the 6th January 1958 my husband and I were appointed houseparents of Ryedale in Shenley Fields Drive.

The home catered for fourteen boys; their ages ranged from about ten years to sixteen years.

We had an assistant housemother, a Miss Merryman, who was an excellent member of staff and invaluable to us. She showed us the ropes and guided us where necessary; the boys had a great respect for her.

The two youngest of our boys were twins aged ten; their father was serving a term of imprisonment for battering them. They were pathetic little things and although they were ten they only looked about six. One of them stuttered very badly. Fortunately they had a teenage brother who was concerned about them and visited them every weekend.

Some of the other children were in care for being beyond their parents control, some for petty crimes. One, and the only one I have ever come across in children's work was an orphan. His parents had been killed in a road accident.

Some of the children had been abandoned by their parents and these on the whole were the saddest.

Apart from Miss Merryman (who was resident at Ryedale) we had four ladies who worked part-time; two in the morning and two in the evening. The two in the morning helped us to get the boys up and give them breakfast. When all that was over they would do some cleaning. The other two ladies would help in preparing the teas; later they would bath the younger children.

Food was a problem when we first arrived; not enough variety rather than a shortage. Six tins of beans for a week, one pound of marmalade and one pound of jam, one pound of biscuits and a similar amount of fats etc. Meat bacon, sausages were also 'rationed' but there was no restriction on potatoes or bread or flour. Eggs — one egg per week per child — two for adults. We were allowed one ordinary sized tin of fruit at Christmas which we were advised to mix with a jelly (saved up from our provisions, I think we were allowed one jelly per month) so that it would be sufficient for all of us. Lentils we could have plenty of; the matron was fond of advising lentils on toast. The biggest laugh of all was our allowance of matches — one small box per week!

Clothes for the children was another problem. The matron came round a couple of times a year to each house and decided whether or not the clothes, vests, under-pants, shirts etc. were worn thin enough for a replacement. When a child grew out of his school uniform or Sunday suit or needed another pair of shoes, then accompanied by one of the houseparents he would have to pay a visit to the stores. The stores was situated in the grounds and in charge was a power mad man. If he thought that the child didn't need a pair of shoes or whatever, then that was it, he didn't get them. If the child was lucky enough to get what he was needing, then the man would decide on the size of shoe or colour of suit. This made the child very antagonistic and hostile, not only towards the storeman but towards anyone he came into contact with. Quite understandable as he had to vent his frustration on someone.

The children slept in two domitories; they had plenty of blankets and they needed them as there was no central heating. This was installed just before we left Shenley in 1960.

The one bathroom, containing two baths, was downstairs and was shared by staff and children alike. Athletes foot was rife.

We had a television and in the evening the children would come into the sitting room along with any of the members of staff to watch the programmes.

We were all very institutionalized; apart from attending school the children saw very little of life outside Shenley Fields.

Bonfire night was celebrated in the grounds with a huge fire, reputed to be the biggest in Northfield if not in Birmingham Sunday morning service was taken in the hall in the grounds with the vicar from the local church presiding.

Holidays were arranged and organised by the superintendant and matron. Coaches were hired and of we all went, to Gosport the first year that we were there. We took over a school hall and classrooms. These were used for sleeping accommodation. The children slept on straw filled sacks on the floor and staff had camp beds. The school canteen provided the food which was excellent and plentiful.

The second year that we were at Shenley, we went to Prestatyn. This time we were in a guest house which was obviously much more comfortable and civilized for both children and staff alike.

During other school holidays such as Easter or Whitsun the superintendent expected the houseparents to take the boys camping. We felt we had roughed it enough and persuaded him to allow us to take them youth hosteling. Without exception, everyone had a splendid three days and on the morning we left Stratford for home there was a lot of long faces. The boys had done their chores at the hostel cheerfully and had been great favourites with the warden who had had a specially large trifle made for them. I don't know what the rules are today concerning youth hostels but at the time we used the hostel, members were expected to reach the hostel under their own steam. Arriving by coach or car was forbidden; on foot or by bike was considered the correct and only way. We for our part took the train from Birmingham to Stratford and then walked from there to the hostel, carrying all our gear.

Other outings we had were provided by 'Girling Brakes' who took us to places such as Windsor; everything was paid for by them and no expense was spared. At Christmas there were so many pantomimes to go to that the children groaned when another invitation came along.

17. Mrs Cooper with 3 of the 5 members of staff at Ryedale Home 10. Elmdene Home 11 is in the background. Photo loaned by Mrs Cooper.

Whenever one of the boys misbehaved they were usually sent to bed early. If it was something serious like stealing then we would stop their pocket money. The superintendant would sometimes cane a boy but that wasn't very often.

When we had been at Shenley for eighteen months a great development took place. Houseparents were given cash each week to buy extra food. It worked out at so much per head. I forget the exact amount but all told it was probably in the region of three pounds. Of course in those days £3 went a long way and we cheated a little.

In the homes we were issued with cleaning materials but the matron considered disinfectant unnecessary, so we used to buy a bottle out of our new allowance and the grocer was quite happy to make the receipt out for the purchase of a pound of sausages.

As far as I know I never met a social worker while I was at Shenley. We did have access to the childrens case histories but it meant applying to the office each time, which was a bit off-putting. Anyway we felt it was best not to go too deeply into their problems before Ryedale, as it may have given us too many preconceived ideas about them.

Personally I felt the intervention of the superintendant and matron cramped our style. We would have preffered to have had more space in which to work, so as to have been able to put over some of our own ideas.

18. Photograph of The Drive with 'The Tree's' on the left and the entrance to the office on the right. Merriland Home 1 is just behind the office. Photo loaned by Mrs Cooper.

Miss Connie Cooper
Melplash.
Late 1960s.

My life at Shenley started off at the age of approximately eleven.

The most striking things I can recall are:

The Homes themselves, it was like living in ones own mansion. I was placed in Melplash. The houseparents Mr and Mrs Neish became and still are people whom I think of as my extended family. I recall not returning on time many week-ends and instead of meeting a flaming row, was met with understanding and care.

We all had duties and I think this went a long way towards team work. Although I met many boys and girls there, somehow names have been erased with the passing of time except Maxine Morgan, for I was sure she was seeing my boy friend Moses.

Meal times were always a splender. Being a single parent, many a night I wish I could just sit down to one of those Sunday dinners. How they ever managed to feed us a dinner and pudding each day, seven days a week is beyond me. But then we did have such a good cook.

I guess what I really was impressed with was the day Father Christmas came through those gates. It was the first time I ever began to see how much I missed out on at home with my own parents and family.

Mr and Mrs Neish, looking back now, although they had a lot to do, I realise Melplash was more than a job to them, They were Malplash.

I spent a brief time at The Trees but that was unpleasant. I smashed up the place and attacked a member of staff. I was later to escape with my daughter while on a visit to see her. One member of staff who I always admired was one who came to work at Melplash, but she went to Switzerland. I think on her leaving she gave me some jewelery and clothing, did I feel like a queen.

It's hard to write on paper all that I felt or can recall. One thing I'm sure of, if the Homes had continued to run with the staff, many children out there now would have stood a chance in life. Melplash gave me a good chance. It was my extended family where no shade of colour or creed was ever mentioned. Each was judged on merit.

Mr G. C.

I was born in 1914 and from 1917 till 1939 lived in Witherford Way which you may know is a road off the Bristol Road between Selly Oak and Northfield. In my early boyhood it was a short road entirely surrounded by farming country, except to the north where Selly Oak Colleges had been established. If you walked across the fields following the direction of Witherford Way you came to a narrow muddy lane (now called Shenley Fields Road) little more than a cart track, which came from Lodge Hill Cemetary and ran roughly southwards till it met another lane where, turning right one came to the Homes. If you turned left the narrow hilly lane led to Northfield.

From the age of 5 till 8½, I went to a kindergarten school operated by Westhill College. My memory may be at fault but I think we entertained some of the children from the Homes at a Christmas party.

My wife remembers some of the older girls coming to Saturday night dances at the school in Station road Harborne. That would be about 1929 – 30.

We had no cars in those days and walks with parents were the usual thing. I remember walking from Selly Oak along the canal to California and presumably via the lanes back home. In the early days the Bristol Road was a single track road. Single decker trams (no 35) came from town as far as Selly Oak, from there you walked or caught the occasional solid tyred open top bus which ran to Rednal.

Surrounded by fields and lanes I found them happy days, though for many they were hard times.

Mr H Cockayne
1916 – 1926
Home 9.

I was in the Shenley Fields Cottage Homes from the age of 6 years to 16 years serving the last two years in the Homes factory learning engineering. I am 79 years old now but I still have many memories of my life there. I went to school at Shenley and 2 of the teachers names was Mr Lock and Mr Dunn. I was in Home 9 which was an all boys home. The foster mother and father were Mr and Mrs Wilkinson and Miss Hatfield was the assistant.

Mr Dunn took us for swimming lessons. I won a certificate for swimming and several prizes for sports. I played an instrument in the band which was run by Mr Grainger. We played on the pier at Llandudno when we were on holiday there. Band practice was held in the Assembly Hall and we marched up and down the drive when the weather was good.

I left Shenley at the age of 16 and went to work at Chapmans which was a circus in London.

Mr Horace Davis (Deceased)
In Care 1924 to 1928 in Home 10.

The following story was passed on to me by Mrs Deanna Bennett who is the daughter of the late Mr Horace Davis. Horace spoke very highly about Shenley Fields Cottage Homes. He had a very sharp memory and often recalled his 4 years spent "In Care". Because of her own interest in the family history Deanna persuaded her father to write down some of his early memories in an exercise book. I am very grateful to her for loaning it to me so I could read his very interesting story.

My first recollection of my childhood was when I was 4 years old. I sat on the steps of number 3 Browning Street Ladywood on a very cold day at the end of November and watched the soldiers on horse back coming home from the war. A week or two before, I had helped the people living in Browning Street trim the street up but at 4 years old I did not know why. Later I realized it was Armistice Day. I remember some weeks later we had a heavy fall of snow and I was playing with other children snow-balling in the street when I had a very bad pain in my back between the shoulder blades. I half crawled into the house and told my mother. She, with a baby in one hand, lifted my jersey and smiled. My braces had broken and the metal dividing part of the braces (no such thing as plastic then) was sticking into my flesh and had fetched blood. My mother soon repaired my braces with needle and cotton.

I remember when I was five years old and started school that me and my brother George was entitled to free clothes from The Birmingham Mail Fund and I was very ashamed to have to go to the Mail offices and have a pair of hobnailed boots and a black jersey buttoned on the shoulder, handed to us whilst being looked at by the lots of other down and out people. Everybody in the school knew they were Birmingham Mail clothes so you had to ride the remarks and insults from the better off kids.

I got myself up to go to school every morning, but we never had anything to eat in the house so I used to run in my bare feet up the street to Perry's the local shop. I asked for ½ pint of milk and a small loaf. If Mr Perry was serving I would say "would you put it in the book and mom will pay you at the end of the week". He would say "I will my son", but if his wife was serving I got nothing and went home with nothing. I had to think of another way to eat, so I would scrounge in the bags in the scullery to find a carrot or swede. If this failed I would run to Ryland Street where I had a friend. I would call for him to walk to school with and his mother would say "would you like a piece (slice of bread) of dripping to eat on the way" so I got my breakfast thanks to this kind lady.

After school or during the holidays I would walk into the town and hold the horses heads at the Masonic Hall in Edmund Street for 2 pennies, and also collect the horse manure into a bucket and walk up Broad Street to Five Ways then into Harborne Road to sell it for 1 penny. When I was very hungry I would pick up apple cores from the gutters and eat them pips as well. I also stood at the factory gates when the workers were coming out and I would ask them if they had any food left. If they had they would throw it to me. When I was about seven I would get up at 5 a.m. on a Monday morning and would stand in the queue at the local pawnshop.

I would save the place in the queue for our neighbours who would come to me at 8 a.m. I charged each neighbour 2 pennies so if I had 3 bundles I made 6d which I spent on food on the way to school. We were never allowed out of the bedroom on Sundays because we only had one of everything to wear and they all had to be washed and dried on Sunday ready for school on Mondays. Can you imagine 2 boys and a girl lying in bed all day every Sunday with no clothes on. I don't know how we passed the time as there was no radio or television then and as the toilets were at the top of the yard we had to practice self control and wait until our clothes were dry.

I remember in 1921 when I was seven years old, the miners were on strike so nobody had any coal. The other lads and myself would dive into the canal which ran at the back of the houses in Browning Street and retrieve the coal from the bottom of the canal. The coal was transported on barges along the canal as road transport, being horse driven was too slow. When I was aged 9 I had some important exams at school (St Barnabies in Ryland Street) but my mother told me I could not go on this day as I was to help her carry a bundle to the pawnbrokers, however I managed to go to school in the afternoon and

19. Mr Horace Davis photographed just before he passed away. Photo loaned by his daughter.

then realized that I was going to get the cane for missing the exam in the morning. I was going to tell the teacher that I had a nose bleed and to prove it I punched myself hard on the nose until it bled. The teacher was very sympathetic and let me take the exam next day in her room.

At the age of 9 I made my mind up to leave home so I walked to Harborne Stiles (now called Tennal Estate) and with some corrugated sheets I built myself a shed. I collected wood for a fire and stayed and slept there for 3 weeks. The police found me and took me home. I had the belt from my father for causing so much worry.

I was in bed one morning (we had no sheets or blankets and covered ourselves with army coats and sacks) and a strange man came into the bedroom and told us to get dressed as they were turning us into the street and nailing the door up as no rent had been paid. We went downstairs into the street and my father was leaning against the wall as white as a sheet with shock, my mother with a child in her arms was crying and the neighbours were looking on. I felt so ashamed. However one of the bailiffs said to me, "take the children that can walk to Summerhill Home on The Parade and tell them what has happened". We went hand in hand George, Dolly, Stanley and myself. We stayed at Summerhill House for 3 days while they investigated us, then we were put into a bakers horse drawn cart and taken to Shenley Fields Cottage Homes.

I stayed in Shenley Fields Cottage Homes from 1924 to 1928 age 10 – 14 years. I was in Home 10 and had a wonderful house mother named Miss Waygood. She taught me many things including darning, a craft I have never forgotten. I used to go into her room on Sunday evening and sing for her while she played harmonium. I remember being admonished by Mr Cohen for stealing fruit from the orchard. I went to church every Sunday in a Norfolk suit. Mr Cohen brought our pocket money on Sunday evening. If we had behaved we had 2 pennies.

I used to get up early to fetch the milk from the rear of the lodge and also to ring the school bell, a chore I used to enjoy doing for headmaster Mr Locke. I recall 2 weeks holiday at Llandudno, sleeping in a school and walking along the promenade shaking a tin and collecting for the school band. I won a shilling for collecting the most money one year. I was also asked to go as a ball boy at the Tally Ho grounds in Edgbaston and was paid half a crown for 6 days work. I thought I was a millionaire. I think all these things moulded my character for life. These 4 years taught me that what you want out of life you have to work for. We had plenty of food, a good education, sport and the love of a house mother named Miss Waygood. We spent all this time in Home 10 except for the first 3 weeks which we spent in quarantine. I remember when we hung up our stockings at Christmas we always got an apple, orange and a new penny but no toys.

When I was 14 I was taken from the homes by my parents and put to work. Dolly, Winnie and Stanley followed later.

Mrs Joan Fletcher nee Kimberley (Deceased)
In Care Home 4 1928 – 1934

The following letter was sent to me in April 1989 after I had an article about Shenley Fields Cottage Homes printed in The Evening Mail newspaper. I was hoping to go out to meet Joan to have a long chat with her about her life in the Cottage Homes but sadly this was not to be as Joan passed away. Her husband said how happy she was about being part of the book about the Shenley Homes.

I would like to print Joan's letter in her memory.

I went into Shenley Fields Cottage Homes for 10 years. Of course I can't remember the date I entered but I do know I was about 4 years old and I was then fostered out. I was in Home 4 and Miss Gent was the Housemother. I remember we used to have 2d pocket money and we would walk in a crocodile to Bartley Green to the sweet shop. You could then buy two bags of sweets for a penny. I learned to swim at the homes swimming baths and went to the homes school in the grounds. Discipline was strict in my home but we were lucky in some aspects as we were well looked after, but for affection we received none. We used to have races on the playing fields. In all we didn't have a bad life only nothing really to me can compensate for parents' love.

I did once return with my husband to Shenley Fields. I found it had changed dramatically. The beauty of the surroundings had been spoilt also the discipline had slackened. My brother is now 71 and I am nearly 65 but I do even now remember names of other children in other cottages and I sincerely hope they too will write. Who knows I may hear of someone who was there at the same time as I was in the 20's and 30's. I hope to hear from you in the near future. I must state however it was a good thing we did have a place like Shenley Fields and I was fortunate to have that start in life.

Second letter.

I have contacted my brother who was in Home 9 and he has helped me answer some of the questions on your questionnaire as he is older than me. I was 4 years old in 1928. I was in Home 11 on the drive for one month to see if I had any illnesses. After this I went into Home 4. My brother Les Kimberley had to look after a 2 year old girl named Doreen Blower. He had the job of feeding her until she went into Home 2 and Les went into Home 9. Mr Wilkson was the Housefather and his wife the Housemother. There was an assistant called Miss Hayward. Mr Locke was Headmaster at the school, he also taught the senior pupils. Miss Powel took small children. Mr Grainger was in charge of the band. Just before my brother left Shenley Fields a Mr Newton took over and he put a show on in the Birmingham Town Hall. It was called Hiawatha.

I would like a mention should a book be written about Shenley Fields. It is a pity we could not sometime have had a reunion. It would have been most interesting to know how some of the ex boys and girls lives have turned out.

Unfortunately Joan didn't live to be able to come to our first re-union but I will certainly include her in our book of memories.

God Bless Joan.

Mr John Dossett-Davies
1957 – 1971

I joined the old City of Birmingham Children's Department in August 1957 as a Senior Care Officer. I came up from Wales where I had been for three years a Child Care Officer in the Rhondda Valley.

My patch in Birmingham was parts of Aston, all of Lozells Hockley, Handsworth, Handsworth Wood, Kingsstanding, Great Barr and Perry Barr and part of Erdington. The old inner city areas hadn't been redeveloped then and the real old Brum of the back to back houses in Summer Lane and Wheeler Street were still in existence as was the exceptionally warm, community spirit and mateyness of these areas. Many of the old houses were located cheek by jowl alongside the small jewellery, gunmakers and engineering workshops and factories which went to make up the City of a Thousand and One Trades which itself had gone to make Britain the proud workshop of the world.

I visited Shenley Fields Childrens Home quite frequently for case conferences at The Trees Reception Centre with Mrs Bowes and Miss Slack. I called also frequently at the cottages on the drive to see the various children I had admitted to care, either on a voluntary basis (section one) or through the courts, and to find children for the foster/adoptive parents I had found in my area of North Birmingham. I recruited the foster parents sometimes by general adverts in the local papers, sometimes by giving talks to church and political groups and sometimes through existing foster parents. These latter foster parents often turned out to be the most suitable because they knew from their friends what the job really entailed and how difficult it could be. The adoptive parents came flocking in throughout the year and were very carefully scrutinized and investigated to ensure they were suitable.

By the mid 1960s, after a period as an Area Officer for a quarter of Birmingham, I had been promoted to be the Assistant City Childrens Officer in Charge of all child care residential establishments in Birmingham. One of my first tasks in my new post was to give the individual units, both at Shenley Fields and at the other big city campus, the Erdington Cottage Homes, more autonomy, and responsibility for their own management. We did this first at the Erdington Cottage Homes when the Superintendent and Matron, Mr and Mrs Wilkes retired to Bexhill on Sea. Later we extended this to Shenley Fields and the Superintendent and Matron at Shenley Fields, Mr and Mrs Ronald Griffin, became advisers in residential care in my department. We kept a small office on each campus and divided most of the management responsibilty for the homes between the four area officers. To symbolise the change of ethos we renamed the Erdington Cottage Homes'The Gardens', and the Shenley Fields Childrens Homes Became just' Shenley Fields'. After some initial apprehension and nervousness on the part of the staff in charge of the individual homes the new system worked well and both children and staff benifited at both campuses, particularly at The Gardens where the previous regime had not been as relaxed as at Shenley Fields.

I had hoped there could have been a diversification of the work of the campuses after the Social Services Department came into operation in April 1971, and day care, family rehabilitation units, pre-fostering and adoption units and adolescent units and units for other client groups (an old people's day centre etc) and voluntary agencies could be set up at both places.

In fact the very last job I did in Birmingham in February 1971 just before I left to become Deputy Director of Social Services for Leicester was to draw up a

"Diversification Blue Print", which looks at the pros and cons of the large childrens campuses and makes a strong case for keeping them in a developed form.) The powers that be in Birmingham did not, however, agree with my recommendations and the rest is history.

The problem with the care of deprived children in recent years is that it has gone in fashions and circles like a carousel. When a fashion has emerged, for example fostering or adoption or small children's homes or day care or intermediate treatment, it has been so enthusiastically taken up as if it was the solution for all deprived children at all times. This has been especially true of fostering and also leaving children at home 'under supervision'. Yet we know that some children do better if they can spend a period in the more neutral atmosphere of a childrens home or special therapy unit. Fostering, adoption, residential care, daycare, intermediate treatment, staying at home with parents under supervision — all these can be valid solutions for some children at some stage in their childhood. However, none is an answer to every problem of every child. I was, myself, responsible for the introduction of some 25 eight-bedded family group homes in different parts of the City, but I certainly did not claim they were suitable for all children in Care.

There is no doubt in my mind that if homes like Shenley Fields and 'The Gardens' could have been kept operational in the modified, diversified way that I envisaged, very many of all too frequent tragedies we read about now affecting children could have been avoided.

Perhaps the final irony in Birmingham is that Shenley Fields with an excellent and enlightened regime under Mr and Mrs Cohen and later Mr and Mrs Griffin should have been razed to the ground and have disappeared completely, and yet The Gardens, a much grimmer place even in its physical aspects, should have survived — physically at least.

Mrs Patricia Eaton nee Telling
In Melplash. Home 8
1953

I was in care with the rest of my family in Home 8 which was called Melplash. Every home had a name as well as a number. There were other buildings on Shenley Fields Drive as well as the actual children's homes. Mr and Mrs Griffin were the superintendant and matron and they lived at Shangi-La which was just inside the front gates. The houseparents got all our food from the stores on the drive also all of our clothing and shoes.

There was a large hall called the Assembly Hall where we had dances, exhibitions, films shows, plays and dancing classes. Every year we had a sports day but I never won any of the events.

There was a small infirmary called the sick bay. I was in there quite a lot.

Life on the drive was O.K. as far as it goes. We had a house mother by the name of Beryl Cullen who was cruelty itself. If anyone came to visit us and brought us anything whether for birthdays, Christmas, parties or for when we went to a do at the Hippodrome and they gave us Christmas presents, we could not open them. Mrs Cullen would take

20. Irene McAndrews wearing the wedding dress first worn by Sue Nicholls in the Crossroads series on Central Television. Sue Nicholls played the part of Marilyn who married the vicar. The photo was loaned to Mrs Pat Eaton by Irene's husband. Sadly Irene has passed away.

them off us. If there was anything in them that would please her own children she would give them our presents.

She would make us kneel down with our hands on our heads for hours on end. We could not sit on our heels to rest. She would also put us in a bath of cold water and make us sit there for a long time then flood the floor and make us mop it up and dry and polish it till it shone. The effect this had on me was to leave me with not much confidence in myself. The only people who took time with us was Nan and Gordon Gough. If it wasn't for them I don't know how I would be today. I don't think I would have a nice home, good husband and two great kids. Mom and Dad Gough really put us on the right road. They gave me happy memories of life in care at Shenley Fields. They did things with us, encouraged us and loved us as far as they could. They were there for us and not for themselves. We had birthday parties and we could invite friends from other homes or outside of the drive for our party treat. Dad Gough helped us build a huge train set in our playroom. All the stations were named after children in our house. Many people came to see it. We won the Mornay Cup for this project.

One of the highlights for us was when The Rocking Berries pop group came to Shenley Drive and performed live for us. They were great.

I am still in touch with many people I knew on the drive including Mom and Dad Gough who are now enjoying their well earned retirement.

Mrs Marjorie Englefield nee Toy
Worked in Shenley Office

I worked in Shenley Fields Childrens Homes for 9½ years in the capacity of Bookkeeper, telephonist and answering queries of visitors etc. I had very little to do with the children who lived in the various houses there but it was interesting to see them on the drive going to and from school. It was very pleasant working at Shenley as the drive and gardens generally were well kept by the head gardener, Mr Collins who was sometimes heard shouting to children to 'get off the grass' etc. In the summer time Mr Griffin the superintendant used to allow me to go and sit on their lawn in my dinner hour to eat my sandwiches which was extremely pleasant. In the winter I often used to go to one of the houses, the housemother being Mrs Beaupre where I enjoyed an hour talking to her.

On one occasion during my time there I arranged an outing for office and staff of the houses to go to Blackpool to see the lights where we stayed overnight. This was very enjoyable. On another occasion I arranged an evening outing for a meal and dancing. There were also several dances held in the Assembly Hall on the drive which I attended.

Not long after joining Shenley I decided it was too long a journey from Hall Green on 2 buses. So then decided to buy myself a moped bicycle actually called a Mobylette — a French model. This was great fun as it took me less time to get to Shenley. Later, as I became "richer" I went in for a mini car which as you can imagine was the tops for me.

The time came however when many alterations took place and I was transferred to Head Office after many enjoyable years at Shenley Fields Homes.

Miss Patricia Faulkner
Suncrest Home 2
Feb. 1951 – Jan 1955
Mar 1962 – Feb 1966

I went into Shenley Fields Cottage Homes when I was a very young child. Miss Longman was the Housemother of our house. I went to the school on the Drive then later went to Harborne Hill School.

I remember several of the other Houseparents such as Mr and Mrs O'Donnal, Mrs Jones, Mr and Mrs Stevens, Mr and Mrs Gough, Mr and Mrs Slack, Mrs Moore, Mrs Bowes and Mrs Poutney. Miss Kendrick was the Assistant Housemother of Suncrest.

I took part in the sports on the playing fields. Shenley children wore blue outfits and the Erdington children wore red. We competed against each other for trophies. I don't know what happened to the trophies.

43

21. Home 2 Suncrest just before the bulldozers moved in. This photograph was taken in 1989 by Jill Plumley. The house was being used as offices by Social Services South District Home Finding Team.

There was a church at Shenley but I had to go to Our Lady of St Rosa Lima in Gregory Avenue. We used the Assembly Hall for concerts and film shows. Once we had the cast from Crossroads come to visit us.

I was in Shenley when our Queen was crowned. We dressed up for the Coronation and had to walk in procession around the Weoley Castle Square. We also dressed up on Mayday and danced round the Maypole each holding a ribbon. We all had white outfits.

The homes were very large but they had outside toilets. They were very cold. Miss Longman was strict about the children having their bowels open every day, and we would have to sit on the toilet until we had opened our bowels, then shout "I've been" where upon one of the older children who would be on loo duty would have to look and let us rise. On one occasion we had a girl who was handicapped and had been sitting for ages on the toilet. When Miss Longman went out to see her because she had been so long she said she would be there till doomsday. Pam Neale who was on loo duty asked Kathy, "How long did she say you've got to sit there? Kathy replied "I've got to sit here till Tuesday".

I feel that we really didn't want for anything. We had all the material things, clean clothes, new shoes when needed, holidays every year, always went to pantomimes and shows. The one thing that always stands out in my mind was that I was always in a large group and people always knew who we were and where we were from. We turned up in coal loads. I felt we were the property of the Childrens Department and placed under a microscope. Everything we did was recorded in our files. We were placed on a list and people would come and look at us as if we were up for sale in a shop window. If they liked the look of us they became our Aunty and Uncle and would perhaps take us out and maybe have us home for the week-end. This I hated. I used to dread the time I was away at week-ends. Most times I stayed at Shenley.

As peers we would have our ups and downs like any large family, and would have our own jobs to do, such as clean shoes, drying up the dishes, make and change your own bed. If you were one of the older children you were expected to help the little ones but this is no more than expected within any family.

The feeling among friends on The Drive was one of comradeship. Sports day was a show of this with Shenley kids in blue against Erdington kids in red.

Apart from the impersonnel side of our lives I was happy at Shenley Fields. The memories will always be with affection and proud to have been one of the Shenley Fields crowd. Above all I'm most proud to have had Miss Longman as my housemother and now I am adult to have her as my friend. Miss Longman has left an impression on my life that will always stay with me. Christmas at Suncrest was like being in Fairyland. The house was decorated by Miss Longman who would spend many hours decorating the stairs and hall. The tree was so out of this world, people came to the house just to see the tree. The two big dining tables were pushed together and we all sat together. In the middle of the table we always had a beautiful centre piece. I think about this every Christmas.

Mrs Joan Firth nee Catchpowle
In Care approx 1938 to May 1943

My brothers Kenneth, Ronald and David and I were sent to the Shenley Fields Cottage Homes at the beginning of the war. Our mother had died and father could not cope. I was put into one cottage and my brothers went into another cottage. My housemother's name was Mrs Vale. Looking back I can see what a remarkable woman she was. She gave to each child love and security.

I remember the playing fields, swimming pool, church and something like a small hospital. We went for walks around the surrounding lanes two by two. I think there must have been a lot of happy children there because I remember a lot of laughter. The things I did not like was the de-lousing when you first got there, because you were already frightened to death, or the lining up each morning for the spoon of cod liver oil.

I was very happy there, in fact I never wanted to leave. I think it must have been about 1940, I remember spending my eighth birthday in the big shelter nearly all day. The war being on we had to be sent to Wales as evacuee's. I remember that train journey frightened me to death.

In Wales I had two homes both with horrid people who did not like children. In fact one only wanted me to polish the floors. I was very unhappy and longed to be back at Shenley with Mrs Vale.

The day came when I went back to Shenley full of hope and joy. Alas it was only for a short time. Our father had re-married and we were to go back to him. Our step-mother only wanted father and not us children, so I was unhappy again.

So you see in a very unhappy childhood I was only happy at Shenley with Mrs Vale. She was the only adult I loved during that period.

Later on I met and married a very kind and good man. I have three lovely daughters and soon to become a grandmother for the first time, so you see life has been good since I became an adult but I have never forgotten those days and I am grateful for the chance to put some of it on paper.

Mr Eric Fisher
In Care 1930 – 1936

In 1930 Eric and his brother went into care on Shenley Fields Drive. He was put into Home 7. He enjoyed many of the facilities including swimming and playing in the boys band. He played the cornet. He remembers the Assembly Hall and the excellent production of Hiawatha put on by the children. Many people came to see it. The hall was used for band practice and church services. Eric also went on holiday with the childrens homes usually to Southsea. He has many pleasant memories of life on the drive but also some not so nice. In his letter he says, my impression of the Homes was the lack of love because of the number of children there. I would hate to think of my children having to go there. I feel I can't ever give the affection I would like to as there was so little love given in the Homes. I think this has affected my relationships with my family at times as I

22. Memories of wonderful shows are all that was left of the stage in the Assembly Hall when this photograph was taken in 1989 by Jill Plumley. The local vandals had no respect for the property and took great delight in repeatedly setting fire to the building whenever they could.

46

find it hard to show my feelings. There was a lot of bullying there by sometimes very sadistic older boys. It was only the fact I had an older brother that prevented me being bullied more. I think most people came across bulling at some time in their life but to have to live in that situation at such a young age must have been very frightening. Others have spoken about punishment inflicted on the bullies but with so many children it must have been difficult to erradicate altogether.

I remember having our special suits made by the tailor on the drive. The beautiful position of the Homes and the surrounding countryside are among my pleasanter memories.

Mr and Mrs Gough
Houseparents at Melplash. Home 8
1962 – 1966

Our memories of Shenley I suppose are still fairly vivid as we have kept in touch with Pat, Maria and Edward from time to time over the years.

We arrived at 'Melplash' in August 1962 just one week before we took the children to Port Talbot in S. Wales for their annual holiday.

Normally we had 14 children, but Melplash still had at that time, some working boys, waiting for hostel accommodation. We were all housed in Timolfa School over-looking the huge steel works. The weather was appalling and one evening we decided to keep all the children in. The school caught fire. We were afraid one of our working boys had been smoking, but it proved to be an electrical fault. The Welsh people were marvellous and came from all over to offer help, and of course we were on television and in the papers. We thankfully returned to Melplash after two weeks and settled in to our new home.

By this time we knew all the childrens names, but not much about their characters or backgrounds. Although we were glad to return from a wet holiday in South Wales, Melplash was not exactly homely.

The houses on The Drive were all substantially built with a grassed area and a playground at the back and a formal lawn in the front, tended by a gardener called Mr Frank Collins.

Inside, the rooms were adequate but rather stark. The playroom so called, was the biggest room in the house with green lino on the floor, battered furniture, toy cupboards and very little else. The walls were a cold green coloured wash. The dining room was next to the kitchen. This was also stark and dull, the only furniture being tables and chairs. The bedrooms were small, girls on one side of the landing and boys on the other. As house-parents our quarters comprised a large bedroom with an expanse of green lino and a sitting room downstairs, with a worn out carpet and very dirty furniture.

That first summer I could not understand why the children got their clothes so dirty, and well remember how I made Pat and Maria do their own washing. Then it dawned on me, everywhere was basically dirty.

The clothing, especially for the older children left a lot to be desired. At the age of 14 they were given a clothing allowance, but this did not go very far or allow them to keep in the fashion. The younger children's clothes was supplied by a central clothing store at the top of the Drive, and was strictly on a one for one basis and the old one had to be really worn out before a new one was supplied.

Food was also supplied from a store and a diet book had to be kept, We were also able to buy extras and a receipt had to be handed in to the office. When the children were at school this was not too bad, but it was difficult giving a varied menu during the holidays.

The grand total with which to buy the Christmas decorations was the old half crown, so we spent the winter evenings making our own out of anything we could find.

By this time we had managed to clean and brighten up the home. The working lads had left us and we became more of a family unit.

Our own sitting room we didn't have much time to use, but one day I set about cleaning it up, and I spent all day scrubbing this filthy carpet. At the end of it I put the gas fire on and the stench of animal urine came up to meet me.

I remember storming across to the Superintendent's office and demanding a new carpet. His wife refused so I said I would buy my own. She said "Buy your own!" in horrified tones. I said certainly I would as I hadn't been brought up in a slum and I had no intention of living in one now. She said some other home could have the old carpet. I took it outside a burnt it. This was not the only time I had a set to with this woman. The next thing to go was the old three piece suite and we replaced it with our own.

Christmas came and in the afternoon we had to endure a visit from the Lord Mayor and Mayoress and various councillors. The children hated it and so did we. The first Christmas we had to have the table weighed down with jellies and trifles, cakes etc. which the family didn't want after a huge Christmas lunch, so other years I fooled them with lots of colour on the table, but very little food — that was all in the larder, and was congratulated by everyone on the wonderful tea-table I had put on!

With the coming of spring we decided to make a garden at the back of the house,

23. The train lay-out at Melplash Home 8, built by Mr Gough and the children. A wonderful project that earned the admiration of The Lord Mayor. Photo loaned by Mrs Gough.

absolutely unheard of at Shenley. We dug around the edge of the grass and found the soil poor so my husband got the lads to dig turf from the field. They were a bit slow so he paid them 2d a load and it all came flying through at a great pace and it cost him a fortune.

We ended up with a very nice garden and the roses were the pride of the plot. A little wall was built and we pressed our dog Betsy's paw mark into the cement. This was the only thing left, when we visited years later.

The bane of our life became the children's social workers. They were very young and had learned everything from a book and most of it was tripe and most impractical.

One girl whose mother was a prostitute was allowed to visit her every week-end. The girl was already promiscuous and we suggested that she would be taught the trade if these visits were allowed. But of course we were not listened to. Another crazy idea was to let a lad of 9 visit his mother in hospital. He had not seen her for years and now she was dying of cancer, he had to go and watch her. The only sensible social workers were retired Police officers.

At this time too, the Children's Department decided that the only punishment, even for quite serious misdemeanours, all we could do was talk to them. This meant that they could virtually put two fingers up to us and go from bad to worse. This of course was the '60s' and we are probably still suffering from them.

Our second holiday was to Exmouth and we stayed at the Y. W. C. A. There we were invaded by Mods and Rockers looking for the girls. After a hair-raising night the Police managed to get rid of most of them and peace reigned.

After finishing the decorating and getting the place more homely we decided to build a train lay-out in the play-room. Dad and the lads did all the carpentry and started buying thr rolling stock. I painted 22 ft of back drop and the villages and halls were named after the children. This was a great success and we were congratulated by the Lord Mayor.

Another winter occupation was competing for the Mornay Cup. Melplash had never had a look in before, but to our great joy we won the cup.

After three years we found that our idea of looking after children and the Children's Department were getting miles apart, so we decided to look for another appointment. The older children had left school and had found jobs and would soon be put into lodgings.

We left with sad hearts but we did keep in touch with several of them for many years.

I hope this will give a brief idea of our life at Shenley.

Mr George Edward Green
Home 2 January 1937 – 1939/40

I lost my father in January 1937. My mother had 3 other children but as far as I know I was the only one of us to spend time in Shenley Fields Cottage Homes as I knew it.

My memories are sad ones though not because of any treatment that I received there for everyone was kind to me, but because of my experiences there. One I remember quite vividly was a nightmare I had. Sleeping in my little bed I saw a big tiger under my bed. Of course I screamed out loud. A young girl in her early teens came to comfort me. I also remember going to the church on Sundays and seeing inside the church a very big light oak chair with a very high kneeler in front of it. I always thought that that was where

24. Another photograph of Suncrest Home 2, photographed from the Assembly Hall and showing how the gardens had become overgrown and wild. This photograph was taken in 1989.

Christ was crucified. Funny looking back I don't know why I should have thought that.

Another incident I remember was being given sea-side spades. I was with a small group of children standing in the drive. One boy lifted up his spade and brought it down edge first on top of another boy's head. I remember screams and blood everywhere. I do not know what happened after that but years later I was on a bus coming along Bristol Road from the city towards Selly Oak and a young man got on the bus. I couldn't help but see a vivid white scar in the middle of his head and I remembered the incident all those years ago at Shenley Homes.

I was there some time before the world war started because I saw my first barrage balloon going up near there. I was 3½ years of age when I lost my father and was a very upset little boy being away from my mother and our home being split up, though I did get back to be with her for a few years during the dark days of the war around 1940/41.

I later got put away for not going to school but that is another story.

I find it very sad that the city have found it necessary to let the drive fall into disrepair with all its good work gone and forgotten. Still, it will live on in the memories of those children who lived out their childhood there. Gone but not entirely forgotten . . .

Ron and Dympna Griffin
Superintendent and Matron
1949 – 1966

We became the fourth of the Superintendents and Matrons at Shenley Fields in 1949. Mr and Mrs Davis opened the homes when the first eight houses were completed in 1887 and they were followed at the beginning of the next century, by Mr and Mrs Cohen who handed over to Mr Blakey and Miss Parry Jones in the nineteen thirties.

Our happy association with the homes continued until 1966 and then, in an increasingly remote way, for the next 11 years. It brought us into contact with many splendid people; adults who gave themselves selflessly to the demands of an exacting job and children whose start in life had been miserable and unhappy but whose spirit was undimmed. So many in fact, that it would be impossible to name them and there will be no names mentioned in this narrative. Suffice to say that, to the great delight of her colleagues, one member of staff featured in the Honours List when she retired and there were others who should have been there as well.

We were to make many a wry jest about our starting date, 1st April, in the years ahead (and we are sure that many others did too) but 1949 was a great time to start.

During the war all classes had shared hardships together and at the end there was a consensus that the nation's resources should be more evenly spread. This feeling was given added impetus in the field of child care by the revelation that maladministration on the part of one local authority had resulted in the death of an unfortunate youngster. Nowadays the public has grown used to one Social Services Department or another producing a scandal every year; but such blunders were rare indeed in those days and public reaction correspondingly greater.

In Birmingham this feeling resulted in the formation of a Corporation Committee — The Childrens Committee — composed of men and women who were interested in child welfare first and were politicians second. Often after a member had been on an official visit lasting 3 or 4 hours we went to the Birmingham Post Year Book to see to which political party he belonged; and as long as 9 years after its formation one member told us that he could not remember when the committee had divided on party lines.

One member unfailingly visited each house on Christmas Day. When he became Lord Mayor we thought that we should not see him but he rescheduled the Lord Mayor's Christmas Day programme so that he could come as usual. These pressures meant that he and the Lady Mayoress could not have their Christmas dinner at home and they arranged for their family to eat it with them at Shenley Fields.

The committee was fortunate also in attracting to its service not only career local government officers but a number who were genuinely interested in its work and some of them remained with it until it was disbanded.

1949 therefore saw a real desire to improve conditions for children in care and the determination and ability to provide the necessary finance. War time conditions and post war uncertainties had resulted in there being about twenty children in each house. It was speedily decided that 12 was the maximun number who could be accommodated in reasonable comfort; energetic action resulted in the lease of additional premises and this target was achieved in about 18 months.

Most homes were in the care of a resident Housemother who had the help of a resident assistant and a part time cleaner who came in each morning. The two resident staff had 1½ days off each week, every third Sunday and 2 hours (if possible) every day but were "on duty" at all other times. Each week we were called on to sign time sheets which showed that they worked 7 hours on their "half day" and even in 1949 it was generally considered that eight hours was a fair days work! Obviously even saints (and Shenley Fields had more than its fair share) could not give proper child care under these conditions and it was readily agreed that staff should be increased by the engagement of non resident help. Through the years non resident help was further increased and the opportunity was also taken to strengthen male influence (in what had until then been a predominately female community) by the engagement of married couples to take charge of homes. In most cases the husband continued with his own employment but in some cases was occupied whole time in the home or about Shenley Fields generally.

Perhaps because Shenley Fields was a largely female enclave in those days, it attracted as an Assistant Housemother an Indian girl striking in appearance and elegantly dressed. But one day strong men and women began to lurk in Woodcock Lane eager to discuss her with anyone who would talk to them. Her composure melted and she decided to leave immediately. On the following Sunday the mystery was explained. "Maharajah's favourite wife flees harem for children's home" declaimed the tabloids, their pages adorned with photographs. Life at Shenley Fields was never a slog and rarely dull but not usually so exciting.

Staffing policy resolved, it was time to consider the amenities of the houses and the state of their furnishings. The ravages of war time made it obvious there was no option but to refurnish the homes almost completely and this was accomplished within two or three years.

But building modernisation was another matter. When the Kings Norton Board of Guardians built the homes in the 1880's, they had done so to a high structual standard, with facilities years in advance of their time, and had set their creation off with some inspired landscaping. Few realise that the eight original homes and school were set opposite to each other in a straight line; they were linked by a winding drive and concealed by artfully planted trees which broke up the institutional aspect of the campus and incidentally made it impossible to make a photographic record of the homes.

But no structural improvements were made after that apart from the provision of one indoor lavatory in each home in the 1930's. In 1949 the accommodation of each home consisted of a staff sitting room, a dining room, a kitchen with scullery, a large hall, a play room, two large bedrooms for the children and two for the staff and one bathroom. The internal walls were largely unplastered, heating (by coal fires) and bathing facilities were inadequate, and toilet facilities impossible. We still shudder when we think of the neat little paths through the snow to the outside toilets where even small children sat and shivered during the winter. But of course it must be remembered that there were, at that time, thousands of houses in Birmingham, including much municipal property, without indoor toilets. It took great thought and a lot of time before plans for a prototype alteration were agreed.

These alterations included plastering all internal surfaces and the partitioning of the childrens bedrooms so as to form six smaller rooms; the provision of indoor toilets, central heating and an additional bathroom and the moderization of the existing bathroom and kitchen. Those who remember would find a visit to the Castle Museum at York which contains a reconstructed kitchen of the period an evocative experience; the bent wood chair and hanging clothes airer could perhaps have come from Shenley Fields.

The first house to be modernized was selected by lot and the builders started work amongst much excitement and anticipation. But the work dragged on much longer than had been anticipated (as most building work seemed to do in those days) and when it was almost completed the builders moved into the next house until, in the final stages of modernization, they were at work in three or four houses at the same time. Such was the pressure on accommodation that the houses continued to be occupied by staff and children throughout the period that the builders were at work. They faced up to the difficulties and indeed hardships, with remarkable cheerfulness; did we not say that Shenley Fields had more than its fair share of saints.

It was always an aim to minimise the impact of institutionlism on the children and a few days after we arrived we let it be known that we thought that official titles had no place in a children's home. Home Office Inspectors made little comment at the time but four years later issued a national memorandum commending the practice.

Food and clothing were originally purchased in bulk and issued from a central store but this limited choice and deprived the children of real life experience of shopping. After a time it proved possible for each of the older children to have a cash allowance for clothing and to close the food store. Groceries were obtained from a local shop but for various reasons, it was never possible for houseparents to buy their food supplies in the way a normal family does.

The search for individuality included arrangements for the children to be photographed regularly and the prints given to them when they left, to form the basis of their own family album. But the young do not cherish photgraphs of themselves taken a year or two before and we often have requests from fathers or mothers for photographs to show their own children. Unhappily we no longer have any.

In 1949 four of the homes at Shenley Fields were used for older boys only, one was a "baby" home and one a sick bay. Reduction in the number of children and the increase in amenities enabled toddlers and even babies to be introduced into the other homes and boys to stay there after they reached the age of eleven or twelve; but as there was a preponderance of boys in care one home had to remain a boys home.

The former sick bay developed into a home for children with special needs. It also became possible for children to stay in their home when they started work (previously they had moved to hostels elsewhere in the city when they left school) until they were able to find lodgings.

A considerable innovation was the conversion of Elmdene into a Reception Centre for the entire city. Curiously Elmdene had originally been used for this purpose when it was built in 1910.

Not for the first time the wheels of local government turned full circle! A housemother and her husband moved from another home at Shenley Fields to run Elmdene and such was their huge success that it was soon decided to move the centre to The Trees, the largest house at Shenley Fields.

When the homes were first opened the school built in the middle was intended for the education of all the children. But as Birmingham spread all around and brought with it many other schools which the children could attend, this was obviously better for them and by 1949 the school on the drive was serving local infant and pre school children as well as those of the same age who lived on the drive.

Opposite the school was a memorial to Shenley Fields children who died in the two world wars. There was a pervasive rumour that a bomb had fallen on the spot in the second war and the bodies of the children killed were buried under the memorial. It was a rumour impossible to stop and we met a man of around 30 only last year who still believed it. Let it be said again; no bomb ever fell there.

25 and 26. Two photographs loaned by Mr Brooke of his parents Mr and Mrs Brooke who were the houseparents in Greenways Home 6.

It became obvious that a high proportion of children required help with their education. In 1950 two part time remedial teachers were engaged; one continued to give highly skilled and devoted service for over twenty seven years and these posts made a valuable contribution to the children's development.

It was a prime objective to encourage the children to seek outside interests and energetic help in this was given, amongst others, by the Vicar of Weoley Castle, the Birmingham Federation of Boys Clubs and many local youth workers and teachers. However, a number of activities centred on the drive, grew up spontaneously. Part time play leaders were engaged to encourage the children to develope skills which they would not otherwise have possessed and a generous benefactor provided a cup for an annual handicrafts competition. A group of benefactors centred on a public house, gave cups for a sports day and there was also a sports day, sponsored by the committee, for all children in residential care. It was always held at Shenley Fields and we could never find out which day the children enjoyed most.

The group who donated these cups had originally "adopted" one of the homes and they maintained a generous interest in the children in that particular home throughout the year; they were gradually joined by other groups who adopted other homes on the drive until at one time every house had its own particular group of friends. This scheme was much more successful than another in which members of the public were invited to become "uncles and aunts" to individual children. For various reasons few of these relationships lasted long.

It was at Christmas that the warm heartedness of the public was most evident. Gifts of toys — new and old — were abundant and so were invitations to parties and entertainments. They came from benefactors who maintained a bountiful interest in the children throughout the year; from others whom we saw only at Christmas but who came without fail; and from others whom we saw only once. Invitations poured in from amateur groups, cinemas and from all the professional theatres in Birmingham. One group regularly gave a film show on Christmas Eve in the Assembly Hall and another on Boxing Day. Those were the days before television.

But the highlight of Christmas was undoubtedly the visit which Santa Claus paid to every house on Christmas Eve. He was rarely able to ride on his sledge but he manfully pulled it behind him. On New Year's Day there was a party in the Assembly Hall for the older and "old" children. Unfortunately it had to come to an end in the early seventies; by then society had failed to come to grips with the lawlessness which pervaded it and a group of teenage yobs from the locality took it into their heads to wreck the teenage party year after year.

Holidays too were a great event. Very few children in residential care in 1949 had seen the sea. The newly appointed Childrens Officer miraculously and within a very short space of time managed to arrange for them to be invited to spend three weeks in his native Gosport. A special train (that was the days of the train!) took about 900 children — virtually all the children in residential care in the city — for what was for most their very first holiday. They were spread over a dozen or more schools in Gosport and given a royal reception by the townspeople. A party almost as large went the following year but then homes began to find their own venues although diminishing numbers continued to go from Shenley Fields to Gosport in 1951 and 52 and again in 1959 and 1960. Those of us who lived at Shenley Fields have equally warm recollections of Tirmorfa School at Port Talbot where groups spent their summer holidays in 1961/2/3/4 and 1965. This despite, or perhaps because of, the fact we made television because of a small fire which occurred

55

27. Mr and Mrs Brooke with some of the Shenley children on holiday.

in one classroom and rapidly filled the whole school with acrid, blinding smoke. One boy whose learning difficulties were marked, covered himself with glory; he alone remembered what he had been told and crawled to safety with his nose just six inches above the floor in the smoke free zone, while every one else held their heads high and spluttered and coughed and staggered to safety. In the early fifties contact was made with the Y M C A at Exmouth and for well over twenty years groups of about 20 children went to stay there for a fortnight. We also used the Malt House at Wick in Glamorgan; Lloyd Street School at Llandudno; the Edgmond Hotel at Prestatyn; the Boys Brigade Camp at Dyffryn Ardudwy, and halls in Scarborough Manorbier, Deganwy and other places.

We are often asked about these holidays and so let us say, for the benefit of the nostalgic, that most of the schools used in Gosport, have been demolished and so has the Edgmond Hotel. But Tirmorfa School still functions and Lloyd Street School is open to all although it is hardly recognisable, it is now a branch of the county library.

The indefatigable compiler of this history asked us to be sure to include details of the incidents which gave us greatest satisfaction. One was the comment made by a distinguished visitor. "These children are happy children" he said. "You can see it in their eyes". We quote it not merely because it was made by the Home Secretary of the time but because as a former teacher he should have known.

Mrs Rose Guest nee Skollin

My first memory of Shenley Fields Homes began in 1927 when I was barely 4 years old. My mother had died and my father had left us to seek his fortune. I was a complete wreck myself. My mother's sister had 4 children of her own and no money so in desperation she took me to Shenley Fields Homes. I didn't see her again until I was 14 years old.

Crippled with rickets and runny sore eyes, by the law of averages of children in those days, I didn't stand a change. But chance did come my way in the guise of dear Dr Aldridge. One look at me and he took me under his wing at the infirmary on Shenley Fields. There every day he would massage my limbs with olive oil, as well as pouring it down my throat. He tenderly massaged my eyes, often carrying me on a cushion during his attendance on other patients there. After six months of this patient loving treatment which also consisted of making me stand between his feet and with me holding just his finger he ordered me to walk towards him. My reward was a bright new shining penny which he put over his one eye. If I managed that seemingly impossible trek he would drop the penny into my cupped hands. That way I was able to stand, walk very unsteadily and also use my weak eyes watching that penny slowly drop.

Came the day at five years of age I was put into the care of a gaunt severe looking woman named Miss Ghent at cottage number 4. She became my one and only "Mother" as we called her till I was 16 years old. Every two months my stay at the infirmary was a must. Oh the time, trouble and money that was used to give me lots of sun ray treatment, Virol and my usual drops in ears and eyes. Sometimes it was a painful process for me, but the many pennies I received off the doctor was an ample reward to look forward to, encouraging me to progress.

Number 4, like the other homes each side of the drive boasted a large dining room where plain but rib sticking meals were dished up to us sitting still under the stern eyes of Mother. She would offer up a prayer, then all fourteen children would eat and woe betide us if any food was left. I had to sit by the assistant mother, she often spoon fed me and kindly finished what I had left behind to save me from a reprimand. Everything was done in an orderly way. The youngest led us in two's out into the hall. A huge staircase grandly took us onto a shiny polished landing where there were 2 dormatories, one for the younger girls and one for the older girls, each with neatly made beds. The beds were made by us every morning. Under doctors orders I had to master climbing those stairs, first on all fours and eventually upright. At the other end of the landing would be Mother's private bedroom, a place no one was ever allowed to enter. Everywhere the aroma of carbolic soap and polish filled the air. Bed-time varied winter and summer but was quite early. Prayers were once again offered by Mother then strict orders of no talking or running about the dormatories. During long hot summer nights when sleep was not forthcoming, we would whisper across the room about the day's events. Rows would erupt, then a shout below stairs had us all obediently hushed, but a few giggles would finalize until next night.

Saturday and Wednesday were our bath nights in a room which had wash basins all around the wall, clothes hooks on polished rails in the middle, and a huge bath that often held 3 of us little ones. The assistant mother let us splash about but "Mother" hadn't the time as many were her chores to see to which we never realized at the time. We often pushed our turn in the line to avoid getting Mother, preferring the assistant mother. Being small I was bathed in a large tub just for me. This was for safety sake for a while.

Our hair was washed once a week with vinegar and soft soap. It was dryed in the play-room situated at the bottom of the grand staircase. This room was all ours where we played whatever took our fancy. Rag dolls were often made with shoe boxes used for pulling them around in by long dirty strings. We all made our own amusements that would amaze many children today. We painted gorgeous patterns on the top of wooden tops to use in the play-ground with long strings to make them whizz round in the play-ground. The lovely colours would spin so fast we had a hard time choosing who's was the best. Our little innocent secrets were told and kept in our play-room. Opposite the play-room was the hallowed quarters of the Mother's sitting room. You entered it only on strict orders either to receive a retribution for a wrong or to see a visitor. Everyone seemed to have someone to come to visit them but I would only have Dr Aldridge passing on his way but still with his usual performance with a new penny and ever watchful of my progress.

While others were at school, I had a boy called John Smith for company in our play-room. Being a spastic in a wheel chair we were both not strong enough for the rough and tumble of school yet. He was older than I was. I listened to his words of wisdom. He told me how he was abandoned and felt the homes to him was a kind of refuge. I too looked upon Shenley as my refuge. Dr Aldridge as usual came to visit, somehow it was at a time we were feeling a little sorry for ourselves. We always laughed together, me on his knee and John telling of any hopes and dreams he had. Mother was always at her kindest when she too found time for us. John would sit me down on the foot platform on his wheelchair and whizz me up and down the room or force me to fetch a soft ball which he tried to throw accurately between two blocks of playing bricks. All was very useful to my legs, eyes and whole being. Sometimes we had a little treat from the Assistant Mother who took us out in the sunshine up that long long drive of the homes. I would manage going up but ended up on John's lap on our return. When the others came home from school, like bubbles out of a champagne bottle, John would protect me from their roughness. Those days and months were really ours, John Smith with his head unable to stay up for long, legs all twisted, but a mind sharp and kind and me with my thick green glasses that hardly stayed on because my nose was non existant. I had braces on my teeth to try to straighten them and hair liked barbed wire that would not lay flat or tidy. My socks used to upset Mother because they always twistd down to my ankles. Yes we were two of a kind and not a very pretty sight but I think Dr Aldridge saw us as a huge challenge to his patience and love.

At 6 years of age I was allowed to go to school at last. What a mile-stone that was for me. I had my very first little bag of books and pencils etc; and trotted up that long drive with the rest. I was sat right in the front row of class because of my poor eye sight and hearing. but I enjoyed and soaked up all the information I could. It was a new vista for me. I heard about places, people through history and geography and was transported to realms beyond belief. I wanted to tell everyone. I told John when I returned. He was the only one who had interest or time for the likes of little me. Mother would nod patiently then tell me to do my usual chores before tea. We all had our chores, mine was to clean the wash basins and put the things in their places.

When I was 10 years old Mother called me into her hallowed room and told me John had passed away. For the first time in my enclosed life I learnt that loved ones leave you forever. Needless to say I was taken to the infirmary once more to learn a little more about how cruel life can be. After tender care with the doctor's usual help I returned a little older and wiser. My one and only play companion as such, had gone with his hopes and dreams unfulfilled.

Every week everyone over 7 years old had 1d to save or spend at Bartley Green tuck shop. We had so much for 1d and we loved the trip to the shop on Saturday with the Assistant Mother.

Sundays held a mysterious time for me. Mother was very stern regarding our behaviour at the breakfast table on that day. We all feared to upset her. Sunday best was rather an uncomfortable affair for me. The clothes were stiff and our long white socks up to our knees were held up with elastic which made my skinny legs itchy and sore. We wore a straw panama hat with ribbons flying behind us as we were marched to church elegantly. I remember how often I cried when the singing started. The choir boys looked so angelic. I stood in awe of it all just like Mother's private sitting room. We sat on polished wooden benches where my itching legs dangled. The parson talked too long, my tummy would rumble so loud that it set the other girls giggling. Mother, in her smart starched dress up to her neck, a straw hat like a boat on her head, would top me on the head. Sometimes I had no pudding for causing such an affray, even though I swallowed hard to control my rumbling stomach to no avail. We would enjoy afternoons in our playground shared with Home 5. Many hours I have spent on the swings, swinging high enough to see gardens of flowers and trees and dream away of what it's like beyond our homes. My horizons opened up for me when selected to go at last to the annual sea-side for a week. Southsea conjured up for me a world I'd never seen but heard so much about. We never slept the night before departure. Bustling with excitement we were all measured for new summer dresses. The seam-mistresses were so busy fitting over 100 children with new clothing. When my turn came one of the seamstresses found the time to sit me on her lap and gave me an enormous hug. The colour I chose for my outfit was heaven for me. On that most exciting day 4 great big chara-bancs came up the drive. With our pillow slips slung over our shoulders full of our personal clothes and items, we scrambled on board. I sat with my nose pressed hard against the windows not to miss anything on our way. Mother counted all of us then climbed aboard and at last we were off. My heart took too many leaps of excitement and I fetched my breakfast up.

After that I had to sit on Mother's lap with a firm hold making sure my excitement didn't overpower me again. We arrived at a huge station and on the platform I became rooted to the floor mouth agape as this huge iron monster, steam being blown from its side and emitting deafening chunting sounds as it rolled to a stop and the doors flung open. This time Mother carried me on and sat me by this huge window. Holding my breath so as not to bring any more meals up, we were suddenly transported, passing fields of sheep, cows, horses and houses that looked small compared to our homes and even trying by now not to fall asleep in case I missed any of these wonders.

At Southsea we slept on mattresses laid out for us in a big school hall. When I saw the rolling sea for the first time it was all too much. Up came my dinner. I do seem to bring up my food during emotional excitements. Now I know why Mother always had me near her more than any other girls on such events. We were still being orderly by the sea and told what to do or not do. I was fascinated by these families of moms and dads and their children who were allowed to do just as they pleased. I crept nearer and nearer on the beach to them until Mother noticed me and ordered me to return to her side. What holidays they were each year. They never failed to excite me.

At the age of eight I had a serious operation at Queen Elizabeth Hospital for a mastoid in my ear. Coming round from the horrible chloriform, head heavily bandaged, I noticed other children had their mums and dads visiting them. I felt so alone , sick with pain and utterly embarrassed, when they asked me where my family was. To my utter, utter amazement who should come striding down the ward 1 penny on his eye, so tall and majestic with white woolley hair and this lovely blue eyes, yes it was my Dr Aldridge coming to see just me. I felt like a princess in spite of looking like a little gnome with a huge bandaged head. I was not to see Shenley for nearly a month. When I returned to Shenley still with my bandages on Mother had made a lovely tea party for me. Doctor dressed my open wound painfully every morning. I do believe he shed tears as I did.

Then my world once more changed, I was now to go to the Royal School for Deaf Children. My education needed more care and attention. The school was so huge, the dormatories stretched beyond belief. I cried all that night with no one to comfort me. All of the girls and boys came from loving happy families and went home during the holidays but I went home to Shenley. I had many tales to tell the girls back there of this huge strange school. I still went along with them to the sea-side, and as I was now growing , dresses were made each time for me. When I was nearly 10 I had another mastoid and once again my dearest friend Dr Aldridge was there. I now had come to realize I had no-one but him, Mother and Home 4.

Returning to school at Edgbaston I longed for my holidays at Shenley. One holiday an outbreak of whooping cough broke out, so I was taken to another group of Cottage Homes in Erdington for my fortnights holiday at Easter. I'm afraid I rebelled for the first time. I would not eat the food, I sat in a corner crying for days. I so wanted Shenley, Mother Ghent and Doctor Aldridge. After a week they returned me back to school. There I felt a little comforted especially when I had some things sent by the doctor to show he was still around as usual.

One sunny day I was called into the school headmaster's office. Wondering what on earth for I found Miss Ghent with him. She smiled then handed me a heavy package. Upon opening it I was amazed to find it full of pennies. Putting her arms around me, something she rarely did and holding me close she told me my Doctor Aldridge had passed away and had left me those pennies. I doubt anyone would comprehend the turmoil I was going through. I was devastated for many days. Fear overwhelmed me, fear for the future. I had no one in the world left. John had gone, Dr Aldridge had gone and I knew soon I had to leave my foster mother Miss Ghent and the only home I ever knew "Shenley Fields".

There are so many memories to recall, so many dramas, joys, humour, sadness and pain. Even though I have mỹ husband, daughter and a home of my own to comfort my autumn years, I will always be grateful and proud to have lived and known Shenley Fields Cottage Homes. I know without its warm refuge, loving care and patient guidance I would not be here today.

Mr Raymond James Guy
Home 7
1940 – 1948

I came from a large poor family and due to the death of my mother in 1935 my sister Jean who was fifteen months older, and myself were sent to live with a step-brother. Jean was then sent to Shenley Fields Homes and at my request I followed, to be with my sister. Jean went to Home 1 and I went to Home 7.

Miss Album was my House Mother, and I am glad to say that she was very strict with me. Her assistant Miss Johnson was the opposite and often disagreed with Miss Album re discipline.

Mr Stokes/Sparkes was the cobbler/storekeeper and was responsible for the distribution of food each week to every home. Mr Brookes (?) was the tailor and band leader. Mrs Southall was the House Mother of Home 4.

The Superintendant's name was Mr Blakey and Miss Phillips was the Matron. She to was a disciplinarian.

I learnt to swim in the homes own swimming pool, and attended church at the Homes Church. I was in the choir and an altar boy at St Gabriels. My confirmation was at St. Lawrences Church in Northfield.

My schools were Jervoise Road Junior School and Ilmington Road Senior School.

During the war I was evacuated to Mountain Ash in South Wales. Before evacuation we slept under the stone staircase during the air raids. This was prior to the erection of underground concrete air raid shelters.

Mr and Mrs Parry were house parents in Home 9 and this is where I ended my days at Shenley. Upon leaving school at fifteen I went to a working boys home in Vauxhall Road, Birmingham 7.

I met my wife when we were sixteen, married at twenty-one and have been happily married for thirty five years.

Jean's house mother was Miss Longman and upon leaving school Jean stayed on as a trainee house mother, but unfortunately she was killed in a car accident in 1965.

Our Sundays were very strict and we always wore our best clothes when we went for our walk around Bartley Green reservoir.

My memories of my life at Shenley Fields Homes are very happy and I owe many thanks to the staff and people there that cared for me in my early years as without their caring I feel my life could have been very different.

Mr Brian J Harvey
Home 3 and 7 Lilac View
1947 – 1957

Our mother could not afford to look after us after my father was killed in the war so we went into care at Shenley Fields Cottage Homes. The Homes were large and in beautiful grounds. There were 11 houses for the children plus a sick bay. We had our own swimming baths which unfortunately got burnt down while I was there.

I remember a small cottage which was on the front of the homes in Woodcock Lane. This was used by the caretaker. During the war they had 4 air raid shelters built. They were left up for the children to play in afterwards.

There were lovely playing fields where we held sports days and played football, cricket, hockey etc.

A Midland Red Bus was given to the Homes for us children to play on. It was great fun.

We had a social aunt and uncle scheme and I would go with my social aunt for week-ends.

28. A sports day photograph loaned by Mrs Steventon whose late husband was in the Shenley Homes.

We celebrated Easter, Birthdays, Christmas and had summer sports days when other homes such as Erdington competed against us.

Life was hard. We all had our jobs to do before we went to school. One of my jobs was to scrub round the drains. All shoes had to be cleaned and inspected before going to bed. I used to clean and bank up the boilers for the night. I did this job till I was 15½ years old.

I enjoyed delivering the groceries to each home in wicker baskets. This was done when I got home from school. I used to take a few sweets out of each basket.

Life was hard but I feel a better person for it. I am now self sufficient and independant. If I had been with my mother this may never have happened. My mother asked me to go to her when I was 12 but I said no because I was so used to the other children around me. I thought I would never see them again.

Mr Barrie Peter Hawker
Home 7
1941 – 1945

My father died in 1936 when I was two years old and in 1941 at the age of seven I went into Shenley Fields Homes and stayed there until I was eleven. I was in the house next to the church during my stay, there was also a swimming pool close to the church where I learnt to swim. I went to school there before going to Jervoise Road School and later to Ilmington Road School. I also remember the little hospital, the sports pavilion and tennis courts.

During the war the dormitories were down stairs so we could get out quickly when there was an air raid.

We had to make our own bed first thing in the morning before breakfast, then we had a rota for preparing meals, washing up, scrubbing the floors and doing odd jobs.

The Homes and land covered a large area, a lot of this was vegetable gardens and orchards as well as the playing fields. During the holidays and at weekends we boys worked helping the two full time gardeners. I can still smell the apple store. When the gardeners stopped for a tea break they would give us an apple.

Mr Blakey was the Superintendant, he would come to church on Sunday afternoon and after the service would give us a talk.

We had pocket money and a house bank, and we could go to the Weoley Cinema on Saturday morning if we had been good.

I learnt to sew, darn socks, knit and cook, but most of all to live in harmony with others. As the war was on most things were very scarce so what little we had we shared.

My academic achievements were very poor when I left school, but I served an Engineering Apprenticeship, went to sea as an Engineer Officer for two years, then went to night school and passed my HNC in Mechanical Engineering and Thermodynamics, and became a Senior Development Engineer at BMC. I an now a teacher of craft and maths at Bournville School.

I do feel that my days at Shenley Fields taught me to stand on my own two feet, and to keep going when things got rough (which I have done despite some severe setbacks).

Mrs Evelyn Haynes nee Stanley
1937 – 1939

I had to go into Shenley Fields Cottage Homes with my brother and sister because my father had died and mother had to go into a sanatorium. I was 6 years old at the time. Mother was very ill and had to have her lungs drained. She was in Little Bromwich Open Air Hospital for 12 months, came out for a few weeks, became ill again and then had to go back for another 12 months (2 years altogether). I remember going to the Homes hospital with all the other kids to have our weekly opening medicine. On arrival at the homes we had to have a bath and our hair washed. At the time I thought I was being drowned as there was so much water and the bath was so deep. I played up the second time we had to go back so mother did the bathing before we went and promised me we wouldn't have to bath on arrival (the health visitor must have had a word with the matron). When we first got there we went into a big house to get sorted out. I believe at that time the homes were designed to take the children in various age groups as the three of us were separated into different houses.

I wouldn't call the House-mother, mother. I must have been very loyal to my own mom or very naughty. When I finally went home, I had steel rimmed glasses with a black patch on one of the lenses and a plaster on my chin. I had wriggled myself to the end of the table

63

and fell off it. I was put on the table in a room on my own for not calling the house-mother, mother. I used to wet my cot so I had a slap every morning for that. I didn't wet my cot on purpose as I wet the bed until the age of 12 years.

I can remember having soggy bread and milk for breakfast. All the children sat round a white scrubbed top table on benches. The house-mother sat at a separate table by a fire. If it was your birthday, you had the privilege of sitting with her.

Oh dear! Happy days, times change and I have got a lot of compassion for orphaned children. I work in a hospital for mentally handicapped now and find it very rewarding. Incidentally my brother didn't want to go home to his own mother, he liked it so much at Shenley Fields Homes. One person I vividly remember and would love to hear from again was a girl about 16 years old called Margaret. She was brought up in the homes and when us three arrived she took to us and reported back to our mother, how we were getting on. Mother took to her and she very often used to say, if she could afford it she would have had Margaret at our home to live with us, but she never did. I would love to know what became of Margaret.

Mrs Violet Hawkins nee Wiltshire
Home 4
1926 – 1932

I was 3 years old when my mother died leaving our father and 3 sisters plus 1 brother. One sister died of scarlet fever in Little Bromwich Hospital aged 7 years. The older sister was 10, the other sister was nearly 5. Our dear brother was just 11 months old and was taken care of and lived with dad's sister until being called up for service in the Second World War. Our paternal grandmother came to live with my two sisters and myself and our father for a few years until she died in 1926. Sadly our father died also in July 1926, so being orphaned, my auntie who already had the care of our brother applied to the assistance board for 10/- a week in order to keep our little family together at her home along with her own daughter and our brother. The request was refused, she was told to send us to the Blue Coat School or some other place of care. We went to Summer Hill Homes near Newtown and from there the selectors sent us to Shenley Fields Homes where we stayed until the latter end of 1932. We have many memories of life there. Mr Hal Cohen and his brother were quite young men who lived at the Lodge with their parents who were the superintendant and matron. My sister was the daily help there. Our home was called Jasmine and was cottage number 4. The school in the drive was my pride and joy and I got to be Head Girl there. I remember Frank Matthews and his brothers and definitely Mr Newman the Head Gardener and also Mr Meredith the Caretaker who lived in the little house still standing in Woodcock Lane. Each day was very much the same as were the weeks, but now and again something different would occur, to break the monotony, such as Spring arriving when the winter clothes, kilts, blouses and blues (knickers) had to be washed then stored away, cotton dresses taking their places. Also visits to the Town Hall to sing in the Choir. Best of all was getting ready for camp at Llandudno.

This cold spell we are in now, reminded me of the time in and around the 1930s when lots of the children of Homes 3, 4, and 5 used to make slides on the icy playgrounds during the winter days. In less than half an hour of fun on them, along would come one or two of the workmen to put sawdust on telling us how dangerous it was. Not to be outdone however as soon as the men had gone we deliberately made another slide exactly parallel with the first one. Of course history repeated itself, once again the sawdust was brought, the scolding given and as soon as the men went we did the same thing over again, ending only when we were called in for our meals, by one of the older girls chanting "All up Home 4, come in at the side door." The boot and shoe lockers were just inside that door with about twenty-four pairs of footwear in little lockers. Many are the times I have had to clean them all before school, informing the Housemother when the task was done only to see quite a few pairs of them thrust on the floor by her, with the remark "Have you forgotten the heels. You will do them every day for a week until they are perfect." The other task I liked even less, was when it was my turn to clean all the cutlery again before afternoon school commenced, so there was a race against time as the school bell rang at one thirty leaving just half an hour from the ending of the mid-day meal to polishing the spoons and forks and having to place them all separately spaced over the big wooden table in the wash-house and again waiting for the Housemother to inspect them, before I could put them away.

One of my rewards whilst in the wash-house was to help myself to a carrot or swede from the big vegetable box in there. Of course it had to be hidden so what better place than just inside the elasticated knicker leg of my blues. I still love raw veg. There were many funny incidents in the dormitories. There were two domitories in each home, with twelve beds in each room. One evening whilst one of the girls, named Vesta was saying her prayers there was such a scuffle caused by a bat flying down the chimney and settling on her hair. She screamed uncontrolably, until the House-mother came with her scissors and cut the offending bat out enabling it to fly out of the quickly opened window. Needless to say there was not much sleep that night in case the bat returned. Church on Sundays was always good, for one thing we could choose who we sat by so girl friends could sit together for a while. The boys all sat on one side of the hall, girls on the other side, but there were many little sly glances passing between the sexes as we picked out our favourites. Mr Cohen the Master who always played the church organ at these times, usually told us all about any eventful bits of news or happenings that might affect us, and once called out all the names of boys who he said had been stealing apples off the trees in the orchard. They all had to stand in front of us to shame them and their pocket money was stopped. Every Sunday two of the older girls had to stay away from church to prepare and cook the dinner. When it was my turn once, the gas temperature in the oven seemed very low indeed. I could see the joint of lamb would never be cooked in time, so I quickly took it to the next home where the girls let me put it in their oven. Of course it had to be done in secret so when I heard them coming back up the drive from church, I had to make a quick dash next door to get the joint. I was a bit too quick and fell up the scullery steps with the tin, the meat rolling out and down the steps into the yard and the fat immediately turning to dripping on the cold bricks. Quickly recovering the joint and returning it to its rightful oven I had to eliminate the greasy mess from the steps and yard with lots of hot water. It was while swishing the last bucketful that the House-mother came round the corner and got the lot over her feet. Of course I got a real telling off for bothering with the cleaning of the yard before doing what I was supposed to do first. She never did find out about the joint and none of us came to any harm.

At Easter-time we were allowed one whole egg and could choose to have it at breakfast or teatime. It was usually the latter everyone chose in order to make the treat last. One girl was chosen to cook the eggs but knowing an egg usually takes 3 minutes and having 16 eggs to cook she multiplied the two figures together and boiled them for 48 minutes. Imagine the effect when we all had an egg like a golf ball to everyones dismay. No pocket money for her that week either.

Now and again we had deputations come to visit the homes, probably from the Council or Education authority. On these occasions our House-mother had the task of preparing lots and lots of salmon sandwiches which had to be taken to the Lodge ready for the visitors tea. The crusts were all cut off and the sandwiches cut diagonally across twice and put on dozens of doylied plates. The remaining crusts were given to us children at teatime instead of the usual slices of bread. Of course we looked on this as a real treat especially if we were lucky enough to find any with a mite of salmon on.

Camping holidays were great fun. A week by the sea. Llandudno and Southsea were the places I went to while at the Shenley Homes. The boys who played in the band always had two weeks and used to play every day on the promenade. A number of us were given wooden collecting boxes and hopefully tried to fill them by politely asking the visitors or residents to spare a penny. The boxes were numbered and when emptied, whoever had colected most that day had double pocket money. I was lucky one of these times, which meant an extra sixpence. Our camping quarters were in a large school, empty owing to vacation time. Two homes shared each classroom and at night we slept on our blankets on the floor. It was all great fun. We used to go to the sand hills and slide down them, with the Master shouting out "Mind the barbed wire".

Schooldays were great. We were given every opportunity to progress. The sporting facilities were second to none and never lacked supporters. Hockey on Saturday afternoon was most welcome even though it meant lots of bruises on our legs. Swimming was also looked forward to but I remember the first time I went on what they called the 'sling', a thick knotted rope on a sort of pulley that went along on a rail high up over the pool for the whole length of the baths. The loop of the rope went around your waist and you were literally pulled along by the teacher walking down the sides of the pool, holding a connecting piece of rope. You were instructed to do the arm and leg movements of breast stroke whilst in the water. It was during this very first time whilst on this contraption that the rope decided to break and down I went coughing and spluttering until rescued by one of the hardy swimmers. It didn't put me off at all in fact I soon learned to swim and have loved it ever since and still go now and again.

Mr Lock our school head teacher took charge of the dramatic teamand put on stage lots of really good plays, mostly Shakespearian. We used to take part in lots of competitions from the school going to Central Hall, Town Hall, Digbeth Institute and the Midland Institute and did win quite a few shields and trophies.

During my days in Home 4, the large dayroom as it was called then, was given over to some artists from the College of Art, who painted the end walls with a picture from a nursery rhyme story. The end product was a very bright, colourful scene of Jack and Jill complete with bucket, water and even the tumble down the hill. It brightened the room up considerably. Each home had a different scene. Once a month the older children of fourteen upwards were taken by coach to a social evening at Harborne where we used to dance. Our dresses were made by ourselves in the sewing room by the Lodge. We were allowed to choose material and styled them ourselves. How proud we felt at actually being able to wear our masterpieces and show off to the boys. These trips didn't last very long though. Perhaps the expence became too great a burden for the orphanage to bear.

Bonfire night took place on what was the bottom field, the fire being lit by the

29. The Shenley heart throb, a real Jack-the-Lad. Note the short trousers which had to be worn till the boys went to work. Photograph loaned by Violet Hawkins.

caretaker. There were fireworks too with lots of oohs and aahs as they soared up into the sky, but everything was orderly and controlled and thoroughly enjoyed.

Christmas was very nice, lots of jelly, fruit, sweets, crackers, mince pies and a xmas cake. There was always entertainment brought in from outside, plus our own plays that were put on. Everyone enjoyed those times.

I used to love reading in bed until the light outside failed. We were not allowed to have lights on in the dormitories after time allowed for us getting into bed, so I had a brilliant idea one night. I obtained a small stub of candle which I lit and fixed on the windowsill at the back of my bed which gave off such a lovely light for reading. A lovely light is more than the right description for it, as it set the curtain on fire causing quite a bit of hurried activity on my part in smothering the fire and cutting off a strip of the damaged curtain and re-sewing a seam up the side next day. Because of the many folds in each curtain and the fact that they were very rarely drawn, the incident went undetected.

We were all so very well looked after when we lived in the Shenley Fields Cottage Homes. We were shielded from the pitfalls of life until able to take our place in the outside world. Although there was plenty of routine work to be done each and every day there was always something we could enjoy among ourselves. Our dress attire was really individual and smart. We had blouses and gym tunics in the winter, then pretty summer

CITY OF BIRMINGHAM
EDUCATION COMMITTEE

SCHOLAR'S LEAVING CERTIFICATE

THIS IS TO CERTIFY

that

Violet Wiltshire

has attended the

Shenley Fields

School

for __2__ years, __6__ months

and is legally exempt from attendance at an Elementary School having reached the age of 14 years, as defined by Section 138 of the Education Act, 1921.

Standard completed __VIII__   Punctuality __Excellent__

Percentage of Attendance __Ex__.   Conduct __Exemplary__.

General Remarks

A very intelligent, hardworking girl.
Member of Junior Red Cross, Dramatic Team
Senior Choir, Netball Team, Band of Mercy.
Needlework excellent

A.B.Lock, Head Teacher.

Chief Education Officer.

May 16th 1930.
Date.

30. School leaving certificate loaned by Mrs Violet Hawkins nee Wiltshire.

dresses in the warmer season. It gave us a sense of pride. There was no spitefulness. We all played and helped each other more often than not so there were plenty of friends around. Thats one thing thats lacking today, personal possessions mean more to people than friends.

It was on looking back, you realised your early teens had gone without being able to embark on an individual career of your own choice. I was 17 years old when I was put into domestic service on release from Shenley. One very good thing that came out of my domestic employment, first as a very happy nanny to two dear girls whom I still have contact with, but while still employed there during twelve years, I met my future husband who called at the house one day to check and repair the central heating system. It must have been love at first sight. We have been happily married now for 45 years with a wonderful family of 2 lovely daughters and great sons in law plus 3 grandsons whom we love dearly.

Mr Peter Henrick
Home 7 Lilac View
1960 – 1963

I came into care with my sister when our mother became ill and had to spend some time in hospital. First of all we went to Erdington Cottage Homes. We were in The Lodge. Mrs Beard was the house-mother. I had my 6th birthday there.

When we moved to Shenley Cottage Homes our father visited us and had us home for week-ends. The name of the house-mother at Lilac View during my time was Mrs Kelly. She and her husband and daughter were the only staff who lived in. The other ladies, who

31. Two small trophies awarded to Peter Henrick for sporting achievements.

lived in the locality would attend the home on a daily basis and were known as aunties. Two ladies in particular I can remember are Auntie Osborne and Aunty Turner. They were engaged in cooking duties, housework and also supervising the children when they were having a bath. They were both very warm and kind hearted people who really cared for us. Mrs Osborne's husband used to collect her from work every evening with their pet poodle called Dinky.

I don't remember being particularly happy or sad while living at Lilac View but there was a time when I tried to run away and climbed through the upstairs window of the sluice room. I fell breaking my arm. I had to stay at sick bay at the far end of the Drive for a few days. We had to go to sick bay every Monday night to have our head checked for lice, also for our innoculations. During the day time all the children from Lilac View had to play outside even if it rained. We used to go into the shed or wash house to get warm and keep dry. I played football most of the time. I played for hours on my own, using the hockey nets for goal posts. There was a large wooden pavilion on the playing fields at the end of the Drive. It was used to hold the sports equipment that was used by Ilmington School. The Homes had their own football team but I was to young to join it.

If we were naughty we had to stand under the stairs in our pyjamas with our hands on our heads until we were told we could go back to bed. It was often freezing cold and we were glad to get back to bed.

There was no television for the children but there was a wireless that was on the shelf in the dining room, and was played during meal times. Mrs Kelly's daughter used to play her records for us in the playroom. Mr and Mrs Kelly had a television in their own sitting room and occasionally would allow us to watch it. I remember seeing Tonto and Juke Box Jury. As a special treat I was allowed to watch the 1962 cup match on the television. During the night I used to get out of bed and lie on the floor to listen to the television through the floor boards. Our bedroom was just above the Kelly's sitting room. Sometimes Mr or Mrs Kelly would hear a noise and come up to see who was out of bed. When they got there of course we were all in bed again. When they asked who had been out of bed no one owned up so often the wrong boy got punished.

There was a Superintendant on the Drive called Mr Griffin. He was a rather portly gentleman with spectacles and I can always remember that any of the older lads in particular who indulged in serious misdemeanours were always frog marched to see him. I can also remember Mr Kelly administering "Justice" to some of the older lads. This would involve taking them into the bathroom and from the sounds emanating from that quarter, giving them a good hiding.

On Saturdays we were allowed out of the home, on our own, without supervision. I spent the time playing football on my own. Some children went to the local shops etc.

The Round Table organized day trips for us. We also went on holiday every year to Exmouth. Every week-end we went to the Weoley Castle Cinema down Barnes Hill. Occasionally we went to Selly Oak and Harborne Picture House.

Mr and Mrs Kelly were very religious. I can remember them singing hymns in the dining room.

There was a school or nursery next door to Lilac View which I did not attend. If I remember correctly the youngsters attending this school were much younger than I was. I was 7 or 8 when I went to Shenley Fields Homes. I and my sister attended Woodcock Hill Junior School in Farwood Road. This was the school most of the youngsters in Lilac View attended.

There was an Assembly Hall on the Drive. This was used for teenage dances etc. I also went there to watch film shows.

Our clothing was collected from the clothing stores. This was a room over the top of the workshop at the end of the Drive by the water tower. We had to climb a steep flight of iron stairs to get up there. You were only measured for your coat and shoes.

We went to church in the local church. I think it was St Gabriells. I don't remember the vicar's name but he was very keen on photography and would call at some of the homes and take photos of some of the youngsters. I still have photographs he took of me whilst I was in the Home.

On Christmas Day each child would get a pillow case full of toys, books, sweets etc and I seem to recall that you also had a birthday party of sorts each year.

In the playroom every child had their own drawer to keep their toys in. I had a train set. I can still remember some of the children's names. There was Thrupps Alston Reed and Frank Grieves.

Every June there was a sports day. Erdington Homes sent some of their children over to compete with our children. It was a very exciting day. We competed for the Shaftmoor Challenge Cup. I still have two of the trophies I won at the sports. They were displayed on the shelf in the dining room and made me very proud.

I often think of Shenley Fields Homes and do not regret having spent some time there. I think it does affect you in later life in quite a number of ways.

Mrs Frances Hornby nee Bowes
1947 – 1980

Shenley, that seems a very long time ago since I started in 1947. That wasn't the beginning of my life though. I lived with my parents who had 9 children on a farm. We lived a very happy and carefree life. Times were not easy for my parents, they worked hard and expected us to do likewise. We were sent to school and Sunday school. I hated school and the first thumping I got was for not being able to spell properly, my first teacher being hard and cruel, particularly to a younger sister who was left-handed.

I struggled through junior and secondary school but my first real appreciation of learning started in the technical school where as a teenager I respected greatly the headmistress and I left with reasonable references but very few qualifications. I went into nursing for a short while at the age of 17, working in a mental hospital in Belfast, which was absolutely terrifying, so I decided I'd probably be better employed by joining up. I was fortunate enough to get into the W. A. F. where I stayed for 4 years and I enjoyed every minute of that time. There weren't any particular responsibilities, mainly as a staff driver driving through England, Wales and Northern Ireland. I was quite aware of the tremendous responsibilities of the people I was driving around. It was at the end of the war that I met my first husband Jack. He was home on holiday from the Palestine police. I had known his family all my life. We married in 1947 and he returned to Palestine where I was due to meet up with him later on when I had got my papers together.

In time I needed a job and a base to work from so I came to Birmingham. I secured a position as Assistant Housemother in the Shenley Fields Cottage Homes and worked at number 9 which was a boys home catering for 27 boys under the care of a Housemother and Housefather. The Housefather went out to work. On the day I arrived I was wearing a nice blue suit and I was made welcome by the Housemother who showed me to my room and told me to start duty at one o'clock that afternoon. I arrived in the dining room and she said "What do you hope to do in that outfit, get an overall on" and I was promptly sent to the linen room to get an overall.

It was the responsibility of the Housemother and myself to cook, wash, clean, repair clothes, and care for 27 boys. The Housemother had total control but I felt like a fish out of water. I realised that without her presence there I could be eaten for supper! I wondered how on earth I could cope with these boys whose ages ranged from 5 – 16 years. I am naturally friendly and affectionate but any kind of warmth was totally unacceptable to the people in charge of that establishment. I used to feel that the little boys would like to sit on your knee or come and have a cuddle but I was always told "you mustn't do that". The home was run under a very strict routine. The children were awakened at 7.00 a.m. and we had to inspect every bed. Normally there were 12 children who wet their beds and they had to take their sheets, bring them down to the bathroom, swill them in cold water and put them out on the line. I used to find this rather horrifying on a cold winters morning and I'm quite sure that when the beds were made up in the evening, quite often the sheets had not been aired, because there was no heating within the home.

Breakfast was at 8.00 a.m. and the boys sat at long wooden tables and had a meal of milk and bread followed by bread dipped in lard and fried and hot cocoa. The staff sat down to cereal, bacon, egg, sausauge and tomatoes followed by toast and marmalade. The table being beautifully laid with nice china. It was totally foreign to me to behave in this fashion and I never enjoyed a meal in that house. After breakfast the boys went upstairs and had to clean their dormitories and then get ready for school and at 9. 00am they promptly went out to school.

Some went to school on the Drive and others went to the local school in the district. At 12.30 everyone rushed in for dinner and the same routine where the boys all sat down to ordinary potato, veg and gravy and maybe rice pudding while the staff sat down at their beautifully laid table to soup and meat and 2 veg and usually apple tart and custard, egg custard and fresh fruit, cheese and biscuits and coffee. The boys rushed of to school again and in the evening when they arrived home to tea each had his clothes to change and put on working clothes. Some had to have a bath before tea, others got bathed after tea. Heads had to be scrutinised each day for lice and any undue blemishes brought to the notice of the Housemother. The evening was spent mainly with boys playing on the yard. Everybody was in bed by 8 o'clock — there wasn't much noise upstairs. I was usually glad to go to my room while the Houseparents and their 2 children enjoyed their family life in their own sitting room.

I was fortunate to get a transfer to another home on the Drive where a Miss Saunders, a kind and loving lady was based. The home did tend to smell of urine but it was warm and cosy and the children were loved. This was a period of very hard work. The children were obviously very disturbed — I had no training in trying to understand their needs and I knew nothing about them. I had no idea who their parents were and if I was lucky maybe someone would talk about them. The Drive in those days was run by a Mr Blakey who was the superintendent and Miss Parry-Jones who was the matron. Miss Parry-Jones was a most formidable lady, big and stern and I recall one day when she came into number 3 where I was working and one little boy rather cheekily asked a question and she gave him such a slap in the face for not having manners that I felt I wanted to give her a kick, but I am sure on the whole she had a very big responsibility to do a good job.

The committee used to come round every so often. I never thought much about them and I didn't understand what their role was. If they came on a wet day and we were sitting round the fire with the children they told us to get these children out in the fresh air and take them for a walk, which to me was absolutely ridiculous when everyone was nice and cosy. The Housemother ensured that when the weather was nice we took the children down to the park and made sure that they had plenty of fresh air. The childrens homes were set in a kind of parkland. The Drive was beautifully maintained and kept to a high standard by the Head Gardener Mr Frank Collins, who was greatly loved and respected. He had 2 assistants John Kettle and Mr Cooper and they worked very hard indeed. It was a joy at all times to walk up the Drive and see the profusion of flowers and flora. They kept us supplied with fresh vegetables and if one was lucky enough to live in a home where this was shared equally with the children, this was a great assett. The gardener was a great source of information and brought in the news to all the homes.

In those days there was a nursery school and also a junior school with its own headmistress. The assembly hall was used on Sundays for church services which were usually taken by the superintendent. I can't recall a vicar coming to take the services. We all marched there and marched back. I can't remember the swimming baths being in use, they were there but I don't think they were safe. The playing fields were greatly used for games, boys played football and girls played netball, but that wasn't so popular in my early days.

Eventually when my husband came home from Palestine, I went to live in Erdington and worked for a period at Highcroft Hall Hospital before transferring to Erdington Cottage Homes where I worked in cottage number 5 with a very cruel housemother. She lived on the premises and she really was monach of all she surveyed and spent most of her time sitting in front of the dining room fire knitting while her 2 staff, Miss Logan and myself came in. The home was so run to time , in that we had to get the children up and make their beds and everything had to be done on the double. I eventually told her I couldn't put up with such cruelty and said I would report her to the superintendent. She pleaded with me not to do so and vowed that she would change her ways but I gave in my notice and left. The week after I left one of the senior boys kicked her and eventually she left which was a relief to know.

My husband Jack knew my feelings about the treatment of children in care at that time and I often said "surely I could do better than this if I was on my own" and one day he saw an advert in the paper and brought it to my notice, knowing I would be interested. The result being that we applied for the post at Shenley Fields Childrens Homes. We wrote to Mr and Mrs Ron Griffin who were now the superintendent and matron and were lucky to get the post. We commenced as Houseparents at the Shenley Fields Childrens Home in January 1950 in House number 4. There were 23 children, Jack was housefather in the capacity that he went out and did his own job during the day and then he was involved during the evening as a father would. I had 1 assistant housemother, who was my sister who had come to join us, and another assistant house housemother who had been brought up in the Childrens Homes. She was a middle aged lady and very deaf. I had been warned that she might cause some trouble because the previous houseparents had left as a result of her problems.

Number 4 was a lovely large Victorian house. Downstairs there was a large sitting room, playroom, dining room, kitchen and bathroom. This bathroom catered for the needs of everybody, children and staff alike. The children slept in 2 dormitories, one for the boys and one for the girls. At night a pail was kept on the landing so that if anybody needed to go to the toilet this was used. My first night there when I went up to empty the pail at 11 pm I was rather horrified to find it very red It looked as though somebody had had a haemorrhage, so I expressed this feeling of horror to Miss Archer. She thought quietly for a while and then she said "My dear, don't worry, we had beetroot for tea" — and so my education began.

I realised we had taken on a tremendous responsibility. Here we were with 23 children. We were all housed together in a large house. There was no central heating and the water ran down the walls.

Quite a number of the children were so very disturbed that they wet the bed, so every morning it was a nightmare ensuring that all the children were made comfortable and all the sheets were put in soak. We had no washing machine or washing facilities, and horror of horror, nearly all the mattresses were full of maggots. The only drying facility was a clothes rack in the kitchen, so that one prayed each morning for a dry day which didn't always happen. We had to have fires on in the dining room, playroom and the sitting room, with clothes racks around them, trying to ensure that the children never had anything that was damp. Our day started at 6.30 a.m. and Miss Archer, Phyllis and myself worked solidly until 11.30 p.m. until we had cleaned every mattress. We never reported our worries to anyone, not thinking that this was something that had to be done. We just felt we couldn't live with the muck and the dirt. I must say the older girls helped as well.

Although we had 23 children they were quite easy to manage and although they had their disturbances there weren't the severe problems found later when things became more open and children were allowed to speak for themselves. The older children enjoyed the work situation with the adults and the younger children having a certain degree of mothering and comfort. The children were going out to school, though at that time it was still an institutional environment. There were a lot of children in the various homes we didn't really have a lot of contact with. We were so busy trying to get our own house in order. At the end of each day the staff sat on the landing because a number of the children had great difficulty in settling down. There were certain problems that we weren't really able to understand. A lot of sexual activities had been going on with the little ones in the bedrooms and we found it very necessary to be on hand on the landing. We sat there every evening and did the darning and sewing until everyone had gone to sleep. Eventually we were able to discuss our worries with the Superintendent and arrangements were made for training programmes. These we found invaluable in helping us to come to terms with our own frustrations. Gradually a training programme began and houseparents meetings were arranged one morning every week. A lot of people found these a bit irksome because we had so very much to do and we were so poorly staffed. Nevertheless it was an extremely good time. Short training courses were arranged for houseparents who were sent away and these breaks gave one a new outlook.

When I first came to Shenley each house had a number. Number 1 to number 11. Gradually they were all given a name. I think most people had a hand in the names because of the shrubs or the flowers that grew outside. The first big excitement was our preparation for the Coronation. Each house was given a period in history that they were to follow, to make a pageant on the big day. We in Jasmine House were to represent Henry V111 and his wives. Everyone was busy for weeks making costumes. Some of the staff and especially Miss Archer who was a great needlewoman, took great pride in getting everybody dressed up. From the oldest to the youngest we all proudly marched along the district on the big day. It was a feast day to be remembered. I forgot to mention we still had Mr Brookes who lived above the workshops at the top of the Drive and up until 1950 he had made all the boys clothing and did all the repair work. Repairs were sent up to him in the morning with the boot repairs and these were done on the premises.

The same happened at the other side of the Drive where Mrs Brookes, not a relation of Mr Brookes, was in charge of the sewing room. There again all the repairs were done, sheets edged and pillow cases made. The children's blouses and dresses for the summer were all made there. Each month we had a condemning session when each housemother took her bundle of clothes down to the sewing room to be condemned. Sometimes it was necessary to send these things back because they hadn't been darned enough. This could be a bit frustrating when one was constantly darning. We were so glad when the day came that the woollen socks went out and we had a mixture of fibres that weren't so difficult to look after or wash.

It was quite a time before we were able to go out and do our own shopping. The stores were sent in from the Drive, we requisitioned in on a Monday or Tuesday for our butter and provisions and if there was something you forgot to put on the order you were very reluctant to go and say so because Mr Brookes was a very busy man and quite often we just went and bought rather than ask him. The only money we dealt with really was pocket money. This was sent up every week and we had to return the form every week to the administrative officer in charge of financial affairs on the Drive. He was always very careful. I'm sure we caused him many headaches with our calculations. The day came when we had Petty Cash and we could go out to purchase certain needs from the shop providing we brought a bill. This was mostly for the benifit of the staff than the children, little extras that it was felt the staff should be able to have.

The event of the year which everybody looked forward to was Sports Day. This was when the Housefathers came into their own. They trained the children. My husband was always delighted when he had good athletes that he could train for Sports Day and took great delight in their achievements. Thank goodness he did, because life was so busy keeping body and soul together and keeping everything shipshape. It was a good thing to have somebody who was interested in the leisure time interests of the children. Indoors we did handicrafts and got the children interested in knitting and doing things for themselves. like encouraging them to write letters home and make contact with their families. It seemed so much better when home visits were allowed and we got to know something about the children and something about their families. The families always enjoyed coming to the Sports Day. There was always the odd horror story. One particular day I looked out onto the field and saw a mother piecing her childs ears with an ordinary darning needle without any sterilising facilities. I recall the first organised holiday for the children. They were taken from Birmingham on a special train to Gosport in Hampshire where we had two absolutely gorgeous sunny weeks and the children had a wonderful time. The accommodation wasn't perfect, we had taken straw paliases and slept on the floor of a school. We were fed in the school canteen but were free to spend our days with the children, going to the seaside. They obviously benefitted a great deal from this as we later learned that it was the first year that Pinewood, or the sick bay as it was still known, did not have an epidemic of colds and flu in the wintertime. It was generally agreed that this had been of such benefit to the children that an annual holiday would be arranged, and thereafter the children were taken on holiday every year. Not an easy task preparing so many children and ensuring they had enough bedding and clothing to last a fortnight.

Christmas was another big event. It was always a nightmare as we did not have enough money to provide each child with a present. People did generously give old toys, but some of these were really pretty useless, so we had to hope for the best and make do and try and provide a good day of entertainment and plenty to eat and drink.

We spent 4 years at Jasmine — happy years on the whole. We all had to work desparately hard but there was a programme of remodernisation taking place — numbers in the homes were being reduced so that there were better facilities for bathing the children, keeping them comfortable, and better conditions for the staff. By this time extra staff were being employed to do the cooking and the cleaning so that the childcare staff had more time to spend with the children. When we moved from Jasmine to Elmdene we took on a short-stay home which was really quite different. The children weren't there long enough for one to be able to make any strong relationships. Quite often 2 or 3 children would arrive in the night and the following morning they would have gone off to court. A lot of departmental changes were taking place and this wasn't an easy time for children coming in and out of care. They did tend to be pushed about from pillar to post. The NSPCC seemed to be picking up children at night and the following morning the department was finding that some legal problem had been committed and the children shouldn't have come into care at all. It wasn't unusual to admitt 12 or 14 children in the week and discharge just as many and it was during this period that one learned of the problems for so many children who were in danger.

During that period the Drive was in a general state of flux. The Houseparents were moving into smaller family group homes in the community and long term children were going with them. As a result those tending to stay on the Drive were the more disturbed children. The department were setting up Assessment Centres within the City. We moved from Elmdene to The Trees and our unit became the Reception/Assessment Centre for Adolescent Girls and Junior Boys up to the age of 16. Previously the Home catered for 20–27 children but now catered for the needs of 17 children who came on a short term basis for assessment. They were on Fit Person Orders or On Remand from the Juvenile Court. This was an extremely demanding and rewarding task. Most of the children were very disturbed, not quite knowing what was going to happen to them. By and large they settled down very well until a decision was made as to whether they should remain in care or return to their own homes.

We were having increasing numbers of coloured children who were finding life in Birmingham very frustrating. I was fortunate most of my time at The Trees to have a very high calibre of staff who were extremely interested in the children and in the job that they were doing although the hours were very long. They had been cut to 48 hours a week. Most people were available if ever they were needed and the staff comradeship made the job so much easier. My first deputy was Ms Margaret Wood who was an excellent colleague. Others that I would like to recall are Bryn Williams, John Dunnion and Linda and one must not forget the continuity of the day staff who came in from their own homes and families to bring a bit of normality with them. Mrs Brown, Mrs Caswell, Sylvia, Mrs Hyness, Mrs Rainbow, Maureen, Jenny, Pauline and many others.

We organised holidays and camping trips for the children taking them to the log cabin or the Bluebell Woods as often as possible and also to the theatre. One eventful weekend the senior staff stayed on duty at The Trees to allow the other staff to go off for a long weekend to Spain. We worked together and we all worked for the benefit of the children. We tried to be outward looking rather than let the frustration get to us. We did not have nightstaff in those days, so it was not unusual to be wakened in the middle of the night 2 or 3 nights a week. Sometimes it was because somebody had absconded and had been missing for a day or two and had been picked up by the police and we would have to get up and go off and bring them back. It wasn't unusual in the summertime to be called to the other side of the county.

I recall one morning we had planned to take a family to Wales to a foster home and were to be off early in the morning. When I woke at 7.00 am, I went to get the children and they were all gone. The whole family had disappeared. The oldest girl was 14 and the youngest child about 3. Eventually we had a call from the police that they had been picked up on the Bristol Road by a lorry driver who had seen that they were in some sort of trouble, picked them up and chatted to them and dropped them at the next police station. They were Birmingham children who didn't want to leave the city but their circumstances were such that it was important that they left Birmingham for their own safety.

There were quite a number of influential visitors who came to Shenley. The first that I recall was the Mayor. It was usually the very pleasant task of the Trees to entertain and provide lunch for these visitors. Edwina Currie who was then a Councillor in Birmingham used to visit on accasion when she was in office. Quite a lass she was then too. I recall the Shaftsmoor Cup and the Morney Cup and remember the occasions on the field when the Shaftsmoor Cup Races were run. I think the Morney Cup was used for the best handicrafts exhibition. We usually had a very exciting evening in the Assembly Hall when Miss Morney and her parents came along. Each house had a display of their handicrafts. We did win some prizes on occasions but I don't think we ever won the cup.

Church Services in Shenley finished around 1950/1 and the children started going out to St Gabriels or the local Catholic church. The children ceased to wear uniforms after the Griffins came. I don't think I've mentioned much about the Griffins. They deserve many tributes paid to them. They were very good superintendent and matron and their interest in the childrens welfare was very obvious. I have never called them, night or day, when they didn't make themselves available. They were very strict about the general care and welfare of the children. Medicals and progress reports were kept to a very high standard, fire drills were maintained and staff training was a high priority with them. They did not believe in corporal punishment although on one or two occasions when this was demanded by a houseparent, Mr Griffin carried this out to the letter of the law but it wasn't a chore that he relished. The Shenley uniform ceased to exist after the Griffins were appointed. As soon as stocks ran out they were replaced by normal dress. The children who were going out to local schools wore a school uniform. The children were dressed as normal as possible so as not to make them stand out as Homes Children.

I think the happiest time at Shenley was when the Committee decided that Mr Bowes and I would be given a house on the Drive and we were allowed to live in Bythorn which was number 16. This was a particular treat and for the first time we had a place of our own.

Naturally, having been in institutional life for so long we were happy to share this facility and found that children who were very disturbed and who were living in The Trees found respite if they were sent to us in the evening and could sit and chat until they were calm enough to return. We loved to do the garden and have time to ourselves to relax ready for the following day.

There was a lot of unhappiness amongst the children, they had their own troubles and traumas and we had to take the rough with the smooth.

At times I wondered if I had any very strong feelings left but the saddest day of my life was the day I left Shenley. I cried for 3 solid days. Fortunately my sister was living close by in Droitwich and we were able to stay there until we got our papers finalised but I felt a great deal of heartache for many months.

Instinctively one realised that Shenley Drive was nearing the end of its days. There was no office at the entrance to the Drive, we didn't have a gardener any more, all the old systems had gradually been whittled away, the sewing rooms closed, vandalism was becoming pretty rife, our lovely Assembly Hall had been broken into and a lot of equipment had been destroyed and the lovely playing fields were gradually being destroyed. Staff were feeling pretty demoralised and it was probably a good time to leave.

28 years of my life had been spent at Shenley and I recall with great affection Miss Archer who was a dear friend to the children. A kind and loving lady. She had been brought up in the Childrens Homes and was a great credit despite her deformities and disabilities, her training and caring was very obvious. During these 28 years I had the very good fortune to meet a number of children who had been brought up in the Homes, for whom life had been very hard and very tough. I had to bear in mind the great difficulties that were experienced by staff, many of whom did a very good job with very little support and without any training, with long hours, very poor pay and very little gratitude. I never did feel that Mr and Mrs Griffin were given the credit they deserved for the hard work they did for the staff and children. It was they who commenced a programme of training for the staff. Mr Griffin was very keen to get better conditions of service and salaries and reduce the working hours. They gave generously of their time and worked hard and loyally for the Childrens Department.

We were very fortunate in our professional colleagues. Educational Psychologist Mrs Priestmoor, Educational Psychologist Tony Pennington and Psychiatrist Dr Reece we found so helpful. Dr Reece was available whenever we were in need of his guidance. His treatment of the children was so wise and sensible.

Without Mr Bowes I could not have stayed so long or so happily at Shenley. He gave so much of his time to the care of the children and was greatly loved by everybody. He enjoyed taking the boys for games and they loved him to play football and the girls used to love him to sit with them during Top of the Pops when he showed a keen interest in their activities and their antics.

Mr Bowes came home from work one day with a twinkle in his eye and was telling me that he and his colleagues had been walking through part of Birmingham and met a group of West Indian girls, and out of the crowd a very tall West Indian girl ran out to him and threw her arms around him and said "Oh it's lovely to see you again" much to the amazement of his colleagues.

I left in 1980 and I continued to work for Social Services Department, mainly with the elderly in the community. This I found a most rewarding task. I met my new husband and remarried in 1987. I had told him a lot about Shenley and was really looking forward to taking him along there, showing him where I had spent probably the happiest years of my life. On arrival at the gate, as we turned in, I couldn't believe my eyes. I thought, where has it gone? There were no sign of The Trees. I got out of the car and walked down the Drive to Bythorn and there was nothing but utter desolation. I felt robbed completely of a lifetime. I can't explain the feeling I had returning there and seeing those lovely houses completely demolished.

I'm sure that many children have suffered hard times there and yet a lot of children have happy memories, but their roots have completely gone. I still keep in touch with some of the children that I knew when I first started so many years ago, and its been interesting to watch their progress over the years. Quite recently as a result of this book that is being discussed I had the good fortune to receive communication from folks that I am so happy to know are still around. One tends to remember the happy events rather than sad ones but I feel a great deal has been lost to the community and many children who need residential care. Shenley Drive was a therapeutic place with its beautiful grounds and trees and I could go and sit by a bush or tree and dream and work off the frustrations that occurred. In these days of enlightenment I do feel that it could be put to better use. It went through such a wonderful time and there was so much laughter and happiness and fun there. I can see groups of children tumbling in the back door from school shouting "What's for tea". I can see children walking out of the front door with their parents and some disappearing when they didn't want to see them.

That's about it, the old Shenley — 11 homes and a sick bay, each home consisting of one housemother, one assistant housemother and some were lucky if they had a housefather. The Houseparents probably having half a day off when a relief housemother came in. The tailor who was responsible for the clothing, the sewing room seamstress who was responsible for the dresses, the storeman who was responsible for giving out provisions, and the superintendent and matron in charge of administration. The olden days were certainly pretty tough. A lot of the children came from very impoverished homes. In 1970 I had an elderly gentleman of 65 come to visit me. He had been brought up in the Homes as an illegitimate boy. As a result of that visit he met up with quite a number of children who had been on Shenley Drive in his young days. The Birmingham Evening Mail did an article about his visit. Things had been much worse in their day and the older boys had ruled the younger ones, but they had no hard feelings. They had all learned a trade and gone out in the world as useful citizens and become gardeners or cabinet makers and suchlike. The ladies had gone into service and did quite well for themselves before marrying and raising a family.

The gentleman I mentioned, Mr Bright, died just a few years ago.

When I first went into Shenley life was pretty hard for staff and children. Gradually the department that dealt with childrens homes in the Education Department changed and the Childrens Department was set up in 1948. Things began to improve, better facilities for children with not quite so much overcrowding. The staffing conditions didn't improve very much and a way this wasn't a bad thing because people tended to live more as a family and got to know each other better, it was a bit more intimate. With time and progress and better working conditions, staff would go away on training courses, and we were more aware that children did belong to their parents.

The 28 years fled, we went through a period of good companionships, the staff used to put on plays, we had staff dances, the children used to have their own discos. There was a great era of happiness and freedom and community living. Most of the houses had their own pets. I remember our dog Sally and cat Seamus at Jasmine. We went through a series of dogs when we were at Elmdene but unfortunately when they were puppies in the Childrens Homes they were teased so much that as they got older they did tend to occasionally misbehave and bite the children and we had to have one or two of them put to sleep.

Gradually we got Shauna, who was a great favourite and lived to the ripe old age of 15. When I retired she came to Ireland with me and is now buried in a grave under the Weeping Willow, where she loved to sit.

32. The Shenley girls on holiday at Llandudno taken around 1922. Photo loaned by Mrs J Jones nee Cooper.

Mrs J Jones nee Cooper
1916 – 1926

My sister and I were sent to Shenley when we were very young in 1916. I was 4 years old and my sister 8 years. I can remember seeing the searchlights going across the sky.

I thought you might like to see the enclosed photograph. It was taken at Llandudno, Happy Valley in about 1922. We spent a weeks holiday there. We were put up in Trinity Road School. We took our own blankets and toilet things. The boys went the first week and girls went the second week. The boys in the band stayed both weeks. They played on the promenade and the money we collected gave us a bit of pocket money.

I found the photograph in the little wooden box we brought from Shenley when we left. The box was made by the boys who worked in the carpenters shop. As it was around 1926 when we left, lightweight cases were not available. Everyone who left the homes had one of these boxes to take whatever they needed for life in the outside world. The box measures 27½ ins in length, 16 inches across and 14 inches deep. It is coloured and varnished in brown. I still have mine today.

One memory I still have of Shenley is of the two big fields belonging to Shenley where every year we had a sports day in the summer. We raced against each other, we did Hop, Skip and Jump and throwing the javelin. Our prizes were always books.

At Christmes we made yards and yards of paper chains to hang on the walls.

On Christmas Day you should have seen our tea table laden with cakes, tarts and mince pies. Our mother was a marvellous cook. We might have been orphans but we were well dressed, well fed and well educated. In fact we were a lot better off than a good many children living in Birmingham at that time.

Life-long friendships were made. My sister and her friend who was also a Shenley girl, still visit each other and they are both 84 years old.

Mr Cohen, the Master must have been very fond of children. He would do his best to get what he could out of those who where responsible for the Homes.

Mr George Judson
House-father at Ryedale
Home 10
1951 – 1955

It was with great interest that I read the article about Shenley Fields Homes. My wife and I were houseparents at Ryedale Home 10 for 3½ years. We left in April 1955 when my late wife became ill.

When we first went to Shenley I had the job of trying to keep the boys cycles in good order. The emphasis should be on the trying, for the horrid things the children did to the bicycles kept me very busy. Some of them were beyond my ability to repair and I had to take them to the Square. (Weoley Castle's round square) There was a very good cycle shop there who were not always very willing to help us because Birmingham authority took a long time to pay. The older children, mostly boys used to go out with the Cyclist Touring Club on Sundays and it was my job to see they had decent bikes. There would be about half a dozen each week. One boy saw a bicycle in Harborne and perloined it. Then he saw a better one and changed it. Then he saw a new one and swopped again. When he got his 'treasure' home to Shenley, the other boys saw it and decided it was too good, so they took it to bits and put the various bits on other bicycles. This all happened just as we were starting. Then we had lots of visits from the police. George had to go to a remand home for a month. Unfortunately (or was it) we had been asked to take over George, as he was not getting on well with his houseparents. We wandered if he would come back and say what a good time he had had at the remand home. However he did not, he came back and said "I'm not going back there anymore". Actually he turned out one of the best boys we ever had. My wife who was a wonderful story teller, would get him to do nearly anything for her.

We always gave the older boys extra priviledges especially things like cooking eggs for their supper. They were much better cooks than I was. They didn't have to be very good to beat me.

When they are bulldozing Shenley are they going to pull all the tree's down. I hope not, as they remind me of one rotten job I had to do on them. It was for the Coronation. I was told by the superintendant that one of the housefathers was afraid to go up the ladders to decorate the tree's on the Drive, so I had the lot to do. Those trees may look pretty but believe me they were absolutely smothered in Birmingham soot. No I didn't enjoy that job one bit.

For the Coronation every Home had to do themselves up as royalty. Our Home did Richard 1 (Lionheart). I made umpteen shields all painted with red crosses.

When my wife and I ran Ryedale there was a Superintendant and Matron called Mr and

Mrs Griffin. Not a long time after we left, each Home was running itself with help and advice from Mr and Mrs Griffin.

Another thing I remember from when I was on Shenley was each Home getting up a show. There was a competition. We won it once. My wife made up the story and I made much of the background scenery. We enjoyed doing that.

Most of our boys went to Ilmington School. Three or four boys went to special schools. There was a lady in charge of them. She had a very difficult job.

In Ryedale we had a full time Assistant Housemother called Elizabeth Hancox, and two part time assistant housemothers. In the mornings we had Clare Raggs who was astounded when she saw two Boxer dogs. She thought she was seeing double, blaming the night before. She made very heavy bread pudding which the boys loved. I called it ducksinker. In the afternoons we had a Mrs leighton, who was a brilliant pianist. There was also a cleaner called Mrs Donnelly, a very respectable woman.

We took the boys away for a holiday each year. The first year we went to Seaview in the Isle of Wight. We stayed in a chapel or rooms at the side of the chapel, sleeping on the floor. I went on ahead with two of the boys. One of them was good at cooking. He told me what to do. I was sure he had not put enough rice in the pudding for the rest of them so I added some more. It was solid. The boys loved it. His name was Lesley Fream. We were visited by the Childrens Officer. I can't remember his name. I have memories of Ralph Lloyd (nicknamed Gas) trying to roller skate. He had a large audience but he never knew. They had a good time watching him.

The second holiday was at Bideford. My groomsman who was headmaster at a Technical College there arranged it for us. We had a boy from another Home with us. He was always absconding and he even absconded from us. I don't think he was, running away just wandering off. He went in a boat on the River Torridge, which has a big tidal bore. We sat on a seat and pretended not to know him, but he came over to us. So did the indignant owner of the boat.

The third holiday was at a hotel called Rosalind in Hastings. The hotel belonged to my sister and her husband. We slept on the floor of course. By that time I had started work as a carpenter for the Birmingham Housing Management. The boys did a 'turn' in a cave with a band.

The Assembly Hall on the Drive was used for choir practice. A Mr Simmonds conducted the choir. I used to go in with them, singing bass and helping Mr Simmonds to control the children. A Mrs Hobbs who was Assistant Superintendant also came in. The hall was also used for a competition amongst the Homes, seeing who could put on the best show. We won that one year. There was a dance done to a dream. One boy named Charlie Mead went really mad in the dance. Mr Mallett told me how good he was, so I told Charlie and he became aware of it and was nowhere near as good in the proper show.

I enjoyed singing and my wife enjoyed telling stories. She used to include the children and me in her stories. That way she could get at their little weaknesses of character. I was never as good a bloke as she made me out to be.

We didn't make a lot of Christmas, but birthdays were very special. They sometimes had to be shared when two boys had a birthday in the same month. Just before birthdays was the only time we locked the pantry door. The older boys understood this.

On the Drive were ten main Homes and a small Home which had been an assistant matrons home, a school (in use), the clinic and the Assembly Hall. There was a little cottage on the main road outside, where the engineer or whatever he was, lived. I can't remember his name. There is someone else I should have mentioned, a cobbler. He had a club foot and was just mad on Aston Villa. I think the Superintendant had a say about what food you got but Mr Mallett was responsible for delivering it to the homes. He and his wife started at Shenley on the same day as my wife and I.

They were nice people. The children went to St Gabriells Church. The vicar was Mr Foster a rather diffident man who was a marvellous organist and a photographer.

We had been in two other homes. One at Newcastle-on-Tyne and one at Bournmouth. Shenley Fields Cottage Homes were much the best Homes for living conditions. We enjoyed our stay there.

Mrs Ivy Kelly nee Bagley
Home 1
1932

My sister and I were placed in care not knowing why. We left when I was 10 and my sister 12. We have had many a chat but we were both too young to remember much of our stay, only that we were well looked after. Discipline was strict, but we were never ill treated in any way. We were punished if we did anything wrong of course usually by being sent to bed.

33. Merriland Home 1 taken in 1989. After the children moved out of the home it was used by Social Services for the Elderly Services Team.

I remember going to the stores on the Drive where we were fitted out with dresses and underwear. I learnt to swim in the swimming baths at Shenley and remember winning a black porcelain doll. I don't remember any birthdays being celebrated, but we used to have the usual Christmas party. Not a lavish affair but we enjoyed ourselves.

As far as I remember there were six houses on either side of the Drive. Boys on one side and girls on the other. There was also the Lodge where the Master and Mistress lived and general administration was carried out. There were 2 bedrooms in each house, each accommodating about 12 girls. I do remember we had the story of Peter Pan in pictures round our room.

Looking back I suppose going on our holidays was my happiest memory. Going to the seaside was an event we looked forward to. Being met at the station by what I presume was the local brass band and being marched up to the school in Llandudno which was to be our home for the next week or so.

As regards how it affected our life, being so young we soon adapted to our new life and soon forgot why we were there or not having a 'real' mother and father.

We regretted leaving there and being fostered out. We did have a brother, but in those days boys were separated from the girls. I regret not knowing what happened to him. After being fostered out we never saw him again, he being 15 years old at the time. We presume he was fostered out too.

Mrs Wyn Kelly nee Ford
Housemother Elmdene, Rosemead and Tree's
1948 – 1953

It was in 1948 that I went to the Homes, just after the Childrens Department took over from the Poor Law.

As I had baby training, I was given the task of opening the first baby home. We had 24 babies under the age of 4 years and it was a real nightmare. We had to carry them up and down stone stairs. The walls in the dormitory were running with condensation and blankets on the cots were damp to the touch. It wasn't long before it was found to be unsuitable for young babies. From then on only one or two babies were admitted with older brothers or sisters and it became a more normal family atmosphere for the children.

The staff were very hard working in those days with 24 children in each home, a housemother and 2 other full time staff. We were responsible for all cooking, cleaning and day to day care of the children. We had a fully equiped sick bay on the drive. All food and clothing came from a central stores each week and the children attended local schools.

It was when Mr and Mrs Griffin became Matron and Superintendant that conditions changed for the better and the number of children started to drop to more normal family units. The children joined local scouts and guides and other groups and attended local Saturday matinee's at the cinema.

The surrounding area was mostly farms and open countryside, we could see right across Senneley's Park and only the odd car or horse passed the Homes going to Mr Strawbridge's farm.

The Assembly Hall was used to put on shows especially at Christmas Time with each home doing their own sketches. There was always plenty of presents and parties at Christmas and each child had a cake on their birthday. I still have many photographs and memories of Shenley Fields Cottage Homes.

Mrs Betty Keys nee Turner
1939 – 1945
Homes 5 – 1 – 11

I was sent to Shenley Fields Homes with my three sisters, Dorothy, Margaret and Jean. I did not go to school at Shenley. I went to Princethorpe Road Infants and Junior School and Ilmington Road Senior Girls School.

Some of the Housemothers I remember were Miss Andrews, Miss Downing and Miss Lawrence from Home 5 and Mrs Vale and Miss Longman from Home 1. We had our own swimming baths where I once swam 100 lengths and received 1 penny for my achievement. The swimming teacher was Mrs Tabbener.

We had a superintendant called Mr Blake. He lived at The Lodge which was right by the big gates where you came in to the Drive. There was a small hospital on the drive. I did not have to go into the hospital.

Our food came from a store room and was delivered to our house each week. The houses were very large. The toilets were outside but there was one upstairs for night time use.

The gardens were really lovely and there were huge playing fields.

All our dresses were made in the sewing room by the seamstresses.

Altogether there were about 12 homes, an office, The Lodge, sewing room, stores, hospital, church. swimming baths and the playing fields.

My sisters and I had a better life at Shenley than we would have had if we had stayed at home. We had a good training for the future.

Mr Edward Kilroy
1953 – 1966
Melplash and Rosemead
Home 8 and 5

I don't really know the absolute facts about why we were put in care but my guess is that our mother felt that she could not cope with four young children without the full support of our father. He was an Irish immigrant who was accustomed to a "go look for work" attitude that often took him away from Birmingham for weeks at a time. I don't believe that during his periods of absence our mother would have an income.

I don't remember life at Shenley Fields being at all bad. There were times when we might have had a rough time but what family anywhere didn't experience those occurrences. We were treated by and large firmly but fairly. One must remember that

34. This photograph of the Kilroy family was taken at Lewis's Store in Birmingham.

society was much more discipline orientated in those times and in fact we were subjected to the slipper or cane at school far more than was the case at the Homes.

I remember the Griffins well. Mr Griffin was a man seldom seen but held in a certain reverence but certainly not fear. Mrs Griffin, a warm and caring woman for whom we had a great regard. Personally I remember her with great fondness.

We were always well clothed and fed. I cannot remember ever wanting for more than I had. I was lucky in having an older sister, Mary, who was particularly motherly, so again I personally didn't go short of affection till after she left. At that time I was an adolescent in the charge of Mr and Mrs Jones at Rosemead. They were not very fond of me and the last couple of years there were quite unpleasant as a result.

One significant thing I recall is that the cameraderie between the children was very good. One thing we never did was tell tales on one another.

We had Mrs Shirley then Mrs Cullen as House Mothers in Melplash and Mrs Jones in Rosemead. One member of staff I remember most clearly was Aunt Molly Harcourt from my early days in Melplash. She lived with her husband the reservoir keeper in a cottage near the reservoir itself. I can't remember exactly how many manual staff we had but there was at least one part time aunty morning and evening.

We went to school at Our Lady and St Rose of Lima in Gregory Avenue and Archbishop Masterson Boys School. We also went to Our Lady and St Rose Church.

We went to Exmouth most years for our holidays and I remember going to Prestatyn when I was much younger.

The stores were delivered from a central store next to the office. It was delivered by the older boys.

One of the most outstanding features about The Drive was the lovely gardens.

Mr Derek Lee
Home 2 Suncrest
1961 – 1967

I was in care on Shenley Fields Drive from 1961 to 1967. My Home was called Suncrest. The house-mothers name was Miss Longman. I went to Woodcock Hill Junior School and then to Ilmington Road Boys School.

In our house there was an assistant house mother whose name was Miss Kendrick known to the children as Aunty Maureen. She later died of cancer. I was very fond of her. There were also two part time ladies named Mrs Bickley and Mrs Cooke. They both did cleaning and cooking and also looked after the children.

The swimming baths on the Drive had closed before I got there but there was a big sports field with an old pavilion and swings and roundabouts. We had an annual sports competition against Erdington Cottage Homes, when awards and presents were given. There was a lovely shield and cup presented to the overall house winners.

We had many holidays when I was on the Drive. We went to places such as Exmouth, Aberavon, Prestatyn and Filey. We usually stayed in schools.

The superintendant and matron were Mr and Mrs Griffin. They had a son and daughter. At the end of the Drive was a small hospital known as Sick Bay. We went there if we had anything infectious such as measles.

Suncrest was a very large house with dormitary bedrooms. The toilets were inside the house by the time I went there but they had been outside across the yard before. Downstairs was a large bathroom with 2 very deep baths in. Upstairs there was a bathroom and toilet for staff use but children were allowed to use it during the night. The housemother had her own sitting room and we had a playroom where we kept our toys. There was a dining room where we had 4 meals every day. During the evening the older children were allowed into Miss Longmans sitting room to play with the best toys which she looked after for us.

Every Sunday we went to church in Shenley Lane for the morning service and sometimes we went to the evening service also. The Vicar's name was Mr Tyson and he would make visits to the homes on his motor bike to see the children.

There were many important visitors like The Lord Mayor of Birmingham, Television and Radio celebrities and many more.

The Assembly Hall had ceased being used for a church and was now used for film shows, youth clubs and New Year's Eve dances.

Life on the Drive was pleasant but strict. Some children would run away only to be collected from a police station somewhere and brought back. All the children from different houses and of different ages would mix together. I think there was a bit of discrimination from children outside the homes towards the children in the Homes. The effect it had on my life was to respect people and behave with good manners and kindness. I also think most of the children from the Drive would make good later in life because they had so much to prove and would work harder. The main thing I learnt was independance and to stand on my own two feet.

There are many happy memories of the Drive. I think most of the long hot summers in the beautiful grounds with sports fields, orchards and lovely gardens. We celebrated bonfire night with a huge bonfire on the fields and a lovely firework display. It was the best bonfire in the district.

Christmas was a very special time as all the children would be invited to many works parties for example Lucas, Girling, Birds Custard, the G.P.O. and many church halls. At Christmastime our housemother Miss Longman would decorate the house up with a large tree and holly and tinsel all up the side of the stairs. It looked lovely and many people came to see it. Christmas Eve all the children would go to the Bristol A.B.C. Cinema in a fleet of coaches for the morning. During the afternoon we would have a film show in the Assembly Hall, usually cartoons. Christmas Day we would each have a large sack of toys and books, which would be opened after breakfast. We would then go off to church. When we returned home there was a beautiful christmas dinner waiting for us.

Birthdays were always celebrated but on a smaller scale. We would have a cake and a present and the other children would sing to us.

I remember there being several childrens homes, about 15 plus a sick bay, stores, reception, superintendants house, the old wooden school which had long been closed and the brick school which had become a nursery school for the children in the homes and from the Weoley Castle Estate. It had a memorial stone outside to remember the staff and children killed in the First World War. Miss Longman used to look after the little garden round it.

A very memorable occasion for all of us was when our housemother, Miss Longman was awarded the B.E.M. for services to children. We had a party and it was a very happy time.

Mrs Lucy Lee nee Shackle
Early 1920's

Lucy was orphaned soon after the end of the 1914/1918 war, while still very young. Her father was killed and buried in France and her mother died soon afterwards. Lucy came to Shenley Fields Cottage Homes with her brother. She had problems with her hearing through having measles. Lucy went into Home 2 and her brother went into Home 7. He was older than her and was not so happy in Shenley Fields Homes. Lucy was

35 and 36. Shenley girls on holiday. Photographs loaned by Mrs Lucy Lee.

too young to remember her parents. Her brother was trained in the Homes to be a tailor and followed in the trade when he left care.

Many people are still remembered by Lucy including Mrs Tabbener the swimming teacher and Miss Castle who worked in the office. A house was built at the end of the Drive, opposite Home 11 for Miss Parry-Jones who was the matron. She also remembers Doris and Elsie Oakley who came with her from Summerhill into Home 2 and also Rose Gamble who was her friend. The boys played cricket on the 3rd field and the Shenley Fields Band marched up and down the drive practicing their music. The band also played at Lodge Hill Cemetary for the Remembrance Day Service. Mr Cohen always took a group of children to the cemetary for the service.

Among her happiest memories are the holidays spent at Wallasey, Llandudno, Southsea and Towyn in Wales. The boys went away first then the girls. They usually slept on the floor in school halls. The boys went to Westwood Ho instead of Towyn. One girl had bad epileptic fits while on holiday.

The children of Shenley Fields had nice clothes. They were made in the homes by the sewing ladies who worked in an upstairs sewing room. The children had a choice of materials and Lucy remembers the beautiful velvet for their blouses which were worn with gym slips. One dress sticks in her memory. It was a very pretty blue colour. Some of the older girls in Shenley were allowed to work in the dress making rooms.

The meals were basic but adequate. Every morning there was porridge for breakfast and they always had fish on Fridays.

The homes had gas lamps for lighting. There was a gas lamp on the landing but not in the bedrooms. A bucket was left on the landing which was used as a toilet during the night. The toilets were out in the yard. Eventually an extension was built at the end of the house which included a toilet. It was really for the use of the house mother but in Lucy's home the housemother allowed the girls to use it during the night only.

The grocery came to each house in large wicker baskets every week. None of the children went to the local shops except for their sweets. Everything was made in the Homes, even their shoes.

The girls would stay in the homes until their 16th birthday. They helped look after the younger children with their house mother. Later the leaving age was reduced to 14 and an assistant house mother was appointed to help the house mother look after up to 24 children. The house had to be cleaned right through and spotless for when the govenors came to do their round of inspection.

Lucy moved about quite a lot when she left care. Her first job after leaving the Royal Deaf School was in Manchester where she trained for 3 years as a dressmaker. She then returned to Shenley Fields Homes and helped with the children. She slept at the infirmary. Birmingham Council found her a job at Handsworth and she travelled there every day on the bus but the wages were low and didn't cover the charge for her lodgings and her bus fare. She then got a job at Worlds Wear in Bearwood. She worked on the cutting machine. The next job was in a factory by the Bull Ring but she only stayed there one day.

The foster mother at Home 10 was friendly with Lucy and got her a job at the Red Lion at Bewdley which lasted for a year. She then worked at Sutton Coldfield for one week. The matron at Shenley Fields was Miss Parry-Jones. She gave Lucy a job at number 11 which was the probation home or pro home as it was called. This was the home the children went to first when entering Shenley Fields before being moved to permanent places in the Homes. Little boys under the age of 5 always went to a girls home first.

Mrs Parry-Jones wrote to Mrs Hunt who ran an agency in London. Lucy moved to a private school to do all the sewing. She enjoyed the work but didn't like the Master and Mistress there. Then Lucy moved to Copthorne in Sussex. Here she heard the first sirens of war. She made the curtains and the blackouts for the school and for the school in Ilfracombe Devon, where the children were evacuated to. She returned to Birmingham just as the bombs were dropping on the town.

Eventually Lucy went to Devon and married a Devon man. She settled in Devon and still lives there today.

Memories of Shenley Fields Cottage Homes are very happy. The food was good and the clothes were lovely. The Shenley children had much nicer clothes than the children at the Royal Deaf School where Lucy spent a lot of her childhood.

Mr Ernest Little
1936 – 1940
Home 9

I was moved to Shenley Fields Homes from the Summerhill Homes. My two brothers and I had been put in Summerhill when we lost both of our parents. The houseparents in my home were Mr and Mrs Aldridge but after they left we had Mr and Mrs Parry. I have happy memories of Shenley. There was quite a good family atmosphere and people were very kind to me. We had good sports facilities and a swimming baths. Miss Tabbener taught swimming and Mr Dunn was sports master. Mr Grainger was the band master. I played solo tenor horn. The homes had their own hospital. I had to go in there once. The sister in charge was Sister Wheeler. We had our jobs to do in the home but we also had leisure time. I went to Weoley Castle and Harborne Picture Houses. We also went to pantomimes at Christmas time. During the summer we went on holiday to either Westward Ho or North Wales. When war broke out we were evacuated. First I went to Malvern Open Air School. Later a boy named Billy Paterson and myself stayed with a family named Rogers at Mountain Ash. I came back to Shenley about 1942. I was then sent to Vauxhall Working Boys Home. They were happy days at Shenley and I still remember many of the childrens names who were in care with me.

Mrs Long nee Hughes
Home 4
1928 – 1932

I was in care at Shenley Fields Homes, with my sister because our dear mother was very ill and unable to look after us herself. Though she was ill she never forgot us and regularly visited us and sent parcels. We were luckier than most of the other children who had no one at all outside of the Homes. On the whole I was not unhappy. It wasn't so free as in later years but we were trusted which was nice. I stayed there until I was 16 and then went to a hostel called Riversdale on the corner of Bristol Road and Pebble Mill Road. It is still there now. I believe it is part of the BBC studios.

The Master and Matron were Mr and Mrs Cohen; the grandest and kindest couple I have ever known. Mrs Cohen made sure children in care were made to feel no different and were treated no different from other children. She helped make beautiful dresses for the girls to attend the Evening Class Socials at Harborne School.

There were about 24 children in each cottage. A typical day was up about 6.30 a.m. The older children did little jobs, I lit the fires. We made our own beds and helped the little children make theirs. School was at nine o'clock till 4.30 on Monday Wednesday Thursday and Friday and 4 o'clock on Tuesdays. The food was good although we all had our moans now and again. A typical days menu was Breakfast; Porridge or bread and milk, bread and butter and cocoa. Dinner varied each day also the sweet but on Sundays we always had jam or treacle tart. Tea consisted of bread and butter and jam with cocoa. We only drank tea on Tuesdays and Sundays and had cake. We always had lovely boiled bacon on Sundays for breakfast. We only had one egg a year and that was on Easter Sunday.

I went to school on the Drive. I loved school and cried buckets when I left. We then went to night school at Station Road Harborne where we had lessons in Cookery, Dramatics and Book-keeping. There was a school social once a month. This is when Mrs Cohen had those lovely party dresses made for us so we wouldn't feel out of place in our gym slips.

Every Christmas we had parties and pantomimes and each year we had 8 days holiday at Llandudno. We stayed in a school and slept on palliasses filled with straw. We thought this was very grand and great fun. The Homes band took over the band-stand and we took collection boxes round. The money collected went towards our outings. We always said we came from Shenley Fields School if anyone asked us. I left school at 14 and worked in the sewing room but I still can't master a treadle sewing machine.

We went to church on the Drive except on special occasions such as Easter and Christmas. I was confirmed at St Lawrence Church in Northfield. We also went to Bartley Green Church. There was a funny moment when we were being confirmed. One of the girls who was not used to the long dresses, fell up the steps as she walked to the alter.

I remember the reservoir being opened at Bartley Green by the then Prince of Wales, later King Edward 8th. We were at the Happy Valley in Llandudno when Amy Johnson flew over the Channel.

Shenley children went in for all the educational events at the Town Hall, Midlands Institute and the Queens Hall such as elocution, reading and singing and won quite a few of the events.

Miss Longman B. E. M.
Suncrest Home 2
1938 – 1967

Miss Longman is in her eighty's and lives quite local to the site which was home to her for so many years. She started work at Shenley Fields Cottage Homes when she was quite a young woman in 1938, and has gained the respect and admiration of many hundreds of people over the years.

When Miss Longman started work at Shenley Fields Cottage Homes there was a Superintendant called Mr Blakey and a Matron called Miss Parry-Jones. Mr Blakey was at Marston Green Homes before they closed. Marston Green Homes were self sufficent and had their own farm etc. They closed around 1935. Mr Blakey took over from Mr and Mrs Cohen. Mrs Blakey did not become matron as she had her own hairdressing business in Selly Oak called Fredericks with her daughters. The Marston Green Homes became Chelmsley Hospital.

Miss Longman worked at Suncrest Home 2 for 2 years then became relief officer for 4 years living in Merriland Home 1. She then went back to Suncrest as Housemother. She had very fixed idea's about how her home should be run and resisted any changes she did not think would benifit the children in her care. Many housemothers changed the pantry into an office but she kept hers as a pantry right up till she left in 1967. Another change she disapproved of was making the large bedrooms into small cubicles. One room was made into 2 cubicles but the children didn't like it and insisted the door be left wide open.

The only books that were kept then were a diet book and a register. There was a small amount of house-keeping money which had to be accounted for every week. Only basic background information on each child was available to housemothers. Every week the children had pocket money. Miss Longman kept very careful records of how much was paid to each child. Every child was encouraged to save each week and Miss Longman kept a little book recording how much they had saved. When they had enough they transfered an amount to the Municipal Bank. One or two housemothers were dishonest about this.

Mr and Mrs Griffin became Superintendant and Matron and brought about a lot of changes. One of the changes was the naming of the Homes. Mr and Mrs Griffin held meetings every week with the house-parents and at one of these meetings it was suggested they all think of a name for their individual Homes. Besides giving the Homes names they also renumbered all of the buildings on the complex. The Lodge where Mr and Mrs Griffin lived became known as Shangi-la or number 1. Home 2 changed into Suncrest, 4 Shenley Fields Drive. Suncrest housed approximately 16 children though during the war this number increased to 24. At first there was only the Housemother and an assistant Housemother to look after all of the children. The older girls in the Home were trained to help look after the younger children. Later more staff such as cleaners were employed.

During the war the children were evacuated to Wales. Some of them came home earlier because they reached the age of 14 years. One of these was Audrey who became a junior member of staff. When she was older she became an Assistant Housemother. Audrey left Shenley to work for a Doctor but came back to work for Miss Longman who also had two 18 year old assistants working for her. They were both around 6 foot tall. One girl came from Norway but her father was taken ill and she went back home. The other girl's parents resented her leaving home and kept sending for her and she eventually gave in and returned home.

Evenings in Suncrest were spent knitting sewing and making peg rugs in the play room. After the little ones went to bed they listened to stories being told on the radio by the Man in Black.

When a child had a birthday they had a small birthday party with some friends invited from school. A cake was baked and decorated but the special treat was going to the shop and choosing one cake for each child. Shop cakes were very special and the children thought it was a marvellous treat and often talk about it even now.

37. The view from the office to the gardens situated between homes 9 and 8. Photo loaned by Miss Longman.

The childrens clothing came from the sewing room. Every summer, girls were measured for 2 new dresses and they were made up for them by the sewing ladies.

The first holiday Miss Longman remembers was when all the Homes went by special train from Snowhill Station to Gosport. They stayed in a school. It was great fun. The last holiday she went on was to Filey in Yorkshire near her home.

After the war, food was very strictly rationed and each home was allocated their exact rations required. Some housemothers cheated on the children by selling some of the rations for children's use, such as bacon, sausage etc, to workman who were working on the Drive.

When the children left school some were found jobs and stayed at the Homes before being moved out to working boys' or girls' hostels or boarded out with families. Every child had to divide wages up between clothing, pocket money and bus fares. This was compulsory. Many went to work at Peyton Peppers a jewellers in Vyse Street. Mr Gerald Lamb who was one of the Directors paid fares to the children to make up for the low wages. Mr Lamb belonged to a motoring club They adopted and sponsored Suncrest.

Mr Griffin once asked Miss Longman to meet The Home Secretary Mr Shooter-Eade. He said he was counting on her to talk The Home Secretary into giving £16000 for Home improvements. She must have said the right thing because they got the money.

There were many activities on Shenley Drive. On the sports fields was an excellent sports pavilion. This was eventually burnt down by vandals in the 1970's. The Homes had their own swimming baths and Miss Tabbaner taught the children to swim and put on wonderful swimming gala's. Miss Stallard gave dancing lessons and put on shows. She also taught netball and matches were played against Erdington Homes. The Assembly Hall was used by many children. The bottom end of the hall used to be used as a church and had lovely stained glass windows while the top half of the hall had a stage where plays and shows were performed. It was also used for film shows and dances.

In the early days the Homes had no heating or electricity. Miss Longman used to light the gas mantle in the bathroom one hour before bath time to take the chill off the room, which was very sparce with a quarry tiled floor and 2 very deep baths. The children were bathed according to age, the youngest being bathed first. When they were bathed and ready for bed, Miss Longman would fill a large copper hot water bottle with boiling water and rub it round every bed just before the child got into it. By next morning ice had formed along the edge of the blanket from the childs breath. The staff used to do upstairs domestic work in coat, hat and gloves because of the cold. Condensation ran down the walls and down the concrete stairs.

All food came from the stores on the Drive. Mr Smith was the stores officer and boot repairer. Boots were inspected every Monday morning.

The Homes had their own Brass Band. They played at various parades including the Armistice Day Parade on Weoley Castle Square and at Lodge Hill Cemetary.

There was a strong competition element on the Drive with cups and trophies to be won. One of these was the Shaftmoor Cup for sporting achievements and the other was the Mornay Cup for handicrafts.

The infimary at the far end of the Drive became known as Pinewood. Originally it was used for sick and infectious children to be kept in isolation and was called The Hospital or Sick Bay. On the whole there was not a lot of infection among the children of Shenley Fields and they were quite healthy. There was a serious epidemic of measles and chicken pox recorded in the old records of 1908. The infirmary later changed to a home for

38. The view from between homes 8 and 9 looking towards the office. Photo loaned by Miss Longman.

mentally and physically disabled children. Every week the Doctor came to Pinewood and children who had just come into care in any of the Homes had to be brought to see the doctor for an F.F.I. inspection (free from infection medical check). They were checked from head to toe and any medical problems were dealt with. These problems often included Atheletes Feet Scabies and Head Lice.

Every Christmas Eve the Police Choir came to Shenley Fields Drive and everyone joined in a carol service usually standing outside the office. The Drive was trimmed with lights especially near the main entrance. The children stood with torches and joined in singing the carols. While they were singing Father Christmas would arrive in a decorated sleigh loaded with presents. The children hurried back to their Homes and Father Christmas came round to each Home leaving a sack full of toys that had been donated by the public and by staff themselves. Mr Griffin used to take photographs of the entrance hall to Suncrest as it was always one of the best decorated halls on the Drive. He also had a Christmas Card made using a photograph of Shenley Fields Cottage Homes.

Only the two baby Homes were mixed sexes apart that is for Elmdene which was called the Probation Home. This was the only Home on the Drive which could be divided in to two sections by a door in the middle of the long corridor. It also had two bathrooms.

Miss Longmans memory for names and faces is still incredibly sharp. These are some of the many people she mentions; Mrs Alma (Hortence) Niblett who worked in the office

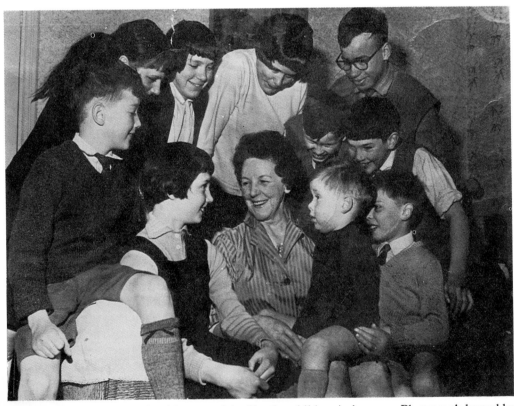

39. Miss Longman B. E. M. with some of the Shenley children in her care. Photograph loaned by Mrs Stallard -Boulter.

as did Sheila Waldron. Mr Taylor's place in the office was taken by Mr Head (Ted). The staff collected their wages from the office every week. Mr Stirk used to be office clerk and store keeper. His wife worked in The Tree's with Mrs Bowes. Mr and Mrs Aldridge worked at the Tree's with Mr and Mrs Parry. Mr Brooks was the tailor and Mr Collins was the gardener. Mr and Mrs Saddler were the houseparents at Merriland. Mr Saddler was an ambulance driver. Mr and Mrs Jones were houseparents in Rosemead. Mrs Bowes worked in Rosemead with Miss Saunders. Her name then was Miss Johnson. She joined the army. Mr and Mrs Mallett were excellent people who ran Melplash. Mr and Mrs Parry ran the Tree's before Mr and Mrs Bowes took over. Mrs Mountford, Mrs Shepherd and Mr and Mrs Stevenson were all houseparents of Ryedale. Mr and Mrs Smith were from Lilac View. Mr and Mrs Thompson were houseparents at Elmdene. They had 2 children. They emigrated to South Africa in the early 1970's.

Mr Grainger was very popular with the boys as he was the Band Master. He was very strict and tamed many a potential delinquent. The band played at childrens concerts on the Town Hall. Mr and Mrs O'Donnal ran the Home next door. They bought a Rolls Royce to take the children out. Mr O'Donnal held gymnastic classes in the Assembly Hall. Mr Pemberton and Mr Kettle looked after the big boilers and Mr Cooper used to empty the outside toilets on Fridays. Mr Fish worked on the Drive as maintenance man. His wife ran one of the scatter homes at Millmead Road.

I believe Miss Longman could write a book on her own. She has so many memories. Every Mothers Day, birthday and Christmas her flat is filled with flowers cards and good wishes sent from many of her 'children' who still remember 'Mom'. How she earned her British Empire Medal for services to children is very obvious. She loved every child in her care and helped them grow into respectable and responsible citizens.

Mr Anthony Lovatt
Home 10 Ryedale
Jan 1974 – Oct 1978

I was quite saddened to hear that Shenley Fields Homes which had featured in a significant part of my childhood, had finally met its demise.

I was in Ryedale between January 1974 and October 1978 under the supervision of firstly Mr and Mrs Stevenson and then later under Mr and Mrs Hopwood. I have a fair memory of the homes and even now I have contact with a person at college who also attended the homes. If my memory serves me well, your home Elmdene was opposite Ryedale and one name that springs to mind who I believe was in Elmdene is Terry Farrelly. There are many more associated with The Tree's, Lilac View, Melplash, Cherry Garth and those whose name I seem to have forgotten. Please excuse me if I appear to be drifting along, but you can't wipe out those times. However I think my most vivid memory of 'The Drive' must be of course Jubilee Day when the whole drive was rigged out in red, white and blue. and sports events were held behind Pinewood. To me that showed the true spirit of the Homes. Occasionally we would grumble between houses but it was never malicious and there was a great sense of loyalty to each other. I was 14 then and I am 26 now. There was a time when I took my daughter along to where her daddy once lived. When you are young you don't appreciate what the staff are trying to do for you but I for one will miss old Shenley.

Mrs Jean Marston nee Drover
1944 – 45
Home 11 (Pro Home)

My sister and I were very interested in your article in the Evening Mail newspaper about Shenley Fields Cottage Homes. In 1944 my younger sister and I had to go into Shenley Fields Homes. Our beloved young mother became ill and had to go into hospital. There was no one to take care of us at home.

We were then Jean and Pearl Drover, Pearl was six years old and I was twelve. We were put into Home 11 or Pro Home as it was called. The Housemother was Miss Groves.

My goodness we had some interesting times. Some happy, some sad, some jolly also some frightening times. The war was on so of course things were very difficult at times but we children were well looked after and though sweets and chocolate were rationed we always had our little share out on Saturday morning and there always seemed enough to eat.

I attended Ilmington Road School and being a 'bright' child was soon put into the top class. My teachers name was Miss Callow. I remember those big girls wanting to befriend me but oh how terrible I smelt. The middle officer in Home 11 used to spray us all over our hair with Sassafras. The smell was terrible and so embarrassing for a twelve year old girl. They asked what disease I had to be sprayed like that for. I had to explain that I was sprayed with this pongy stuff to prevent me catching head lice from them and taking it back to the other children. Once they knew this we all soon became friends.

An interesting couple of sisters were Winifred and Margaret Chillingworth. Margaret was only sixteen when I went to Shenley and she was the Junior Officer in our Home. Winifred worked in the little hospital belonging to the Homes right at the bottom of the Drive. I think those two sisters had been looked after in the Homes for years and then when they came of age jobs were found for them. They were both very friendly. There were two sisters in our home, June and Gladys Byford. Their mother was ill too. I wonder where they are now.

I learnt to swim while in Shenley Homes. They had their own swimming baths. They also had their own Sunday School and I won first prize for writing an essay on 'Drink'. Ha Ha What did I know about the evils of drink. Our lovely mother never recovered. She was a young widow left with us children and worked herself into an early grave. She died aged 39 years. The only drink she enjoyed was the occasional stout.

Shenley Homes also had their own shoemaker/repairer and as the war was on we all had to line up one day to be measured for clogs. I had bright red ones.

We all had little bunk beds for safety in case of bombs dropping. One day workmen arrived and dismantled all the bunks as the war was almost over and it was decided to give each child a separate single bed again. It was lovely. All the toilets were outside. Only the Officers had an indoor toilet.

We only drank tea on Sundays at tea time the rest of the time we had cocoa to drink. How we looked forward to our big jugs of tea on Sundays. I must tell you about the Weoley Castle Cinema. Every Saturday afternoon the balcony was given over to the Shenley Homes Children. Flash Gordon-Buster Crabb, he was my screen hero at the time. The Flash Gordon serial was screened after the main film every Saturday afternoon. I remember that our Saturday lunch every Saturday was sausage soup with big lumps of sausage floating in the gravy.

All the children from the Homes would then assemble outside the Superintendants office and off we would all go in an orderly fashion marching down to the cinema. When we returned later during the afternoon, Miss Groves used to let just us four big girls get into the kitchen and make the little cakes for Sunday tea. Two cakes allowed per child. We loved those Saturday afternoons as it was like being at home.

Big children or should I say older children at the age of 12 years were allowed 4 old pennies pocket money per week paid every Saturday morning by the Superintendant. He carried the money around in a big blue cloth bag. We felt very important. The trouble was though, it was 2d each to get into the cinema and I had to pay for my sister who was too young to get pocket money. How I begrudged paying her entrance fee. What an unfair rule. Surely they could have paid for her.

I was in the Home when V. E, and V. J. day was celebrated. What a happy time. The officers took us bigger children down into the village and we all joined in the dancing and merrymaking.

I have many memories of Shenley Fields but I will never forget the shock and trauma of suddenly being taken from our lovely mother and a poor but loving happy home and being left in those strange large buildings. We went to Erdington Homes first then transfered to Shenley Homes after one month. I learnt a lot from this and swore that my own children would never ever go through this. The first day we arrived at Home 11 at Shenley my sister and I were given numbers. She was number 6 and I was number 9. Miss Grove was a kind person but strict and aloof. I felt so lonely, but of course this is how things were done in those days.

You may be interested to know that our top class at Ilmington Road School did Housewifery and most Thursdays (Miss Groves day off) the whole class used to go to Home 11 for the day and 'take over'. We all split up to do jobs with our teacher in charge. We cleaned the place, made the beds, chopped wood for the next days fires, cooked the midday meal, usually stew and a steamed pudding to be ready for when the children came in at twelve midday. We prepared tea and usually made rock cakes or sponges. The officers used to vacate the premises that day. My friends used to ask me to show them my bed and how things went on etc.

I remember knocking the sitting room door at eight oclock one school day morning and when Miss Grove called me in I said I would not be emptying the chamber pots anymore as it was an unpleasant job. She told me to get up there and do my job as everyone had to pull together. Well I went upstairs and looked again, and then I went down and knocked again at the sitting room door and trembling I told her that my mom would not like me to be doing this unpleasant job. She told me to get out of her sight but I never did that job again.

Every month a van called to each home bringing the months supply of sweets. We celebrated our birthdays with a huge home made cake decorated with chopped boiled sweets. People sent little gifts to the homes to be shared out. These were kept for Christmas and Birthdays.

There was a Home especially for tiny babies. I think it was Home 6. We loved to see those lovely little babies.

Besides Miss Grove the Housemother we had Miss Lawrence the Relief Housemother and Margaret Chillingworth who was Junior Officer. She was 16 years old. Her sister Winifred Chillingworth worked in the infirmary.

I returned home in September 1945 as my mother needed me to nurse her. She died six weeks afterwards.

99

Mr Frank Matthews
Home 9 and 11
1922 – 1930

During my research for this book I met a wonderful man called Mr Frank Matthews. He lived in the Shenley Homes between 1922 and 1930. He was a very small child and was given work to do in the garden as it was felt the open air job would benifit him. He really took to gardening and took great pride in his flower beds. When I went out to see him he spent about 2 hours talking about his life in care on Shenley Fields Drive. Like everyone else he told me of the very firm discipline. He felt it was very necessary and helped children develop themselves and have respect for others around them. This he feels is something that is sadly missing from the lives of youngsters today.

Frank came into care with his brothers when his father died and mother became to ill to look after them. He had 2 brothers in the homes, Lesley and Albert. An older brother was too old to stay at the homes and he lived at Aston. Frank was first taken to Summerfield Receiving Home in town then transferred to Oaklands which was just opposite Selly Oak Hospital. He was 9 years old when he first came into care going into Home 11 first then moving to Home 9. Mr and Mrs Squires were the Houseparents. Mr Squires worked in the office and Mrs Squires ran the home with the help of an assistant house mother, who lived at the Home and a cleaner who came in daily. Frank was not very keen on Mr and Mrs Squires. They went to the boys hostel at Vauxhall to work. Frank met up with them again when he left care when almost 15 years old to work for Mr E. C. Keay of Edgbaston for 2 years. While in the Homes Frank did most of the greenhouse work and spent hours planting asparagas beds by the Assembly Hall. This job made his fingers very sore. The Drive had many fruit tree's, apples, pears and plums. The orchard was at the back of the school and the Assembly Hall. There were also fruit tree's at the back of The Lodge by the greenhouses. Tomatoes and cucumbers were grown in the greenhouses. These were for the Housemothers not the children. There was a large potatoe patch by the hospital, that grew many tons of potatoes for use on the drive. He used a little machine to plant the seeds. The garden beds were done twice a year by Frank. Cabbages and peas were also grown. Each home had a small garden patch at the back of the house to grow their own selection of vegetables and flowers. There was an Assembly Hall on the drive. When there was a concert held there Mr Newman and Frank did beautiful flower arrangements using huge pots of plants out of the greenhouses. If any of the boys were caught scrumping any of the fruit they were punished. Mr Newman used to live by the Cock Inn at Bartley Green either in Clapgate or Jiggins Lane. Frank remembers pushing a wheelbarrow full of old cuttings and planting them in Mr Newmans garden for him. Mr Newman gave Frank a book about gardening when he left care. He still has that book and the references he was given when he started work. He considers himself one of the lucky ones being taught gardening as he feels it has given himself and others a great deal of pleasure. Frank remembers several people from his days on Shenley. Mr Kettle did the guttering along the drive for the water. Frank lodged with Mr Kettles nephew Jack before he got married.

Mr Meredith lived in the cottage on the Woodcock Lane side of the drive. He was the engineer. His daughter was killed while riding her bike. Mr Cooper and Mr Rose were also gardeners. He felt Mr Newman was not the nicest person but he had great respect for him. Frank was nicknamed Little Two Foot Nothing and Robin Red Breast by Mr Cooper and Mr Rose.

40. Mr Newman who tended the gardens and greenhouses in the 1920's and 30's. He taught many boys the rudiments of gardening and set many on the road to a life-long career in gardening. Photo loaned by Mr Frank Matthews.

Frank remembers the Cohens. Mr Cohen was the Superintendant. The whole family were very nice and caring.

One of Franks favourite people was Mr Henry Grainger, the band master. He conducted the band at Erdington as well as Shenley. He describes him as a very large man with a heart of gold. Frank played the E Flat Tenor Horn, not excellently but good enough to be in the group. Every year they went on holiday to Llandudno or Wallasey. They stayed at a school. He remembers the school at Llandudno best as it had wonderful borders of large white daisies in front of it. The boys slept on the floor on straw filled mattresses. Their clothing went into a pillow-case and was used as a pillow each night. The staff slept on camp beds. The band played on Llandudno pier and had collecting boxes. The money collected was shared between the boys for pocket money. Frank usually got about 1½d, which was a lot then. Sometimes the band was allowed to stay an extra week. This was the week the girls came down for their holiday. Mr Grainger played every instrument in the band. Back home the band practiced in the Assembly Hall and in the room above the workshops at the end of the drive. On Mondays and Fridays they practiced after school but Tuesdays, Wednesdays and Thursdays you got up early because band practice was before school and you also had your chores to do before the school bell went. In summer the band practiced marching up and down the drive, but in winter it was done in the Assembly Hall. They also marched to Lodge Hill Cemetary on Armistice Day and played The Last Post at the Rememberance Parade. Christmas time they played Carols along the drive.

He remembers the Assembly Hall being built in 1923. Two men were killed while working on its construction. It had an altar with carved altar rails and an organ. Mr Cohen used to play the organ while the boys used to pump it. Sometimes the boys were late starting and the organ wouldn't play. Mr Cohen used to shout Blow Donkey Blow. Everyone laughed when no music came out.

In 1929 several children went to St Lawrence Church Northfield for their confirmation. He also remembers going to Northfield early one morning to watch the eclipse through coloured glass. That was very exciting. He also went to the opening of the Woodlands Hospital. He thinks royalty performed the opening ceremony. There was an outbreak of dyptheria while he was in the Homes. He remembers lying in the field not caring if he lived or died, he felt so ill. He went into the homes hospital and had to sleep on the balcony. The matron was a lovely person. She used to ask them if they wanted to swim the Channel. He felt it was said to encourage them to get well.

The fields were used for sports practice and every year they had a sports day competing against Erdington and Marston Green Homes. Shenley usually got licked. Frank wasn't much good at sports, he prefered to spend his time in the gardens. They also had a huge bonfire on the field on November 5th. When it snowed Home 9 and 10 built forts and had snowball raids on each other.

There were several workshops on the drive, tailors, shoe repairers, carpentry and maintenance workshops. At the end of the drive there was a large water tower. He once climbed all the way up the ladder. He played a few practical jokes. Once he dangled a piece of string out of the bedroom window and into the pantry windows with spoons attached. They rattled in the salt box and the assistant housemother used to think some-one was in the pantry.

The boys used to take the housemother a cup of tea in bed and have one themselves as well. Frank's brothers ran away once. Albert ate bacon that had been cooked on a shovel and earned the nick-name Shovel. Les used to catch birds under the riddle. They nicked-named him Spuggy. Les later became a boot repairer.

The children from Shenley Fields sometimes used to go to a little church in Bartley Green. The vicar's son worked for the B.B.C. The Assembly Hall was most often their church.

Some of the boys and a few girls were clever enough to attend a school outside the Homes. It may have been King Edwards School. Frank was educated at the homes school. He remembers being stood up on a desk one morning because he was so clean and tidy. There was a large picture of Sir Walter Raleigh on the wall at the back of the room. The children used to have a story read to them immediately after lunch. One Frank remembers very well was Peter Pan. Discipline in the school was very strict. If you scraped you chair when you stood up, you had to sit down again and keep doing it till you could stand silently. The Head Master Mr Locke, wrote The History of Kings Norton and Northfield. The Assistant Master was Mr Dunne. He was very much against smoking and a very good man.

There was swimming baths on the drive. Children were put into a harness until they could swim unaided.

Christmas was a good time. There were concerts given in the Assembly Hall by the children. They had a party in the school where huge tables were laid covered in food. It was very enjoyable.

The Shenley Homes were surrounded by farms and farm land. Frank remembers Ledsams, Hintons and Speedwells. Someone from Hintons was courting the assistant housemother at Home 11. Some of the boys used to walk to California to escort house mothers returning from Harborne.

The homes were well furnished though not lavish. The walls were painted and had to be washed with soft soap. When the housemother was out of the way the boys had great fun splashing the soap around. There were no lights in the bedrooms, they used the light from the landing to light the bedrooms. The bedroom floors were wooden and had to be cleaned with Ronuk on a bumper. There were no curtains up to the windows in the bedrooms. The hall floor had to be scrubbed. If you missed doing the corner the bucket was kicked over and you started again. Frank usually had outside cleaning jobs such as sweeping the yards and the spud bashing for 30 people. The children did most of the

41. Mr Frank Matthews as a young man ready to leave care and start his career in gardening after being taught for many years by Mr Newman. Frank later became known as the Wizard of Sparkhill Park. Photo loaned by Mr Frank Matthews.

domestic work and all of the washing up includung scrubbing grates etc. Water was heated in an outside scullary in large boilers. The meals were filling but basic. Every morning you had porrage or bread dipped in lard. You only drank tea at weekends, during the week it was cocoa only. This was made with only water, no milk. At the weekend if everyone had been good you got a cake. The children at Home 8 swopped their cake for a bar of soap as the housemother would not let them have much soap. There was oilcloth on the dining room floor. The sour milk was used to scrub the floors with. The boys did as much domestic work as girls and learned to sew and darn their own socks. They used to make soup out of vegetables cooked in an old tin over the stove. The training was all very useful to them when they left care.

Each house at Shenley Fields had coal fires. Every day the ash was collected and taken to a spot by the workshops. Here it was riddled and the clinkers used again in the stoves.

Home 9 had 30 boys in it. Mr Squires used to have them running round the yard at 6.30 a.m. each morning. There were several wild cats living along the drive at Shenley.

In the 1920 Mr Alan Cobham (later Sir) came to the district with his Flying Circus, giving flights to folks in that area. Frank doesn't remember any of the homes children having a ride.

Shenley Fields had a very nice doctor from Northfield. A big man with a rich deep voice and a very pleasant manner.

In 1929 some of the children went to Cadbury's about jobs but Frank can't remember if anyone was accepted.

Other gardeners who worked at Shenley were Mr Bennett, Mr Cooper and Mr Rose. All very nice country folk.

There was a girl called Dorothy Wood who worked in the office, and Frank fancied her very much. He always liked blondes but fortunately met the beautiful auburn haired Marie. A lovely lady he later married.

Frank Matthews is a very happy contented man. He enjoys his life and puts most of the thanks down to Shenley Fields Cottage Homes. He said they taught him to respect himself and others and by introducing him to gardening opened the door to a very worthwhile and fulfilling career that gave him and many thousands of people great pleasure. He spent most of his working life at Sparkhill Park and had an article printed about him in the newspaper. They called him The Wizard of Sparkhill Park.

Mrs Barbara Maullin nee Green
Home 4
1939 –

I am very pleased to hear that you are writing a book about the Shenley Fields Homes but sad to hear that they are being demolished.

I have many happy memories of the homes and the people who worked there. I was fond of the cook who worked at our house and I loved the matron who was very kind to me. The handy man who cleaned our shoes in the out house was quite a character. I was four years old when taken into care just before the war, so it was a very frightened four year old who walked up that drive, past the rose beds and beautiful pine trees. Even in

104

fear I noticed the beautiful gardens, but my fear grew as the war became real, adults always whispering about 'The Germans' and being woken in the night during air raids and lying on the cold floor under the stone stairs. Later we had air raid shelters in the yard. I always felt the panic in the adults even though they all tried to be cheerful. For years I thought Churchill was God. I was very confused between religion and the government. I did not like wearing the same dresses as the other children or walking in a 'crocodile'. We had remarks like, "There go the Homes children". I was put into Home 4 with my older sister Vera. Leslie my brother lived across the road. We were well cared for, but the food was awful. I went to the nursery on the drive and later to one of the local schools.

We were taken to Shenley Fields because our parents separated and mother suffered a nervous breakdown. She later remarried and had another family. I was captivated by the beauty of the drive as we passed through the gates of Shenley Fields on that hot summer day in 1939. There were roses every where, climbing and tumbling over bowers in superb pink and white abundance, combined with deep green luxurious pine trees, meticulous velvet lawns and scented lavenda borders. The colour and perfume of that scene has never faded for me.

I was one of several distraught children travelling in the van, which stopped outside the hospital. However my spirits lifted when I saw my sister Vera, waiting in the door way. I had missed her terribly. Her hair had been cut off and covered by a ghastly smelling rubber cap. Vera saw me staring at her and became very angry. She continually complained to the nurses, fiercely defending our mother and insisting she had always kept us clean. My sister tried to stop the nurses from separating us. Seeing Vera so upset I panicked. Eventually after giving the nurses quite a run around I was caught and carried away. My hair was cut and I was forced into a bath of water so hot I found it difficult to breath. Some days later I met the housemother of home number 4, who very kindly explained to me that I would be living there with my sister and that soon I would be seeing my brother again. I was taken to the lawn across the drive, where the younger children were enjoying a picnic tea. I was so excited when I saw Leslie. I ran to him almost knocking him over. He did not fuss me because he was with his friends, but I knew he was pleased to see me. Later Vera came for me. As I was only four years old I had to go to bed early. We went upstairs to the dormitory. Vera told me her bed was near the door because she was the oldest, so she had to get up earlier than the other girls to help with the breakfast and also to help get every one out quickly in the event of an air raid. I settled into the routine of Shenley Fields and gradually became very happy.

Never taking for granted the beauty of the gardens, I followed the gardeners around and learnt the names of all the flowers. I enjoyed the nature walks down the lanes at the back of the drive. We saw many red squirrels and rabbits.

There were sunny picnics on the lawn and trips to near by farms.

I attended the nursery. Every afternoon we collected our canvas mats and laid them on the floor for our nap. I can still remember the smell of the canvas. We always slept well in the afternoons because many of our nights were disturbed during the air raids.

We used to peep through the fence around the playground to watch the Air Force men working on the barrage balloons. I secretly wondered if these men were the Germans the cook was always talking about.

Sadly the happy days did not last, we were separated again. My brother and sister were evacuated to Wales while I was in hospital. Without Vera and Leslie, living through the air raids, the sirens, the horrible smelly shelters was unbearably frightening for a lonely child.

42 and 43. The 'Love Tree' photographed around 1989 by Jill Plumley.

Mrs Irene Mcfadyen nee Woodfield
1952 – 1961

I first came into care when I was 5 years old. I went to Middlemore Homes first then moved to Shenley Fields Cottage Homes in the Home called Merriland which was Home 1 and the first Home on the Drive. The houseparents were Mr and Mrs Platt. They had a son and daughter. They were not very nice people. No one in our home was allowed to have sugar. Mrs Platt always said she had to save it. My sister June was afraid of Mrs Platt and jumped when Mrs Platt shouted for a cup of tea. One day June got her own back and put about 16 spoons of sugar in Mrs Platts cup of tea. She got into trouble for it. Mrs Platt was very religious and inflicted her religion on everyone. One night the children raided the pantry. We ate a whole tray of biscuits. Mrs Platt hit us with the back of a carving knife to frighten us. She was very cruel.

I remember 9 of us running away together. We had a marvellous time. We did it to rebel. The police stopped us in the street. We said we was going skating and had permission. We were returned home and as a punishment I had to scrub the long corridor in sick bay with a toothbrush. I used to wag school a lot often spending my time in the outside shed until I was discovered. I went to Woodcock Hill Junior And Infant School then Ilmington Secondary Modern. Later I went to Harborne Hill. I was in Merriland for 6 years and left after an accident with the Platts. I had to go to Pebble Mill House on Bristol Road until it was sorted out. I probably stayed there for about 3 – 6 months. It was a lovely place. I returned to Merriland when Mrs Saddler took over the Home. I played up quite a lot and eventually had to move out of Merriland. I stayed at sick bay while something was sorted out for me. No-one wanted me but Mrs Moore agreed to give me a trial. I stayed with Mr and Mrs Moore. They were lovely people and I really enjoyed living at Ferndale.

Christmas was a wonderful time for kids in care. There were dozens of parties and pantomimes to go to and presents from everyone. On Christmas morning we woke up to a pillow case full of toys on the landing.

The food was always very good. Our cook was Aunty Kath. She lived near Weoley Castle Square. I was very fond of her. She fostered 2 children from Shenley. My favourite meal was sausage and mash which we had every Saturday. The food wasn't so nice or so plentiful when Platts were in charge at Merriland.

I remember a Midland Red bus being brought to the Homes for the children to play on. It was parked on the playing fields for years. There probably wasn't much left to tow away.

There was a pavilion on the playing fields. It held all the sports equipment etc. It was used a lot by the pupils of Ilmington School who also used the playing fields for their sports.

Every Thursday a teenage dance was held in the Assembly Hall. You had to be 13 years old before you could go to it. I couldn't wait for my 13th birthday and felt I was the cats whisker with my stiffened underskirt and beehive hairstyle. Mom Moore used to go mad at us for pinching the sugar to stiffen the net in our underskirts. The boys were dressed in tight trousers like Teddy Boys. It was a great night out and looked forward to every week. It was the ultimate punishment if you could not go to the dance. Some of us also went to the Square Club on Weoley Castle Square, but it wasn't as good as our dance in the Assembly Hall.

The Homes went on holiday every year. Usually each Home went on their own or teamed up with another Home to help with transport costs. We usually went to Exeter or Exmouth. I remember how envious we were when Ryedale went on an exchange visit to Jersey.

The Assembly Hall was used for many things such as dancing lessons, gymnastics, film shows and of course our teenage dance. Every year there were presentations given out from the Assembly Hall. These included The Morney Cup, The Shaftmoor Cup and individual cups and shields. The Morney Cup was presented to the Home that did the best project and The Shaftmoor Cup was for the Home that did best in sports. The smaller cups and shields were for individual sporting achievements at the annual sports day. My husband Bob who also lived and grew up in Shenley, was very athletic and won several cups and shields. The Sports Day was an annual event shared by Erdington Cottage Homes.

I remember having a Pictorial Auntie. There was a Sunday newspaper called the Sunday Pictorial and they sponsored a scheme called the Pictorial Aunties which was like part time fostering. I was 6 years old when I got my first Pictorial Aunty. They must have thought I was 6 months old because on their first visit to see me they brought me a baby-gro suit. They later brought me a Cinderella Watch which I treasured.

I don't know for sure where our grocery came from but I think it was collected from the office. I used to collect our sweets and ice cream ration from the office every week. One week just before Easter, I saw an enormous egg in the office. It had been donated to the children. After Easter every child had a great chunk of chocolate from this egg.

We all had our jobs to do in the Home and took it in turns in helping with jobs such as washing and drying dishes etc.

Every Sunday we had to go to church, morning and evening. We always got out of the evening service by making the weakest person go to church for us. She had to remember what the service was and what hymns were sung. We used to go off down the square to play Thunder and Lightning. We eventually got caught and were punished.

In 1953 we all had a Coronation Mug but I can't remember how we celebrated the Coronation.

There is a tree in the orchard called The Love Tree. It has hundreds of initials carved into the trunk. They are now right at the top of the tree. As it has grown the initials have grown with it.

My favourite memories are of the games we played such as Kick the Can. I later left Shenley and went to The Limes but Shenley will always be my childhood home.

I married Robert McFadyen who also lived in Shenley Fields Homes and shares my happy memories.

James Mclean
1980 – 1983
Elmdene Home 11

Life really started for me at Shenley Fields Drive in 1980. I was only 12 years old and one of three brothers. I telephoned Social Services as father had left home. He could not cope with the three of us children and a sick wife. We had already been in a childrens home before when father was unemployed for some years and money was hard to find.

Mother and father split up and father got custody of us. Then mother had a serious accident. We moved to Rednal to live. We all had to try and start new lives which wasn't that easy. You see by then I had already been to two secondary schools and thought that my education was suffering. Then things started to get worse, my older brother wasn't going to school and began staying out all night. Social services became involved and started asking questions. I told them what had happened and they were very understanding. They said that we couldn't stay at home on our own and that mother would have to go back into hospital and us three into care. We all understood what was about to happen.

We were then taken for a medical and then to a Childrens Home called Elmdene. It was on Shenley Fields Drive. The Officer in Charge was Mrs Jill Plumley. She was very nice and welcomed us with open arms. I found some sort of loving warmth there. She was always very keen on seeing us do well at school, also in the home. Many times she would take us all out on day trips etc. We would never have had this at home. We had new clothes, shoes and the best of food. These were all things our father could not afford to give us.

When we first moved into Elmdene it was just a boys home. Someone decided that it was unnatural having just boys so it was decided we should become a mixed sex home. The older boys faces gleamed with pleasure at the thought of girls coming to live with us. We had to move to one of the other homes down the drive. It was called Greenways and had previously been a baby home. I remember the day we moved very well. All the lads helped with the moving and carried things up and down the drive all day. Aunt Jill as we called her, thought we had all worked very hard and took us on a trip to Stourport as a reward.

As time went on we started cooking for ourselves on Saturdays. The staff felt the training would help us prepare for when we left care and had to look after ourselves.

As I was getting older my social worker thought I would benefit from being fostered as the chances of returning home were very remote. I was found a very nice family in Hall Green.

When I went back to Elmdene for a visit I was told the homes were closing down and would eventually be pulled down. I was shocked and thought to myself 'what are you doing, that's my background and all my memories you messing about with'. I was very upset and so was everyone else in Elmdene. The homes were lovely old buildings, late Victorian I think. There was about twelve houses altogether. They don't build houses like that now. I was angry that they were pulling them down and felt they could have been put to better use. They said they were too expensive to run. I thought they would have used them for all the homeless people.

Well I think I had a good start in life thanks to The Shenley Fields Homes and all the staff who looked after me. I feel a better person for being there.

Mr Robert McDermott previously Robert Oakley
1950's

I was in the Shenley Fields Homes back in the c1950's with my brother Brian Oakley. The only thing I can remember about my brother Brian is his habit of putting two fingers in his mouth.

44. Robert McDermott nee Oakley on board ship while in the Merchant Navy.

I was given a silver coloured metal toy plane just before being taken away to my new parents. I do not feel the woman who took us was our real mother as she had no photos of my father or any of the family. We went from Shenley Homes to Kings Heath on the bus.

We lived in lodgings for goodness knows how long. I do know we moved to Alum Rock (51 Collage Road) and my mother was living at this address with my gran and grand-dad. I know I moved around a bit and lived in Saltley, then Washwood Heath. That is where my school was.

One day I asked mother for photos of my father. She almost screamed the place down. I ran away a few times and started to live with the Alexandra Family who had two children. One day my Mother came to see me with a Christmas present. When I opened it I found a Red Book and a Christmas Card. I still don't know where that book came from to this day. I wish I did because I would travel round the world to thank them. I have a funny feeling it was one of my family. Maybe my father.

I left my mother when I was sixteen to make my own way. I moved to Northfield and to Selly Oak. I joined The Royal Army Corps, then volunteered my service in the Royal Pioneer Corps and did my service in Cyprus.

I came out in 1961 after doing 3 years and went to live in Selly Oak. I started to look for my mother. I found her working in The Rock Public House in Alum Rock. I remember the first words she said to me was "Have you got a cig". I was hurt at her response. I had taken her flowers and gifts. My welcome was like talking to a brick wall. A few days later I went to see my sister Joan. My welcome there was no better. I went to see my brother Eric who just wanted to be left alone as did my other brother Brian who was married with two children.

All this took place in Birmingham and I now live in Cornwall. I am still trying to find my brothers and sister or their families.

This is a rundown of what I know. I was born at The Ridings in Yardley Birmingham on 21st March 1940. My mother left my father when I was 3 months old. He was in the Royal Airforce as a lorry driver. His name was Eric Oakley. My other brothers were Edwin Oakley, Eric Oakley and Brian Oakley. My sisters name was Joan Oakley and I know she married a Canadian.

When I was first put into care I was put into a home in Wales then Erdington before moving to Shenley Fields Homes.

I have never married. I am now in the Merchant Navy and have been for 28 years. My one dream is to be united with my family again and to find out a little more of my background. Perhaps this book will help.

I am very happy to be able to add a conclusion to the above story from Bob as he has now managed to make contact with the missing members of his family and plans to hold a family reunion very soon. May I wish them all good luck for the future.

Mr John Mead (deceased)
Home 10
1940s and 50s

I was one of the lads that was in care in the Shenley Fields Homes. I was in Home 10 which was later named Ryedale. Also with me was my brothers Harold, Les, Charlie, Derek, Patrick and my sister Elsie in another home. These are a few of the names that come to mind when thinking of Shenley, Leslie Freem, Bill Bosworth, Cedric and Brian Dent, David North, Bert Moore plus many more.

There were 11 homes on the drive plus assembly hall, swimming baths, school, cobblers shop, tailors shop, hospital, matrons house, offices, superintendents house, food stores and sports pavilion.

Each of the homes had a small staff group. In ours we had Mrs Poston, the cleaner, Mrs Rugg, the cleaner and Mrs Leighton the afternoon tea lady. Some of the homes house parents or foster parents were Mrs Coe, Mr and Mrs Chester, Miss Thursfield and Mr and Mrs Lunn. The superintendent was Mr Blakey and the Matron was Miss Parry-Jones. Later we had Mr and Mrs Griffin as Superintendent and Matron. I took part in the sports and won several trophies but I don't know where they are now. We had a lovely party on the drive to celebrate the end of the war.

Life was very strict but we still had plenty of fun and it stood me in good stead for life.

Sadly John died suddenly before I managed to do a taped interview with him. He attended our reunion and was a very happy man. I know he would have related many of his escapades to me had I managed to visit him. However he spoke several times to his family about life in care at Shenley Fields Drive and they have written to me with some of those recollections which they would like printed in his memory.

Since my father's death we have tried to remember as many things as possible about his

45. This photograph was loaned to me by Derek Mead who had quite a shock when it was produced at our first reunion.

life in the Homes and know it would have been important to him to contribute to this book. We hope this will be a small way of cherishing his memories and parts of his life forever.

My father told us about the chores that he used to do while he was in the Home. He said that each child was given a set of chores that had to be done before going to school in the morning. The chores ranged from waking the smaller children and getting them dressed, to cleaning all the other boys' shoes, washing clothes and worst of all the emptying of the buckets that had been used during the night as toilets. He said that as the boys got older the better the chores they were given and best of all was the lighting of the boiler which my father did in his last year at the Homes.

Pocket money was given out on a Saturday and if they had been good all week they used to get 2d and two hard boiled sweets which were handed out by housemothers. If they volunteered to sweep the drive down on a Saturday, as my father did, then they got an ice cream as a treat.

Not uncommon practice was to get into fights with other boys at school as certain children "did not like" children from "The Homes" and there was a great deal of rivalry between what they called the "insiders" and the "outsiders".

Most of the boys used to say that it was very frightening in the winter when they had to walk home in the dark.

My father also told us about the time he broke the gramaphone. He had been told by

112

the Housemother "not to touch" but he kept winding it up and making it go faster and faster and he over-wound it. The spring snapped sending the record flying which promptly broke. He was punished for this by being given extra chores and his sweets and pocket money were stopped.

On one occasion the boys were on holiday in Gosport and he and another lad "ran away". They went to the ferry port and waited for a couple with children to get on the ferry. They walked along side them and ended up in the Isle Of Wight. While in the Isle of Wight they bought an ice-cream and sat on the beach. When a passer by asked who they were they told him that they had run away from the Homes. A short time later they were collected and taken back to the others.

Miss K. R. Mead

Mr Frederick Meredith
1907 till 1932

Mr Meredith senior was an engineer in charge of the boilers at Selly Oak Hospital.
He was a fit man who never had to go to the doctors except when he crushed his fingers after trapping them in the boilers. He worked alone at night when this happened.

In 1907 Mr and Mrs Meredith moved from their home in Selly Oak to the engineers

46. This little cottage still stands on Woodcock Lane and is the only part of the Shenley Homes to survive. Mr Meredith lived here as a child with his parents. His father was the engineer for the homes. The cottage is now privately owned.

cottage at the Shenley Fields Cottage Homes. They moved in a local butchers pony and trap.

The cottage had 2 bedrooms and had to be decorated every year because it was so damp. Mrs Meredith eventually had 8 children to bring up in this cottage. In 1908 it is recorded in the ledger that the Meredith children caught chicken pox. Fred tried very hard to get chicken pox, he even slept in his little sisters bed but he did not get it. In 1909 Mr Meredith Snr had a raise in his wages of 1/- per week. This brought his wages up to 36/- per week less 4/- per week for rent on the cottage. They raised 8 children on these wages. Mrs Meredith made the childrens clothes herself. There was an official post box set into the wall of the cottage.

Mr Meredith Senior was the engineer for the Cottage Homes. He was responsible for the pumps that pumped the water from the water tower to the single taps on each sink in the cottages. He also used to light the boilers that heated the schools etc. Early every morning he would light the boiler under the school to get the rooms warm. The teachers would arrive at 9 a.m. and complain of the heat and throw open all the windows letting the heat escape. By 11 o'clock the school was cold again. The church services were also held in the school. A partition was folded back to make about 4 rooms into one large room. Mr Cohen used to play the organ which had to be pumped by one of the boys. There were two services, one was held with the vicar from Bartley Green or Northfield and Mr Cohen took the other service.

Fred Meredith went to school on the campus then went to Bartley Green School. Mr Cohen was not happy about Fred going to Bartley Green School as it was not very clean and he was afraid Fred would bring diseases such as whooping cough, measles etc, back to the homes children. So Fred came back to the Shenley Fields School where he stayed till he reached standard three. He then moved to St Peters School Harborne. He walked 3 miles to school every morning which took about 1 hour. It took about 2 hours to walk back though.

One of the teachers he remembers well from the Shenley School was Mr Freeth the schools headmaster. Mr Freeth brought a frog to school in his pocket to help him with a lesson but the frog jumped out of his pocket and the children nick-named him Froggy Freeth. He was a good teacher who walked to school every day from Harborne.

Shenley Cottage Homes had their own swimming baths. When Fred was very young he would ride piggy back on the back of the older boys. One of them went under the water and really frightened Fred. He never did it again. He actually learnt to swim in Bournville Baths. The children of Shenley learnt to swim by wearing a harness around their middle and being pulled across the baths on a pully.

The Cottage homes had their own band as did the Cottage Homes at Marston Green, Erdington and the Industrial School at Harborne. The band master responsible for these bands was Mr Grainger. The band practiced in the school first and later in the Assembly Hall. They played outside Curzon Street Hall helping to recruit soldiers and then marched with them from Curzon Hall to the railway station. Many people remember them playing on Rememberance Day at Lodge Hill Cemetary and also on the Pier at Llandudno when the children from Shenley went to Llandudno for their annual holiday. The band also played every Sunday at St. Peters Church Harborne and the boys from the Industrial School used to march from Balden Road to St. Peters in their hob nailed boots. Mr Grainger was a very strict man.

Every year many of the children went to the pantomime. They walked to Harborne

Railway Station where they caught the train to Navigation Street. The train stopped just outside the station platform. There was a flight of steps straight up to the rear of the theatre.

For many years the bread for Shenley Children was baked at the workhouse in Selly Oak and the laundry was done at the infirmary. Woman used to travel in from Bartley Green, California and Harborne to help the foster mothers do the laundry. Mrs Meredith was helped by a lady named Mrs Lee. Mrs Lee was a very nice lady who lived in the row of cottages in Adams Hill. Fred Meredith used to visit her at her cottage and he can remember Miss Mumford who was known as the tallest woman. She lived in the end cottage and when she passed Mrs Lee's cottage window the room went dark. She was about 7 foot tall. When she died her remains were buried at the little church yard at Adams Hill in Bartley Green.

Fred Meredith can remember many of the names of people who lived and worked at Shenley Fields Cottage Homes. There was the Master and Matron, Mr and Mrs Cohen. They were in charge of the homes. Mr Cohen was a strict disciplinarian but Mrs Cohen was the sweetest woman around and everyone loved her. She had silver hair.

Two of the homes had married couples in charge of them. Mr and Mrs Morgan ran home 7. Mr Morgan was also the carpenter. Mr and Mrs Burdle ran home 9. They had a daughter. The infirmary on the Drive had a nurse and an assistant nurse. Mr Meredith senior was on call 24 hours a day as the homes engineer. There was also a Painter. He lived at 33 Harborne Park Road. There was a tailor who made suits of workhouse grey, a bootmaker who also lived in Harborne and the head gardener who had 4 men working for him one of which had the unpleasant job of emptying the closets and disposing of sewage.

Many boys in the homes followed the trades of shoe makers, tailors, gardeners or joined the armed services. The girls usually went into service as maids or nannies etc.

Until the Poor Law was abolished in 1911 sanitation was very crude. In the back yard of each cottage there was a row of closets with a passage at the back. There was a lavatory seat with a bucket underneath reached through a door off this passage. This was emptied by Mr Jack Brown the gardener. He emptied this into a water barrow. Mr Webb the local farmer had the liquid sewage running on his land. The solid sewage was poured into a trench at the back of the field and buried. When Birmingham Council took over and services improved. They had gas for lighting and cooking and a modern sewer. Jack Brown was relieved of bucket duties and promoted to general handiman. Jack was not a very clean man who only shaved once a year for the annual staff party.

There was a tower at the far end of the drive. This contained 2 huge water tanks. There was a well at the side of the tower. A boiler house housed two Lancashire Boilers which drove the pumps which pumped the water from the well to the single taps on the sinks in each cottage.

There was a fountain and a spring in Cromwell Lane. This served all the nailmakers cottages in the locality. Beautiful water cress grew on the spring in Cromwell Lane and Bangham Pitt.

There was a public house just outside the back gate of Shenley Fields Cottage Homes. It was called The Welsh Go By and was run by a man called Mr Hemus. It was a small farm house with a beer licence.

Ilmington School was built on a piece of land where a plane crashed during the First World War. The pilot telephoned the M.O.D. from the Merediths cottage.

There was a local man called Squire Ledsam. He was a strange man and very solitary. His house stood where St Gabriels Church now stands. The house was surrounded by

47. Mr Meredith talking to me at our first reunion. Photograph taken by Ken Dunn.

high walls and was protected by dogs. He had one of the few valve radio sets in the district. Fred Meredith had a crystal set.

Mr and Mrs Cohen the master and matron lived in the first house on Shenley Drive. It was called the Lodge. They had a nurse maid for their children called Sarah Bufton. She lived at Home 11 Miss Ford was the foster mother of Home 5 and Miss Harris had Home 6.

One day Mrs Meredith sent Fred to Miss Harris for a bunch of flowering currants instead he asked for some flour and currants. There was also Miss Field at Home 3 and Miss Gent at Home 4.

There was a small wooden school at the back of the Meredith's cottage. This was the infants school. It was also used for the weekly staff dances where a professional M.C. taught dance steps.

Palethorpes lived in the big house at the top of Ley Hill in what is now the Neighbourhood Office. About 1908/9 they had a very large and heavy motor car which they used to drive past Meredith's cottage early every morning. There was a grass verge on both sides of the road outside the cottage where 2 goats were tethered and Merediths chickens ran free. Occassionally one of the chickens got hit by the Palethorpes car. Mrs Meredith used to run out to get the chicken and it was used for lunch that day. The Palethorpe family would always stop and pay 2/6 for the damage on their way home.

The Merediths had a female dog which kept attracting a lot of attention from the male dog that belonged to Mr Mountford at Yew Tree Farm. After the dog had hung around all day, Fred would tie a piece of string around its neck and take the dog back to Yew Tree Farm. Mr Mountford paid him for returning the dog. Fred was quite an enterprising fellow and also earned 6d for a dustbin full of horse muck which would be used on the gardens.

Mr Jack Brown was also an enterprising fellow. He emptied the toilet buckets but also entertained the children with his gramaphone and records and delivered the Sunday Newspapers.

Mr Beard was the gardener. He came from Evesham and kept lovely strawberry beds just past Homes 10 and 11 and asparagus beds around the Assembly Hall Stretching from the infirmary to the Long Nuke ditch which later became Long Nuke Road, was the playing fields. These were used for the annual sports day also for the maypole dancing and bonfire night party.

Fred remembers standing outside the infirmary and looking across the fields to Lodge Hill Cemetery. At dusk the rows of headstones looked like washing on a washing line. He could also see Chamberlain Tower at the university.

There was a pony belonging to Mr Cohen and a donkey that used to graze in the lower fields. The were often tormented by children.

Pigs have also been kept by the Meredith family and it didn't always meet with the approval of the committee. Pig wash was collected in Hogs Head barrells. The committee met on alternate Tuesdays at the committee rooms on the Drive. The pig wash was collected every week by Thomas Thornton and taken to Shenley's Farm owned by Mr Ward. One Tuesday when Mr Thornton was moving the barrells the committee complained about the awful smell it created and ordered Mr Cohen to have it burnt in the boilers in future. Mr Meredith was given permission to keep pigs again during the war. He kept the pigs very clean.

Fred Meredith has a very good memory and enjoyed attending the reunion of SHENLEY "CHILDREN" on 10th December 1989 where he met many people who remembered him from their SHENLEY DAYS.

Mrs Moore
Housemother at Ferndale
1953 – 1968

Mrs Moore or Mom Moore as she was known to staff and children is a lovely warm friendly lady who ran Ferndale Childrens Home which was number 5 Shenley Fields Drive. She was there for some 15 years.

The home was extremely comfortable and homely thanks to Mrs Moores efforts to create home for all her "children". She is now retired and lives in Harborne. Her memories of Ferndale are very precious to her.

The home had many pets including Judy the dog. The children had guinea pigs, rabbits, mice etc.

Every year Shenley had a huge bonfire on the top field. Shellmex supplied the fireworks and Mrs Moore provided a buffet. The staff brought their children along and everyone had a lovely time. One year Midland Red donated a single deck bus to the

48. A photograph of the staff who lived and worked at Shenley Cottage Homes. The homes in the background are homes 4 and 5. Photo loaned by Mrs Moore.

49. Ferndale Home 5 which later became known as Cherry Garth. Photo loaned by Mrs Moore.

50 and 51. The tree's on Shenley Drive turn into a winter wonderland after a heavy fall of snow. Photo's loaned by Mrs Moore.

children of Shenley Fields. Children in care were not allowed to be photographed or used for advertising so the staff were asked to bring their children in for the photo. The bus was parked on the playing field and gave a great deal of pleasure to the children over the years.

Shellmex sponsored Ferndale and were very good to them providing the children with Easter Eggs, birthday presents, Christmas gifts, panto tickets and a television.

Ferndale went on holiday every year staying in schools or YWCA hostels. Once they stayed in a church hall at Scarborough. The vicar was very good to them while they were there. The staff made custard one day which turned out very lumpy. When the children complained the staff said it was Holy Custard. The vicar found this very amusing.

Mom Moore played the piano, and many evenings were spent in her sitting room listening to her music.

Ferndale changed its name in the 70's to Cherry Garth but it will always be Ferndale to Mom Moore and her staff and many many children.

52. Greenways Home 6. Note the extra rails across the windows in the bedrooms. This home was one of the baby homes and these rails were used to prevent the toddlers falling out of the windows. Photo loaned by Mrs Moore.

Mrs Alma Niblett
The Office
1963 – 1978 approx

I worked for Social Services for a total of 30 years. The last 15 of those years were at Shenley Fields in the Office as a Clerical Officer. There were a great deal of records and accounts that had to be kept as you can imagine with over 300 children and staff living and working in the twelve childrens homes. Every child's admission and discharge had to be recorded as did many other details. The staff brought time sheets, petty cash returns etc that had to be dealt with and sent in to head office in town. Then we had the weekly hand out of wages and petty cash. In those days the drive was beautifully kept, with flower borders round well kept lawns and very elegant trees that were many years old; some probably planted when the drive was first opened back in 1887. I used to enjoy spending my summertime lunch break in the little garden just on the left of the entrance gates. It was the private garden of Mr and Mrs Griffin who were the superintendant and matron at that time.

Every Christmas my husband Chas and I had a very special task that we really enjoyed. Chas became Father Christmas to all of the children still left in the homes over Christmas. The Police Male Voice Choir used to come to the Drive on Christmas Eve. They stood with the children and staff by the front door to the office, and sang carols, this was when Father Christmas used to arrive with his sack of toys. Chas and I went to every home on the Drive and left a sack of toys. The toys had been donated by kind people who wanted to bring a little extra happiness to the children. I always remember one little boy who only wanted a train set for Christmas. This was the one toy we had not got. I was sad that we could not make his wish come true for Christmas but decided that we would buy him a train set as soon as we could after Christmas. When we were locking up to go home that evening a car drew up outside with four lads from a youth club inside. They had brought some toys for the children from other members of the youth club. We were delighted to find a train set in the parcel of toys and quickly wrapped it up for the little boy who was so looking forward to a train set for Christmas. Who said miracles don't happen. I think we had a little miracle that night.

I was often having phone calls from people who were trying to find out information about their own admission to care in Shenley Fields or their parents admission to care. One day I had a phone call from a young lady who wanted details of her fathers time in care. Her father seemed reluctant to talk about his care days and she wanted to help him. It appears he came into care at the age of 5 and was admitted by his aunty who came from Bromyard. She had more children of her own than she could cope with and felt this extra child was too much. He stayed in care until he left school. He was put to work at Paynes the shoe repairers. Paynes took a lot of the Shenley children and continued the training that had been started at Shenley Homes. Her father, Mr Smith, really took to shoe repairing and later set himself up in his own business. He moved to Hockley to live and later married. He and his wife had two boys and a girl. The daughter got married and went to live in Bromyard where her husbands family lived. When Mr Smith retired he decided he would also go to Bromyard to live. At this time Mr Smith and his daughter knew nothing about the aunty who had admitted him to care so many years ago.

When I mentioned this fact to Mr Smith's daughter she was very interested and decided to try to trace her. I suggested she contacted the local registry office or undertaker etc. It turns out they had a cousin living just round the corner from where they themselves were

53. The decay sets in. This photograph shows the entrance to the office around 1989. The office was last used by Social Services as a base for Social Workers and Home Helps. Photographed by Jill Plumley.

living. She let me know about this and I invited them over to Shenley. They arrived one Saturday afternoon. Mr Smith was a little reluctant to come back to the homes as he thought things would be just as they were when he was in the homes all those years ago. He was more than a little surprised to see all of the children in Greenways enjoying an egg each as it wasn't even Easter. He had been allowed one egg per year and that was on Easter Morning. He was very impressed with the home and the furniture, and how happy the children were. It was a very pleasant afternoon and he presented me with a lovely bouquet. At that time Mrs Bowes, who was the officer in charge at the Trees, was having a reunion party for men over 60 who had been in care at Shenley. Mr Smith was invited. He was reluctant at first but then came for two years running and really enjoyed it. He met old friends and enjoyed having a good natter with them. Unfortunately he died soon after his second reunion. I had many requests from people trying to trace their back-grounds.

One request that I will always remember was from a man who rang up from Papua New Guinea. He had been in Shenley as a child and was one of the children sent out to Australia to live. He desparately wanted to return to England but had not got a passport and could not obtain one because he had not got the necessary papers giving details of his birth etc. I tried to find out the information for him and had many phone calls from him at all hours of the day and night. I never did hear whether he got back to England or not.

Mrs Sheila North nee Birkenhead
Home 1
1939 – 1950

Sheila first went into Shenley Fields as a baby in 1939. She went into Home 6. She later moved to Home 5 but the Home was transferred to Home 1 for some reason not known to Sheila. She stayed on Shenley Drive for several years till she was 11 years old. She was then fostered by the House-mother called Miss Tonks from Home 5. Miss Tonks married Mr Bradley and moved south to Hastings with Sheila. Sheila could not cope in the small bedroom without her friends and after 2 years the fostering broke down and she returned to Birmingham to Millmead Road Childrens Home with Mr and Mrs Spencer. At 15 she left school and went into domestic work.

I have many memories of Shenley Fields especially of the people I met. There was Miss Longman in Suncrest Home 2. Mr and Mrs Cox ran Merriland Home 1, they then went to one of the scattered homes in Kings Heath. Mr and Mrs Platt then took over Merriland followed by Mr and Mrs Saddler. Miss Ray and Aunt Margaret Salt were staff at Merriland. Mr and Mrs Bowes ran Jasmin Home 4 then they moved to The Tree's Home 9. Winnie Archer was brought up in the homes and worked in the sewing rooms before becoming an aunt (this was the title given to the care staff). The tailor was Mr Brookes. Mr Smith brought the provisions round to each home in a wicker basket on wheels. The baskets were then used on sports day to hold the sandwiches. Sports day was in June and I used to take my own son and daughter back to see them. The provisions came from the stores by the office. The cobbler was Mr Cooper. His workshop was by Home 5.

Every home did a project for the Mornay Cup. Merriland did a show on the stage in the Assembly Hall. It was all the Nursery Rhymes acted out by the children under the guidance of Mr and Mrs Platt.

I remember the white cross of Rememberance outside the school and also the Midland Red single deck bus donated to the Homes for the children to play in. It was great fun. I enjoyed my life on 'The Drive'. Easter had special memories of hand painted hard boiled eggs.

While in Home 5 Miss Tonks the housemother made us sit with our head down on the table for 1 hour after lunch for a sleep. The infants school was at the back of home 2 and 3 and was like a wooden shed.

Mr and Mrs Pemberton lived in the engineers cottage with their son John and dog Scruff. Mr Pemberton looked after the boilers.

The tailoring was done in a workshop at the end of the Drive opposite the Infirmary and the cobblers workshop was next door. The children played out in clogs instead of shoes.

When I was in the 'Big' school we had to sing "Now the day is over", every evening before going home. The classrooms were divided with tall shutter doors. The nursery school had little camp beds for the toddlers to sleep on after their dinner.

Every year we went to Gosport for our holidays. We travelled there by coach and everyone slept on sacks of straw on the floor.

One of the Homes had a Boxer dog and it got lost. It was mentioned in the news-paper and a breeder saw it and felt sorry for the children. He gave every home a boxer dog. The original dog returned. Mrs Bowes had one of the boxers. She also had a Bull dog called Sally.

54. Sheila North then Sheila Birkenhead photographed on the field near the homes hospital in 1952. Photo loaned by Sheila North.

55. Shenley Children dressed up for the Coronation 1953 photograph loaned by Sheila North.

I spent a lot of time in sick bay. The bedrooms were open air with metal bars on the windows to stop anyone getting in.

I had ring worm and had to wear a white hat to walk up and down the Drive in.

Every child had their own number on their peg and clothes. Mine was number 6. We had the Gibbs block toothpaste. One night I climbed out of my cot, got the toothpaste and got back in the cot to eat it.

The food was quite good. Most of it was home grown. The milk came in big churns from the local farms. I still have a slice of bread and margarine with all my meals. This is something I have always done from Shenley Fields. My children have never been able to understand it.

I remember a big black Labrador dog called Queenie that used to visit Miss Longman. The dog lived with her owner in a caravan in Cromwell Lane. Miss Longman had a cat herself.

The inside of the homes were painted brick. The top half was painted yellow and the bottom half was painted green. There was an orange stripe round the middle of the wall. My first job was bed-making at the age of 5. Everyone went to bed at 6 p.m. If you talked you stood in the corner with your hands on your head. The rooms were freezing so you was glad to get back into bed and go to sleep. The boiler house was in the garden by the outside toilets. The toilets had to be emptied. During the night there was a bucket put on the landing. The older girls had to wake the little ones to take them to the toilet during the night. During the day no one was allowed to go into the house only at meal times or to do chores. You either had to play in the yard or if it was raining you stood in the shed. Everyone made their beds after breakfast. Mr Griffin waited at the top of the drive to inspect our hands and nails for cleanliness every morning. After church Mr Griffin gave the cane to those who had played up. The vicar was Mr Foster from St Gabriels Church.

My mother-in-law and father-in-law were social aunt and uncle to me from when I was 4½ years old. They had me at their house week-ends and took me on holiday. I knew them as Aunty Violet and Uncle Bill.

Everyone at Shenley wore the same sort of clothes. The girls wore navy knickers, liberty bodice, buckle shoes and green check dress or navy gym slip. Boys wore grey. Everyone knew where you came from. You had to walk hand in hand to the shops and on walks. I enjoyed sport especially football and cricket with the boys. I had some piano lessons but wasn't much good. There was a girl called Joan Tracey who played the piano very well. She didn't read music so played by ear.

Bonfire night was a very good night. Everyone walked up the drive with a torch.

Merriland went on the Radio and was interviewed about what they wanted for Christmas. I wanted a book about animals especially cats and dogs, but I received a book about nature study and was very upset. Everyone had a golliwog for Christmas. I think Christmas time was good for kids in care.

I particularly remember the scrubbed tables and benches. We did not have chairs. It was a good life and I would be happy to do it again. I feel I may have disciplined my own children more because of the strict upbringing I had. Good manners and discipline was instilled in everyone. I still knock on doors and wait to be called in.

I did have my moments of naughtiness. On Sunday we were given 1d which we should have put on the plate in church but I had the 1d off my friends and took them to Aunty Violets and Uncle Bills.

I went to Princethorpe Road School. Mr Goldberg was the Head Master. One day I played truant from school with my friend and we went to the duck pond (a local park with

56. Sheila North and friends at the first reunion in 1989. Photograph taken by Mr Ken Roberts nee Dunn.

a pond in). A lady asked us why we were not at school. We said we had been ill. She asked us to collect conkers for her handicapped son. She then took us back to school. We had to forfeit one sweet as punishment. After that I went to Bristol Street Special School. Uncle Bert drove the school bus to take us to Bristol Street School.

Doctor Clarke was the Homes doctor for many years.

My memories of Shenley Fields Cottage Homes are still very clear and mostly happy. I am very unhappy about it being pulled down.

Miss Christine Noxon
Residential Child Care Officer
Home 8 Melplash
1969 – 1972

I worked an Melplash as a Residential Child Care Officer or R C C O as we were called. The work was varied to say the least. We did everything from bathing babies to cleaning and stoking coke boilers, to cooking and washing clothes for up to 14 children. Try squeezing 4 babies into one pram. The children were in care for all sorts of reasons and were all ages from birth to 16 or 17 years old. We tried to make the 'Home' as nice and homely as possible, My main surprise when I worked there was the different races in care.

57 and 58. Christine Noxon with some of the Shenley children taken just before she left Melplash for a new life in Australia where she became an 'Angel'.

When my mother worked in the 1950's at the sick bay with Sister Tolley, there were only white children in care.

I knew the area well as I was brought up in Weoley Castle and went Ilmington School, I remember the children from Shenley well especially on Mondays when dinner money was collected. The Homes children had free dinners. I always felt so sorry for them.

I knew a little about the children from my mother's stories of the children in sick bay on Shenley. So I was surprised to find myself working at Shenley years hence and taking the children to school meeting the same teachers as once taught myself.

I once cared for a young girl in Melplash and when her mother visited her I found she had been to the same school as myself. This helped bring me a little closer to the girl but of course we could not show favouritism.

One of my most precious memories was when I helped care for a 4 week old baby. Whilst bathing the little one in a bath tub in front of the fire one cold winters day, I looked up from the baby and saw the other children were sitting on the floor, wide eyed, looking at the baby. It was so natural. I thought that's worth all the hard work, to catch that glow of amazement in the eyes of the other children seeing such a little child being bathed. A beautiful moment shared.

I am now living in Australia but often think of Shenley Fields Cottage Homes and the many people I met there.

126

Mrs Marjorie Nutt nee Staveley
Home 6
1923 – 1928

I was in Shenley Fields Cottage Homes from 1923 to 1928. I was only 4½years old when I left there for another home, yet I remember Shenley very well. Most vivid in my memory is the day I ran over the cricket pitch during a cricket match and was hit by the ball. The ball hit me so hard it broke my left leg. I am disabled to this day with it. I was taken to the homes infirmary and remember the building very well. We had our own swimming baths at Shenley also. You were strapped to a board and guided across the water to teach you to swim.

Outside our home was an old wash house with old metal tubs.

On Mayday we had a Punch and Judy Show and dancing round the Maypole. I seem to remember seeing cows and goats too but I would love to know if that was true or imaginary.

Every evening before we went to bed we would stand in front of a big white table and say our prayers and sing 'Gentle Jesus meek and mild' and then we had to say "Goodnight Mother, Goodnight all. May the Lord bless you all. Amen".

I remember I was in the hospital with a septic toe on Guy Fawkes Night and the nurse telling me he was waving to me.

Just before I left the first boy was brought in to our home. His name was Bill Bishbone. That was what I called him because I couldn't say his proper name. I had a car, he had a pencil and we swopped them to remember each other by. I often wonder what happened to him. He would be about 70 years old now.

One thing I do remember about the clothes we wore was the little red muffs we had to keep our hands warm.

I would love to see Shenley again, for however bare it was with no luxuries I was never as happy or as loved again as a child or as a teenager until I married in 1960. Alas I was widowed in 1980.

Mrs Irene O'Donnell
Houseparent
Rosemead
1950 – 1953

I was housemother at Rosemeed from 1950 to 1953 when I moved to the then new family home unit in Kings Heath where I stayed for 24 years before retiring. When my husband and I moved from Shenley we took eight of the Shenley children with us.

There is a book called "The First Four Years" — a report by the childrens officer 1949-1953. There is an interesting chapter in it about Shenley Fields — how it was founded by the Kings Norton Board of Guardians etc.

Mr Chuter-Ede the then Home Secretary in September 1951 visited Shenley. At the end of the visit to Shenley he said, "These children are happy children. They have clear eyes and you can read a childs happiness in its eyes". (Mr Chuter-Ede was an ex-teacher).

I have enclosed some photographs for your book. I am happy to say the dog was found again.

ANYBODY HERE SEEN GUSSIE?

NOT so long ago, 17 small boys in a children's home near Birmingham begged their foster-mother, Mrs. Barbara E. Smith, to get them a dog—not just any dog, but "one with a pedigree a mile long."

Eventually Mrs. Smith and her husband got one, a fine Boxer (pictured here), which was quickly named Gorgeous Gussie.

For a year Gorgeous Gussie was the pride and joy of every boy in the Children's Cottage Home, Shenley Fields, Birmingham. Then, on May 19 this year, she disappeared.

Every day the boys organised search parties for their pet. Notices were put on trees, walls and police-stations—without result. So now they have written to the Editor of the "News of the World."

"We had Gussie when she was two months old. She was like our baby," they write. "We miss her very much. Please, sir, could you help us?"

They say that their pet, a brindle bitch, is now 20 months old, is 20 inches high at the shoulder, has a white flash on her muzzle, white brisket and white paws.

And the letter is signed—

Edward Wright.
Colin Stone.
Ernest Law
Philip West
Tommy Law
Dennis Wall.
Tony West
Brian Harvey

Victor Deeves
Kenneth Moore.
JOHN WEST.
John Bayen.
Joe Stone.
Thomas McCloskey.
Sandra Smith
Clifford L. Wall.
Richard Foster

59. This newspaper cutting appeared in a local newspaper when the childrens dog went missing. Some of the 'children' have been to our reunions and will be very surprised to see their signature here. The cutting from the unnamed newspaper was sent in by Mrs Irene O'Donnell.

60. Dancing lessons in the Assembly Hall around 1952. Photo loaned by Mrs O'Donnell.

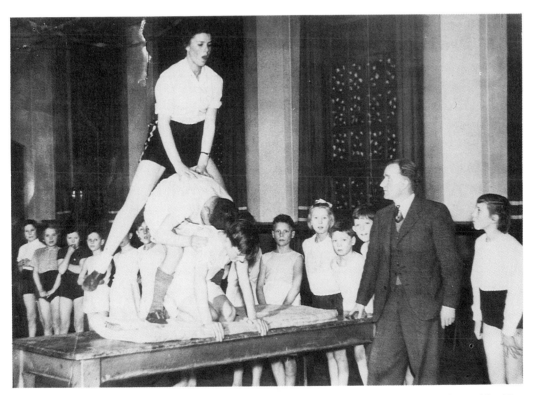

61. Mr O'Donnell takes a gymnastic class in the Assembly Hall around 1952. Photo loaned by Mrs O. Donnell.

62. This photograph appeared in the Evening Mail on June 3rd 1974 after Doris Oxley and friends met up with Mr Fred Bright (deceased) for tea at 'The Trees'. The photograph was sent in by Doris Oxley.

Mrs Doris Oxley nee Perks
Home 3
1915 – 1924

I was in care at Shenley Fields Cottage Homes from 1915 to 1924. My name then was Doris Mabel Perks. I was in care with my sister Evelyn Constance Perks, my younger sister Edna May Perks and my brother Leonard Harry Perks. The girls were in home 3 and our brother was in home 7. We were taken into care when our father deserted us.

We all went to school on the drive. The headmaster's name was Mr Freeth and some of the teachers were Mr Bowers, Mrs Ward, Mrs Rapp and Mrs Palmer. The school was also used as our church and the vicar's name was Reverand Taff. We had our own swimming baths which were only for the homes children. The swimming teachers name was Miss Hands. I won a certificate when I was 12 years old for swimming 12 lengths of the baths. I also took part in the sports events. The Homes had their own Brass Band but this was for the boys. The band master was Mr Grainger.

I remember the names of some of the house mothers. They were Home 1 Miss Dewey, Home 2 Miss Bennett, Home 3 Miss Field, Home 4 Miss Gent, Home 5 Miss Ford, Home 6 Miss Harris and Home 7 Miss Waring. The wonderful gardens were managed by Mr Newman who taught many a boy how to become good gardeners. Several followed in the gardening profession when they left care. Mr Meredith was the engineer and handyman and Mr Brown made and repaired the boots and shoes. The boots were inspected every Monday. There was a Superintendant and Matron called Mr and Mrs Cohen. They were very strict but quite nice.

Every Monday a lady came to our house to do the washing. Her name was Mrs Wimbush. We had no electricity in our house when I lived there and the toilets were outside, Every week the grocery was delivered in wicker baskets.

I went to church in the school. There was a visiting Vicar named Reverend Taff. I did not learn a trade except how to do housework but all the boys learned a trade. Life was very strict and we did not have much pleasure so we didn't laugh much. Christmas was not too bad, anything was better than the strict routine of daily life.

My happiest memory is of visiting day which was about every 6 months. Then I saw my mother for about 2 hours.

Mrs Laura Palmer nee Sayce
1936 – 1949
Home 2 (Suncrest)

I went into Shenley Homes with my brother and sister. We went to Summerhill first. Our foster mothers name was Miss Longman. She was a very caring person and looked after us very well. At one time there were 24 children in our home and only three staff to look after us. We were always well clothed and kept spotlessly clean.

I was a delicate child and had to go to Baskerville Residential School in Harborne. I came back to Shenley for my holidays etc. Sometimes I arrived home for my holiday a few days before the Shenley children started their holiday. When this happened I used to go to the office to help Mr Taylor. I collected and delivered letters etc from the other homes and took them to the office. I also took the sweet ration round for Mr Brooks and collected and delivered the sewing for the sewing ladies. Mr Taylor used to give me a piece of cake on a Friday as a reward. All the post including our birthday cards went to the office and was delivered to the homes by the office staff. The only thing that came straight to our homes was the bread. We had to leave a wicker basket at the end of the path and the baker put the bread in it. The bread was baked by Hardings. I spent a lot of time in the hospital at the end of the Drive. The owls used to really frighten me when I was in the open-air wards. If I was poorly when I came from Baskerville I had to go to the isolation block in the hospital. This is where the open veranda was. The children from Erdington came to Shenley at week-ends because Erdington was getting all the bombing. They had to see the Doctor before being sent to several of the homes on the Drive. One thing that really sticks in my mind is the very hot water we had on Saturday for our bath. The Doctor was a lady doctor called Dr Roberts. There was another Doctor called Dr Aldridge. He was a tall man with a moustache and a monacle. He played Father Christmas every year. I used to see Dr Roberts at Baskerville as well as Shenley.

During the war we were evacuated to Mountain Ash. My sister and I went to one lady who we didn't like. My sister liked Mrs Edwards who lived round the corner and I liked Mrs Moon, so we split up and went to the different ladies. I got scabies when I was there, not because the place was dirty but because I had poor health. I was in bed for quite a time then and a Doctor Scales came in to see me.

I first went to Baskerville on August 6th 1942. I remember it very clearly. When we were at Shenley we had picnics on the lovely fields down by the hospital. We loved this even though the picnic was only a lettuce leaf on bread or a jam sandwich it was still very exciting. Sometimes Miss Longman took us to Sennerley's Park instead. I remember having the cane once. I might have been classed as delicate but if you did wrong you had

131

the cane. A note had been sent round warning all the children that they would be punished if they threw stones at the apple trees. I ignored this warning and threw a stone at the apple tree by the air-raid shelter. It missed the apples and hit a boy who had to go to hospital to have stitches put in the cut on his head. Miss Parry-Jones the matron caned me across my knuckles. She was a very strict lady. On Sunday evening we had to go to church at Weoley Castle. It was a little Methodist Church by the Post-Office. On Sundays we had to read or sew. No-one could play games or make a noise. We used to go for lots of walks with Miss Longman.

The school felt I should learn to swim. We had our own Swimming Baths at Shenley. The swimming teacher was Miss Tabbener. She taught us to swim by putting a harness around our waist and pulling us along in the water. I only went once. It frightened me too much. My sister and brother were champion swimmers.

Our mother was allowed to visit us once a month. I remember having a Cadbury Cream Egg for Easter. They were larger than they are now and we had one every Easter Sunday. This started just after the war.

The bathrooms were freezing cold because of the quarry tiled floors. The potatoes were peeled in the brewhouse. This was a cold job also. All the laundry was kept in here as well. When I first went into Shenley there was a lady called Mother Hawkins in charge and Miss Longman was her assistant. There was also a junior to help out. When Mother Hawkins retired Miss Longman took over. There were 24 children in each home during the war. It was a tight squeeze at the table. We used to think Miss Longman's room was a palace and loved doing her dusting. I remember Christmas at Home 2. Miss Longman decorated the home up really lovely. I remember one Christmas in particular, Miss Longman put the two big tables together. She placed a large mirror in the centre and covered it with small home made trees and artificial snow then placed some glass swans on it. It looked really lovely. The older girls in the home went round to some of the other homes to see their decorations etc. Mrs Parry at Home 9 had made a beautiful cake which looked like a thatched cottage.

Mr Blakey the superintendent used to have a little black dog. My brother used to take it for walks. Miss Longman had a cat and one year it had kittens in the wardrobe. While in the home you had a number. This was on your clothes and your peg etc. My number was number 13. This number never changed all the time you were in that home. Our clothes came from a room above the office, where the sewing ladies worked. I can remember in 1937 when the King and Queen were crowned, we had two sets of dresses. I had a blue dress with pictures of little children playing and also a pink dress with cats on. The little children had Princess Margaret Bonnets and the older girls had Panama hats. I remember going for a walk on Coronation Day. We walked as far as Lodge Hill and then turned back. When we got home there was a lovely party laid out for us. I remember another party but this one was to mark the end of the war. We all went to Woodbines Farm which was a large farm opposite the Castle Pub. We had a huge bonfire at this party.

All the land round the Homes was farm land. There was a farm called Strawbridges Farm down Cromwell Lane close to the spring. The tall blocks of flats that were built in Woodcock Lane had to be pulled down eventually because they were built on a spring and it made the flats very damp. The same thing happened to the houses built by our hospital. I remember a real gypsies caravan standing in Moores Lane. There used to be two very old houses standing in Woodcock Lane. They were on the right hand side just before the entrance on the left into Shenley Homes. We used to believe they were both haunted.

During the war we had lovely pantomimes in the Assembly Hall. They were put on by the people from Weoley Castle including the air-raid wardens. They did rehersals in the air-raid shelters. I used to see them twice because they put the show on at Baskerville School also.

Every Christmas we always had a doll. We woke up early and had our breakfast, which was usually a boiled egg. Then we opened our present, did our jobs then went for a walk. We walked a lot in those days.

During the war our beds were downstairs in the playroom. This was so we could get out quickly if there was a raid during the night. We had a coat monitor who had to make sure our coats were placed across the bottom of our bed every night and our shoes had to be placed in the right position to get them on quickly, ready to run outside to the air-raid shelter on the drive. The playroom had to be moved upstairs. We had a large table in the playroom that had a drawer at each end. The drawers were full of wooden building bricks for us to play with. There were cupboards down the side of the room and we had a small cupboard each. Miss Longman kept the best dolls and books in her own room. You were only allowed to play with these if you had been very good. The loveliest doll I remember was at Baskerville School. On my first day there I went into this big hall. There was a table full of dolls because everyone had to leave their dolls there when they got up in the morning. There was a chair with what I thought was a naughty girl sat on it. It turned out to be a life size model of a Shirley Temple doll. It was a really lovely doll that had been given to the school. I remember a shed in the grounds of Baskerville. It used to intrigue me because I didn't know what it contained and it was kept locked. I found out later it was a huge dolls house that had been put in there during the war.

The most memorable feature of Shenley Fields Homes was the size of the houses and the wonderful grounds. A lot of our vegetables were home grown. After the war Ilmington Road School used to come on our fields to use them for their sports. There was a large sports pavilion.

We were very lucky to have so much space. I enjoyed my life at the homes because I knew no other way of life except at Baskerville.

I still keep in touch with Miss Longman. She is a wonderful person who dedicated her life to children.

Mrs Parry (deceased)
Home 9
1940's

I worked as a foster mother for over thirty years. My two daughters were brought up with the children in care. Both were married from Shenley and had their wedding reception in the Assembly Hall there.

My husband and I were the first married couple to be appointed, as 'Mothers' were all single women. We lived in the largest house opposite the office. Miss Castle was the secretary and when she started she cycled from Shirley where she lived, to Shenley. Mr Blakey was the Superintendant, When I started, Mr Newman was head gardener, Mr Pemberton was engineer, Mr Smith was store man and Mr Brookes looked after boys suits and shoes.

One of my family of boys lives in the next village to me and visits me often.

We had a happy but hard life at Shenley and I feel sad to hear it is starting to close down.

63. Mr Parry who was housefather of Home 9 with the Shenley football team. Photo loaned by his daughter Mrs Astbury.

Mrs Asbury (daughter of Mrs Parry)
Home 9
1940's

I have quite a few memories of Shenley, as I grew up there with my sister when our parents were houseparents of Home 9.

They had a carnival once a year when house mothers and children paraded down the Drive, and a pantomime once a year. There again most house mothers and children would be in it. This was at the Assembly Hall. Then there was the swimming gala that was held in the Homes swimming baths on the Drive.

I was married from Home 9 and had my reception in the Assembly Hall. The wedding service was at St Peters Church in Harborne.

Mrs Margaret Payne nee Barker and
Mr Harold Barker
Home 4
1911 – 1918

After reading of your very pleasant memories of Shenley Fields Cottage Homes, I had to write to give you mine, which to say the least were far from pleasant.

I was admitted to Shenley Fields in 1911 at the age of 7 together with six brothers and sisters. My father left my mother to emigrate to make a better life for us at that time and we never saw him again. My mother was of the impression that he had gone down with the Titanic but we had nothing to confirm this.

When my family was admitted to Shenley Fields, we had very little to eat and I myself have lived on bread and water there for at least a week on many occasion. The homes at that time were run by Mr Cohen. I can still remember my brother Harold, at the age of 5 scratching for a carrot in the garden. For this he was strapped with a 2 inch wide leather belt. Harold is the only other member of my family still alive. These were truly not very happy times.

I had nothing, no treats, no special occasions, nothing to enhance the seven years I spent at Shenley Fields, and as far as I am concerned that very miserable existence my family and I suffered there is well best forgotten and not a place to remember with joy.

Three of my family died of blood complaints which the doctors diagnosed as neglect from childhood. Shenley Fields was a roof over our heads but it was a roof I could have done without because during the time I was there, there was no feeling, no warmness and as I said before very little to eat. My brother Harold can verify everything I have said, in fact it was he that had the strapping for eating a carrot.

I do say thank God for the welfare state and I also state that I thank God my own children did not have to suffer the misery that I did. I say good riddance to Shenley Fields although I realise things and facilities have changed a great deal since I was there.

My House Mother in Home 4, was a Mrs Black, not a very nice mother. Our treat for a year was a scabby apple, rich people's wind falls. I am 85 and still remember Shenley Fields with horror. I have not a single good memory of the place.

Mrs M Payne.

I recieved the above letter from Mrs Payne and as it was the first letter from someone who was not at all happy with Shenley Fields I felt I must go to see her.

Mrs Payne has been quite poorly following a fall and a stroke but agreed to me going to see her in her lovely home at Shirley. Her brother Harold was also there and contributed a lot to the discussion.

Margaret and Harold had to go into care when mother who had been left with 7 children and an invalid mother, had to go into hospital for an operation on her varicose veins.

The children were first taken to a workhouse for a bath before being transferred to Shenley Fields Cottage Homes. Margaret went into Home 5 with baby Harold who was only a few months old.

She had to look after him all the time she was there. The children were taken to the infirmary to see their mother and remembers all the old ladies saving their sweets to give to them. When mother came out of the infirmary she could not have the children straight home but came to see them at Shenley Fields. She could only afford to come once a month because of the bus fare.

All the children had to play outside during the day unless they had chores to do. Margaret was allergic to the sun though at that time no one knew what was the matter with her. Her face and hands were a terrible mess. One of the nurses from the Shenley infirmary even took her to Selly Oak Hospital for treatment but it did not get better. She had to wear a mask to cover her face because it was such a sight. It was not diagnosed as sun allergy till after she left care and was in service. She had to carry a letter saying she was not infectious. She missed a lot of summer schooling because of this complaint. The

64. St Michaels Church at Bartley Green where now stands a group of new houses. Photo loaned by Mr Perry.

nurse at the infirmary was very nice. The infirmary had open air balconies all along one side.

The church was in the hall of the school. They went twice on Sundays. Mr Cohen played the organ.

They never had holidays while in Shenley. The war started while they were in the homes. Harold remembers a Zepplin crashing in the fields outside the homes. Margaret remembers doing a play for a group of wounded soldiers. She played the fairy godmother in Cinderella and also sang "Come buy my Calder Herrings" in another play.

There were a few nice children in care in the Homes. Nellie Smith is one that sticks in Margaret's memory also the washer woman. The cobbler Mr Cooper was a very unpleasant man and was bad to the little girls. Her sister got into trouble for hitting him when she found him touching her sister. He was a crippled man with a clubbed foot. Harold remembers seeing young Hal Cohen with his wheelbarrow and thought he was a very privileged child.

The drive was roughly tarmaced and just after it was re-surfaced Margaret got into serious trouble because she got tar on another girl's dress. She had the slipper and was on bread and water for 3 days. Another incident which caused her to have bread and water for 3 days was when she vomited at the breakfast table after seeing maggots in the porridge. Miss Black the house-mother was not a very nice person. Harold got 6 of the best from Mr Cohen when he was caught taking carrots out of the garden because he was hungry. There was a swimming baths on the drive. Harold remembers learning to swim there with a harness around his waist which was on a pulley over the water. You learnt to swim on the floor before going into the water.

Everyone learnt to darn socks and sew on buttons. Harold found this very useful when he was sent into the Navy. He had no choice about going into the Navy when he left care but seemed to take to it. His brother did not like it at all. Harold went to Newport Docks after Shenley Fields.

The one thing both Harold and Margaret remember with pleasure is the walks along Cromwell Lane to Bartley Green and the Bartley Green Reservoir. Margaret recalls the lovely primroses along the lane. There was a little church on Adams Hill with a small church yard next door, where the 'Giant of Harborne'was buried. Margarets son now has a house built on the site of the old church.

Another very pleasant walk was to St Lawrences Church in Northfield. The area has changed a lot since they walked in long lines with head held high and backs very straight.

Eventually the Barker children went home to mother. Times were very hard and money was scarce. Margaret was often sent to buy 3d worth of bacon bits to make dinner for all of them. Boiled onions was a regular meal. Poverty together at home with mother was better than life in care at Shenley Fields Cottage Homes.

Mrs May Pearson nee Griffin
Home 3
1914 – 1929

I went into care when my mother died and father could not look after us. I had 3 brothers, Tom, Ted and Albert. They went into Home 7. My sister and I went into Home 3 with Miss Field as our Housemother. I did not realise Millie was my real sister for several years as we were all like a huge family and everyone was sisters to me. I was very spoilt while in the Homes because I was crippled with a spine injury and spent many years in a plaster caste. I also spent several years in the Woodlands Hospital or the Royal Cripples Hospital as it was called then. Miss Field was wonderful to me. She bathed me in a tin bath in the kitchen so my plaster would not get wet. She then carried me from one room to another. I had my hair washed over a bowl in the kitchen. Even the Housemother next door used to spoil me. She called me "Smiler" and would often say "Come on Smiler come over to see me". She was a very nice lady. There were 24 children in each home. Every home had 1 Housemother at first but later a relief housemother was appointed to give the housemother a ½ day break. It was quite a task looking after so many children but the older girls were taught how to do housework and helped look after the younger children. We all had utmost respect for our housemothers. They were all called Mother. Discipline was strict but very fair. Miss Field was a wonderful woman and looked very elegant in her blue dress and crisp white apron. All the housemothers wore the same uniform and looked very distinguished. Our relief mother was Miss Horsefield.

When children first went into the Shenley Fields Cottage Homes, they first went into Home 11. This was called the Receiving Home or Pro Home. They had to have their heads and bodies cleaned of lice and fleas. They were scrubbed with carbolic soap. They moved into the other homes according to age and sex. The girls went into houses on the right and boys on the left. Home 5 was the only mixed sex home at that time.

I was taught to darn sew and embroider while in Home 3. I made a cotton nightdress when I was about 12 years old and I still have it today. I can still get into the nightdress as I haven't grown much at all because of my spine trouble. As I grew up in the Home I became a prefect and it was my job to take the younger children to bed. We would all kneel down on the huge landing to say prayers before jumping into bed. When the little ones were in bed the older girls would sit down stairs with mother to do our sewing and darning. If there was no sewing or darning to be done we did some embroidery on a huge table cloth. The cloth covered the long table that we sat at for our meals. It was printed with a Willow Pattern transfer and we embroidered it in several shades of blue and white. When it was finished it was really lovely and was shown at exhibitions in and around Birmingham. I would love to know what has happened to it now and if it still exists.

We all wore navy and white in the winter and pretty blue cotton dresses in summer and of course we all wore hats. The girls used to darn the boys socks as well as their own stockings though some of the boys learnt to darn as well. While we were sewing and darning the house mother sat at her sewing machine sewing cloths for when the girls had their periods. We didn't have nice soft sanitary towels then.

I went to both of the schools at Shenley Fields. One was a little wooden building at the back of Home 3. The other school was much larger and was used for our church on Sundays, as the classrooms could be opened up to form one large room.

I still have my school certificate signed by Mr Locke who was our Headmaster. Some of the teachers were Mr Freeth who we called' Froggy'. Mr Dunne, Mrs Wrapp and Miss Palmer. Some of the teachers lived in the teachers cottages which were just outside of the Shenley Homes. I missed a lot of my schooling while I was in the Woodlands. One of our christmas parties was held in the large school. The other party was held in our individual homes. One year Mr Cadbury was the Father Christmas and he gave everyone a ½d bar of Cadbury's Chocolate. I spent three Christmases at the Woodlands Hospital altogether. I don't remember many toys except my first doll. My brother sent it to me after he left the homes. I was 12 years old. It was a beautiful doll with a green dress and blonde hair. I can still picture it now. The schools choir took part in the Birmingham School Choir Competition and we sang in the Town Hall Birmingham. There was lots of things to do if you lived in the Shenley Fields Homes. The homes had their own swimming baths. Miss Tabbener was the swimming instructor. We used to dress up as flowers and ducks for swimming displays. I got a penny for passing the swimming test. Competitions were played against Erdington and Marston Green Homes and sometimes Barnardo's Homes. Footbal hockey and cricket was also played against these homes. We had very good football, cricket and hockey teams. We also competed against them at our annual sports day.

Shenley Homes had their own brass band and boy scouts band. The military brass band used to march to Lodge Hill Cemetary on Armistice Day for the Rememberance Service. They also played on the pier at Llandudno when we went on our annual holiday. The girls went for the first week then the boys had the second week. We all stayed at a large school and slept on the floor of the hall. We each took a pillow case with our clothes in. This was also our pillow. The Shenley Fields Band played to the public on the pier and collected money in tins. This was our pocket money for spending in the week. In front of the school was beautiful white daisies. Llandudno was our favourite holiday resort and we had many a giggle in the big hall during the night.

The Homes gardens were beautiful and very well kept by Mr Newman. We each had a little plot of garden by our own home to cultivate but the large gardens were tended by Mr Newman and his men providing us with fresh fruit and vegetables and a wonderful array of flowers and shrubs.

The grocery came from the stores at the top of the drive and was delivered to each home by the older boys in large wicker baskets. These same baskets were used on sports days to take the sandwiches and cakes to the sports field. The milk was collected in large churns from the local farms. On Easter Sunday we all had a whole egg for breakfast. On May Day we dressed horse and carts up and rode into Harborne. There was a Maypole on the top field and we did Maypole Dancing with coloured ribbons on the Maypole. I always wanted a red ribbon.

One year we went to Wallasey where the Queen Mary was docked. We were shown over the ship and then had to write an essay about it. I won a leather bag embossed with acorns. It was the first prize and inside the bag was 5/-. I treasured it for ages.

The homes children were very priviledged to have excellent medical care. We had our own hospital, doctor and dentist. Dr Aldridge was our doctor and later his son became the doctor. The hospital with its open air wards was right by the playing fields.

There was a donkey kept on the bottom field but he did not like anyone riding him.

In 1923 our Assembly Hall was opened. It was a large building and served as a church on Sundays and during the week was used for many activities including amatuer dramatics and dancing. The far end of the hall had an altar with beautiful stained glass windows which were designed by Birmingham University Students. All the chairs were turned round on Sundays to face the altar. Boys sat on one side and girls sat on the other. Mr Cohen played the organ for us. The vicar was Reverand Wilton. During the week the chairs were turned to face the stage. We put on several plays which were performed in front of the Guardians. These were the people who ran the Homes in those early days. Each Christmas every cottage put on a play for the Guardians. I was once a Butterfly Queen on the stage and can still recite the verse I had to say.

While we were in care our uncle paid for our keep. My father and uncle layed the Tarmac playgrounds at Shenley. My brother worked for Mr Newman the gardener and when he left Shenley he worked at Cannon Hill Park. One of my brothers played in the Homes Military Band. I won several school prizes at the Homes school. At that time the schools were for children in care only.

Mr and Mrs Cohen were the Superintendant and Matron of the Homes. Mrs Cohen was a lovely lady. She walked very upright and had silver hair and a very small waist. Miss Field, Miss Gent and Mrs Cohen were all very much alike and very elegant ladies. Mr Cohen was strict and he gave out the corporal punishment when required. This was done every Monday morning in the office. My brother got four of the best for stealing fruit from the orchard. He went to the office with dusters down his trousers so he would not feel the cane so much.

Non of the houses had electricity. They had huge coal ranges. All the floors were stone including the stairs. We had a toilet indoors which we were allowed to use during the night but daytime we had to use the outside toilet.

I was confirmed Easter 1925 at St Lawrences Church in Northfield. I still have my prayer book which was given to me at my confirmation. Reverand Hassan was the minister then.

I really enjoyed my life in Shenley Fields Cottage Homes and remember the wonderful gooseberries we picked from the orchard. It was a very happy place to be. Many names of friends are still remembered by me including Florrie Dutton, Marg Scrivens, Maud Nicholson, Ivy Sharp, Gladys Winters, Dolly Highley are some of the girls. There was a little boy in our house called Douglas. Everyone loved him. Gwen Archer was very deaf. They kept her on as a sewing mistress. Many children went on to university from Shenley Fields. Harry Cockayne went abroad to do some work with animals. Rosy Gamble was

65. The group of Shenley children who walked to Northfield to see the eclipse. Photo loaned by Mrs Pearson.

66. Country dancing on the fields was always popular. May Pearson who loaned the photograph is in the front right hand corner of the group.

one of my many friends also Jessie Cooper. Miss Castle worked in the office. The stores where we had our food from was by the office. Mr Smith was the cobbler and worked in the Homes for 35 years. He taught the boys how to make and mend boots and shoes. He taught my brother who then became a cobbler when he left care.

I still have my bank book with 3/6 in it. We used the Municipal Bank in Harborne and walked there through the Weoley Castle ruins scaring each other about ghosts. Cyril Scott was a boy I really liked.

I still have a table cloth that was made by Miss Field. It is white cotton with a deep lace border.

I left the homes in 1929 and went to Riversdale House on the corner of Pebble Mill Road. It was later called Pebble Mill House. I had a wonderful time there. I started work at Southalls Chemist in Bull Street. My wages were 10/- per week. I had to divide that up for savings, rent etc. I saved quite a lot of money there. Riversdale House was looked on as a finishing school where you stayed till you were 18 or 19 years old. Then they found you a position where you lived in. I went to Lady Reynolds at Knowle to look after her little daughter as a nanny. I went into hotels with them and I had a uniform. We were so well trained in the Homes we could be taken anywhere. When we left the Homes we all had two sets of clothes given to us. I still have the little suitcase Miss Field gave me with my clothes. It has C. FIELD on the front. She bought me some grey silk stockings also. After I left she invited me to her sisters house in Stourbridge.

They were happy days and I owe a lot of my happiness to the care I received in Shenley Fields Cottage Homes. Many everyday things remind me of my happy youth.

Jackie Pearshouse
Rosemead

There seems no need to look at a clock or even rack my brains too much, to imagine what it was like — the time I spent in care at the Shenley Fields Homes. The only childhood I can remember is one of fun, love and warmth. So many thoughts come to mind when someone asks "what was it like in care". The naive seem to conjure up all kinds of thoughts: — Bars on windows, locks on doors and no end of punishments. Well I can assure all those people who ask and all those people who'd like to, but wouldn't dare! that it was nothing like that.

My years in care are my treasured memories that through hard times since, no-one could take away. The stigma that you carry through life just by saying "I was brought up in care" is incredible. Many assume that you committed a crime to be put away in a Childrens Home.

My only crime was that I along with my four sisters and a brother were born to a woman who didn't want us. My mother left us, the youngest 8 months and the eldest 6 years old. My father couldn't cope alone and my grandparents bravely managed for 6 months. Hence the start of my eleven years at Rosemead.

We were all kept together, so we never had the problem of families trying to trace lost brothers and sisters.

Life was grand in that big house where pear trees grew up the sides of it. There was so much happiness and warmth. We were never cold or hungry.

Shenley Fields School, Northfield,
Birmingham.

SCHOLAR'S
LEAVING CERTIFICATE

This is to Certify that.....

Mary Griffin

has attended the Shenley Fields School

for ___ 8 ___ years, ___ — ___ months, and is legally exempt from attendance at an Elementary School, having ~~either passed an examination by H.M.ᵃ Inspector of Schools, in Reading, Writing, and Arithmetic in the 7th Standard or~~ reached the age of 14 years, as defined by Section 9 of the Education Act, 1918.

Standard completed ___ VI.

Attendance ___ V.C ___ Ruth Ruisons

Punctuality ___ Excellent

Conduct ___ Exemplary.

General Remarks ___ A remarkably refined and well-behaved girl. Extremely neat and painstaking. An excellent needlewoman.

A. Lock

Head Teacher.

Date 24ᵗʰ July ___ 1926.

67. Scholars Leaving Certificate belonging to May Pearson nee Griffin.

142

Our independence grew in little tobacco tins with our names scratched on the lid. It was from there our pocket money would be handed out on Saturday morning, and every birthday it would go up just a little bit more.

Christmas time was beautiful. Santa would ride his sleigh down the Drive ringing his bell for all the children to come out and see him. There was a present for every one. Christmas was made special for the children who hadn't any family to go to. Letters would be written by each child addressed to Father Christmas. Eager faces awaited every tear of Christmas paper on Christmas morning. We always got what we wanted.

Mrs Elaine Platt nee Higgins
Home 5 Ferndale
1953 – 1971

I went into care on Shenley Fields Drive in 1953 when I was 5 years old. The Home I went into was Ferndale, (this was later changed to Cherry Garth). My housemother or foster mother as they were sometimes called was Mrs Moore. She was a lovely person, very warm and caring. When you first go into care you feel very frightened but she soon helped me settle down. I shared a dormitory with several other girls. There were about 14 boys and girls altogether in our Home. The house was large but very friendly and warm. We had our own playroom with television. There were lots of boxed games. We each had our own locker which we had to keep tidy. Mrs Moore had her own sitting room, but she often came into our room to play the piano for us and to play cards with us. We had 4 good meals every day, and at week-ends we had sweet ration and ice creams. Every day we had an apple or orange for school. During the week we had school dinners. Sundays was special, we had cakes jellies, pop and ice-cream.

It was nice being brought up with lots of 'brothers and sisters' and you never had time to be lonely as you always had friends.

We used to go scrumping for apples and pears on the Drive. We would have been in trouble if we were caught. There were swings on the playing fields so we didn't need to go the park. Our garden was like a park. We had dancing lessons, ballet and country dancing etc on Thursdays and picture shows on Fridays in the Assembly Hall. I think we had more fun and entertainment than most kids not in care. I had boy-friends on the Drive too. Although we didn't get much fuss or attention as other kids do, it didn't deter me from becoming an affectionate warm person.

Our punishment for being naughty was very fair, even though you didn't think so at the time. We either had to go without our pocket money (8/-) for the week, stay in every night for a week or do extra jobs. We all had a job a day to do on a rota basis, before school and at weekends. If we were naughty at night we'd have to stand downstairs in the hallway for an hour (it didn't do me any harm anyway). We were never hit at all. The worst you could get was a slap on the back of the legs. The other punishments were usually effective without being hit.

Kids from other Homes always told us our housemother was one of the best on the Drive. She was one of the most lenient and gave you extensions if you went out some-where special at night. If you came back late she would put her foot down and you would loose your extension time for next time. I was very happy living there thanks to a fabulous 'mom'. We were taught how to save and handle money, which has helped me a lot in later life.

Being in care has affected my life now in many ways. I can handle money well and take care of myself. I am a very sociable person due to being brought up with lots of 'brothers and sisters' like a realy family and find it easy to mix with both sexes. I am now very understanding, caring and thoughtful towards less fortunate people than myself because I can relate to them. Being in care taught me independence. I find types like us find it easier to cope in life than someone from normal families. We have to make sure we don't fall down as we have no-one to fall back on to help lift us up again. This helps make you stronger.

Being brought up in care also has its draw backs for instance, when one is brought up in a large family and have to go it alone for the first time it's more lonely and hard. If the going gets tough one has no one to support or help in times of trouble. You really miss your big family at Christmas. It's so lonely. When you get older you envy families. I never envied families when I was in care but I do now. Even if you are invited to someones house for Christmas you still feel on the outside of things. You feel intimidated sometimes if people offer pity. Yes it's a harder and lonely life when one goes out into the big wide world. You feel a stigma about your past. One misses having a mum around and no one visits you if you go into hospital. Your own children lack a Grandma and Granddad, aunts and uncles etc. Some relatives (if you have them) welcome you when you're young but when you get older they reject you. My past upbringing taught me how to deal with children and bring them up properly. How to deal with the discipine side of things. I also learnt to love animals as we all had our own pests in the Home. I had guinea pigs. I learnt to be a good all rounder in sports, dancing, swimming etc also to be a good mixer. I learnt to cook, clean and do my own washing, ironing and generally look after myself.

My happiest memories of the Drive were the Christmases. We went to parties wearing pretty frilly dresses (the rest of the year our clothes were quite drab). There were also lots of pantomimes to go to. We had dancing lessons and I was thrilled when I won bronze and silver medals. We went swimming every week in the school holidays.

Being in care has given me a lot of benefits. I feel a better person for it. I consider myself very lucky to have had such a wonderful housemother and a great group of friends that I still keep in touch with today.

Mrs Jill Plumley
Melplash and Elmdene
1971 – 1983

I started work at Shenley Fields Cottage Homes on 2nd June 1971. I had never been in a Childrens Home and did not know anything about the Shenley Fields Childrens Homes though I had lived in Weoley Castle all my life and attended local schools with some of the homes children. When I went to meet Mr and Mrs Neish who were in charge of Melplash I really did not know what to expect. I think I was expecting a place like the films picture the old orphanages. Huge rooms full of miserable half starved children. What I did find was totally different. Shenley Fields Drive was beautiful. The gardens

68. A group of Officers in Charge (new title for housemothers) enjoy a rare night out. Photographed at The Nite Out Theatre in Birmingham.

were very well kept by Mr Collins and made each of the homes look very pleasant. There were many pine trees that were obviously quite old. At the back of some of the homes was an orchard. Not many children played on the drive-way but each home had a large back garden with swings etc, for the children to play on. Melplash was a 12 bedded unit with quite a wide age range of children. Mr and Mrs Neish were very homely and the children loved them. I started work as a domestic cleaner doing 15 hour work each week. My son Steven was at school and daughter Helen was being looked after by my neighbour Betty. I was very upset when Helen wouldn't settle with Betty and I thought I would have to give my job up but Mrs Neish helped me by speaking to the Headmistress of Shenley Fields Nursery. Helen was allowed to start nursery school just for the hours I was at work at Melplash. Other members of staff I remember from these early days are May, Edna, Dorothy Williams, Pat Smallman, Jean Killingworth, Lily Craddock and Christine Noxon. Christine emigrated to Australia when she left Melplash. Her place was taken by Margaret Mitchell. Mr and Mrs Neish left and their place was taken by Mr and Mrs Kiczma. I got on very well with them and enjoyed working for them. Mr Peter Kiczma offered me the post of childrens attendant. I enjoyed this job more than the domestic post as it involved me working more with the children and their problems. I made up my mind that this was what I wanted to do most and decided I would not rest until I was Officer in Charge of a home of my own. For the valuable experience I took the post of cook at Melplash before applying for the Deputy Officer in Charge post. By this time Mr and Mrs Kiczma had left and Mr and Mrs Poray had taken over the home. I saw many children come and go from Melplash and still have many photos of trips we went on with them. Most of them were lovely children and I often wondered what happened to them, especially Maya, Sandra and Jeanette or Frizzy as we used to call her. I have shed many a tear when they all left.

After Melplash I moved to Elmdene as Officer in Charge or Housemother as we were called then. My Husband became Part Time House-Father. This meant he worked at his own job during the day and worked for a minimum of 10 hours a week in the home. He did not receive a wage for this but had his meals free. Believe me he did many more than 10 hours work in that home each week. I was warned that it was a tough home and the boys there were still upset about the previous Houseparents leaving. I went there expecting the worse. The boys met us at the door and told my husband and I not to unpack as they would be getting rid of us quick. I felt like running but it only made me more determined to stay. They really gave us a hard time. There were 10 boys in the Home. Only 2 of these were orphans. Some had been in care most of their lives. Several were non school attenders. Others were in care because they could not cope in their own home for various reasons.

The previous Officer had emigrated to South Africa. She had been at Elmdene for several years and most of the boys regarded her as their mother. She was the only "mother" most of them had known and when she left they felt deserted.

I think the big test came when I had to go court with 6 of the boys. They had robbed the milkman of £10 and the dairy decided to prosecute them as an example to others. I think all of the boys had decided they would have to move to Forhill Remand Home. In court I had to stand up and say why I felt these boys had behaved this way. I said I felt it was because of the upheaval the boys had been through and I also felt it was done to test me out. The magistrate asked me if I wanted to keep the boys at Elmdene. I insisted that this was what I felt needed to happen as another rejection would be very detrimental to the boys and to the relationship I was trying to build up. The magistrate allowed 5 of the boys to come home with me after a stern warning and the oldest lad who had actually taken the £10 was sent to Forhill Remand Home for only 3 weeks. From then on things improved a great deal. We struggled to improve the general conditions in the unit which was quite run down. The staff gave us a lot of support and brought in many nice ornaments and pieces of furniture. Soon the home started to feel comfortable and homely and many of the tensions went. Most of the boys clothing was old and shabby so it was replaced with new more trendy clothes which made the boys feel better and more confident. They started to settle down and accept the basic rules of the home which made life better for everyone. I am not saying they were little angels because they most definitely were not but they could be spoken to and reasoned with, which made life a little easier all round. We were on the way up the ladder.

Shenley Fields Drive was like a little village. Originally it had been built to take the children that were in the workhouse in Selly Oak. At first only 5 Homes were built but this soon expanded to 11 Homes 1 hospital, 2 schools, 1 engineers cottage, 1 superintendants lodge, several workshops and store rooms 1 swimming baths 1 office and a church/assembly hall. When I started in 1971 the swimming baths had already gone, the engineers cottage was derelict, one school had been pulled down and the other had become a nursery school used by children from the local estate. The assembly hall was no longer used for church services and the children from the homes went to local churches of their own choice. The hall was used for a few functions and discos but was fast becoming vandalized. The hospital had now changed its function to a home for mentally and physically handicapped children, and had been renamed Pinewood. All of the children went to Pinewood for their medical checks. Two of the Doctors then were Dr Clarke and Dr Ireland. Mr and Mrs Griffin lived at the Lodge which was called Shangri La. They were the Superintendant and Matron and contributed enormously to the well being of every child in care and member of staff in the home. They were very supportive to all of the Houseparents and always offered advice and encouragement when problems presented themselves. Next door to Shangri La was the office. Everyone went to the office for their wages and petty cash float. The shoemakers shop had gone but above the office's the seamstresses made curtains and covers and did repairs for each home. The children had more choice in what they wore. The uniforms had gone. Clothing was purchased on clothing orders from a select number of shops who would accept the orders from Social Services. They often had to wait some time for payment.

I used to shop at the Weoley Castle Square Shopping Centre, at a shop called Lawrences. They were very good to us and gave me a good discount which enabled me to get more for the boys out of their clothing allowance. The clothing allowance was one of our nightmares. The department made us an allowance for so much per year per bed. They did not take into account that the beds could be used several times a year by different children who each arrived with just the clothes they stood up in. We had to buy school uniforms and casual clothes out of this budget, and some of the boys were in adult size clothes. We also had the problem of clothing that went missing. When new boys arrived and had new clothes bought for them, several pairs of shoes and trousers belonging to the other boys mysteriously went missing. We found 2 hiding places, one was the old air-raid shelter in the garden and the other was up the chimney in the outside shed that used to be the wash house. We often laugh at some of the antics the boys got up to with their clothes. One boy named Terry wanted to wear his best green flares (trousers with very wide legs and a lot of buttons at the waist) for school. He was only allowed to go to school in straight legged grey trousers. Every day he sneaked his green trousers out of the house and changed into them behind the shed, hiding his grey trousers in the bushes. When the school phoned us one day to ask why he was wearing green trousers instead of grey we searched and found his grey trousers. They were brought indoors and Terry was afraid to come home because he knew he had been found out. We solved the problem by buying grey flared trousers which he contributed half the cost. The same boy was a fanatic for bicycles. He used to creep out during the night, steal a bike and hide it in the orchard then be back in bed before anyone woke up next morning. I wonder what he is driving around in now. I bet its not a bike. He was a real charmer. An Arthur Daley in the making, and one of our most popular boys. The youngest child we had in our home was 2 years old and the eldest was 17 years. They all had different problems and very different personalities. Even the toughest character had something nice if you took the time to get to know him. This was brought out by different members of staff. If a boy did not get on with one member of staff he did with another. I have always felt that a Home was only as good as the staff who ran it. I was lucky to have lovely people to help me run my home. Everyone contributed something different to make the place feel homely and very secure. This was a compliment I had given to the home by many councillors, parents and social workers and something I was very proud of. All the ladies were called aunt by the boys and my husband Roy was called 'unc'. I inherited 7 lovely ladies that each had something different to offer the boys and the home.

Aunt Lil who baked the loveliest cakes and sounded very strict and sharp but underneath was very caring. The boys knew where they stood with her. Aunt Eadie wore big bloomers down to her knee's. The boys used to have hysterics when she bent down. She would chase them with the mop afterwards.

Aunt Nora, always elegant and refined but a good listener if you had a problem. She had a habit of exaggerating the s's at the end of her words. Terry had great fun imitating her and was very fond of Nora. She loved walking the children to the park or local shops and believed in fresh air.

Aunt Doris lived for the children. She could only see the good points in any child and refused to condemn them no matter how naughty they were. She got very upset about some of the problems the children came in with especially if they had been badly treated. She always knew before anyone else if someone wasn't well, and she never forgot anyone's birthday. Her family was also very involved with the boys and her daughter Yvonne used to cut the boys hair. Doris and husband Jim ran the home for several months when the previous officer first left.

Doreen was the comedienne of the team. The boys could have a laugh with her and sometimes good naturedly played her up. She brought her two children Sharron and Steven to Elmdene during the school holidays. Sharron played with my daughter Helen and Steven played with the lads.

Rose was the D.I.Y. lady. She was always mending things. She walked so fast you had a job keeping up with her. She gave the boys a good telling off when they made a mess of 'her' bedrooms but they knew she held no grudges and still tidied up after them the next day. Did we find a few surprises when she turned mattresses and cleared out drawers and wardrobes especially from Hugh and Delroy. Her sense of humour was great.

Dolly or Aunt Will was everyone's mom. She heard everyone's troubles including mine. She was everyone's strong sympathic shoulder. You could tell her your inner most secrets and they went no further. She was famous for getting her words mixed up. One day one of our 14 year olds was playing her up. She said to him, "I will give you such a wanking if you don't stop". This was a combination of walloping and spanking but came out as wanking. Robert just smiled at her suppressing his laughter. I had to take her to one side and explain what she was promising him. We have had many a laugh over this since.

A few new staff followed as the older staff retired. I was fortunate to be given a deputy officer. The first deputy I had was Lydia but she only stayed for a little while and left to look after her mother.

The second deputy was Ann. She was a lively person, very young with fresh ideas. She loved the children and worked very well with them. She eventually left to become Officer in Charge of one of the 8 bed units.

My last deputy was Monica. She started at Elmdene just before it closed and is now Officer in Charge at another home.

The boys insisted on us having a male member of staff as Roy was the only male staff they saw and he wasn't around during the day. We employed Mike as a childrens attendant but the boys only wanted him as a punch bag and I don't think Mike was cut out for changing soiled underpants off our incontinent 4 year old. He left to work in a teenage unit.

Another person who only stayed for a short while was a domestic called Ann. She had a very young family and found it difficult coping with a family and a job.

The last member of staff to join Elmdene was our cook Stephanie. She was big and very jolly and scared stiff of our donkey Matthew. He used to wait round the corner and frighten her to death when she crossed the yard. She was a great cook with a lovely personality. Everyone contributed something to the home to make it a nice place to live and work I couldn't have managed without any of them.

Roy my husband was my biggest support. He had been a difficult child and could see that many of the problems the boys exhibited were really cries for help. We had children in our private sitting room at all times of day or night. Sometimes the only way to get to the bottom of their problems was to make them become angry and often abusive. Then they calmed down and began pouring out their problems. Roy and I have lay awake through the night talking about some of these problems and how they can best be dealt with. Roy has endles patience and great understanding. Roy and our two children had a lot to put up with. Because Helen was the only girl in an all boy unit she had a little more protection and attention from the staff who were very good to her. This often made the boys jealous and they could be quite spiteful to her, but she could cope with this and became quite bossy in defence. Most of the time the boys helped her especially when they all had home-work to do. Helen excelled with the little children and kept them amused for hours. She still has contact with many of the boys from Elmdene. Steven was very quiet and reserved. He kept himself to himself and never got involved in the boys arguments but was always ready to help if they needed bikes repaired.

Elmdene was sponsored by the Birmingham Junior Chambers of Commerce. They supported us in our fund raising and in arranging the childrens holidays. Every week we had table tennis competitions between the Junior Chambers people and our boys. They had little silver cups made to present to the winner of the competition and to the best new player. Junior Chambers helped with transport arrangements and pocket money for the annual holiday. We considered ourselves very lucky to have such dedicated sponsors.

We had some lovely holidays while at Elmdene mostly to Great Yarmouth or Weymouth. We have also been to Butlins at Phwelli and Barry Island. I think the favourite was Weymouth. We stayed in caravans at Blue Water Caravan Site, which is midway between Weymouth and Portland. If the weather was very hot we went into Weymouth on the beach but if it was too chilly for swimming in the sea we went up towards Portland. There is an underground prison there called The Verne and a huge Borstal Institute. The borstal used to facinate the lads. Once, when we were walking by the borstal, two of our younger boys were really playing me up. I noticed one of the security guards watching them and when I got near him I suddenly asked if they had any vacancies for naughty boys. He immediately said "yes take them to that office". The boys were scared stiff and never moved from my side till the guards were well out of site. One night towards the end of the holiday we decided to go for a midnight drive in the mini bus. We first went down into Weymouth where the boys were thrilled to see army tanks driving along the front, They were from the local army camp. Then we went up to Portland and drove up by the Prison Gates. It was very spooky and even I felt nervous. The boys loved it and talked about that night for weeks after the holidays. We did have one bad holiday however. We stayed at Great Yarmouth and on the Friday went to the Model Village. I had a movie camera with me and intended to film the village as I walked around. After explaining to the boys the need to stay on the path and not touch the models I allowed them to walk on ahead. When I was half way round a security officer tapped me on the shoulder and asked if the boy with him belonged to me. I said he was one of our group and he informed me he had 5 more in a shed. My heart sank as I followed him back to the shed were the boys were being held.

The boys looked very guilty and worried. The man explained the bigger boys had lowered the youngest boy down the Wishing Well to get at the money that had been thrown down there. They tried to deny it but just looking at the wet state of young Jason told me different. I made them empty their pockets of any money they had including their own pocket money and gave it all to the man. He said we had to leave the village and not go back. He then escorted us off through a side gate. I was so angry and humiliated. The guilty boys missed the party disco that night at the camp. We can laugh about that incident now and several more of our more difficult times but thankfully they were not that frequent.

An important part of our Home was the pets. We had guinea pigs and tropical fish to begin with. Our first dog was Goldie a lovely little whippet bitch. She was found abandoned in Balsall Heath and was barely alive when the boys from Ryedale Home asked me to look after her. The vet advised us to have her put down as she was very old and ill. She looked at us with great big brown eyes as though pleading for a chance. We decided she was worth the struggle and she stayed for 8½ years till she died. She was so faithful and placid. Then we had a donkey called Matthew. He was a real character and refused to be ridden by anyone. He often escaped into the road and had to be rescued. The local boys from the community kept letting him out in the middle of the night and we were afraid he would be injured so we had to let him go to a local farm. He knew Stephanie our cook was afraid of him and he waited round the corner of the building till she came out then he chased her round the garden till we rescued her. The other dog we had was Hannah a retired greyhound. He was a big softy and loved the children. When the home closed he came to my house to live. He broke his leg one night when he slipped on the ice while chasing a cat. He could not cope with his leg in plaster and became very viscious. It made it impossible to do anything for him and eventually he had to be put to sleep. It broke my heart as he was a lovely dog.

The majority of my time as Officer in Charge was spent at Elmdene 17 Shenley Fields Drive where we had 10 boys. In 1981 we had to move to Greenways 6 Shenley Fields Drive, so we could accommodate boys and girls. This was a move I wasn't happy about as I had great reservations about taking in girls in a unit that had always taken only boys. Boys with problems can be difficult enough but girls and boys with problems was something I preferred to do without. However the powers that be decided we must become a mixed unit and that's what we became. We never really settled in this house mainly because of the problems we had with local 'Skin Heads' (these were a group of local youngsters who shaved their heads and went about as a gang often causing trouble). They used to come on the Drive when the police chased them from Weoley Castle Square where they had been causing trouble. They hid in the long grass in the orchard at the back of our house and lay there till the police had left, then they would come into our gardens and break the childrens slides and swings and break into our sheds where the bikes were stored. It was this same group who kept letting Matthew the donkey out of his stable and out onto the roadway. One week-end in particular they really caused us problems and it cost us our caravan and a great deal of upset for the children.

During the week-end Roy and the boys had pulled our caravan down the drive and sited it in the back garden of the new Home. The boys spent the whole week-end cleaning it up ready for our eldest lad to start minimal care training using the caravan as a flat. On the Sunday evening after spending the whole day cleaning and polishing the caravan the boys went to bed very tired but happy that the caravan looked so nice. Between 10.30 p.m. and 11.30 p.m. some of the local youngsters came into the garden and pushed the caravan through the back gates and rolled it down the two grass banks at the back of the house, wrecking it beyond repair. The boys and staff were very upset. The incident featured in the Evening Mail Newspaper the next day with a photo showing the damaged caravan. The day after, we had a phone call from a man who said he was at the Royal Agricultural Show. He offered the boys his small caravan to replace the one they had lost. He said he was a farmer from Cornwall and offered free holidays on his farm to some of the boys.

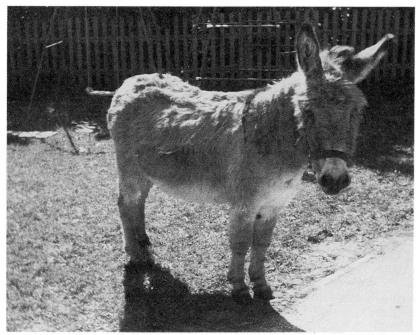

69. Matthew the donkey. The biggest problem of them all. He would have been on permanent washing up punishment if he was human. Photographed in the back garden at Greenways by Jill Plumley.

The caravan was to be brought over on Sunday. Some of the boys cancelled home leave so they could meet him to thank him for the caravan. Sadly it was a hoax and no one came or phoned again. The boys were both heartbroken and very angry.

It was not a success mixing boys and girls. The staff found it difficult to adjust to having both sexes. The boys hated the girls invading their domain. We had some very unpleasant situations to deal with. The boys became devious and the girls became viscious. When we finally got them settled down and friendly we had other problems then like keeping them out of each others bedroom. Life was never the same again.

In October 1982 the Home had to close. It was a very sad time for every-one, especially staff and children who had been at Elmdene for many years. Having a complex of eleven childrens homes situated together had many good and bad points. I personally feel the good points outweighed the bad. We often helped each other out with staff and when we celebrated bonfire night, Easter, Christmas etc we had a wonderful time. I remember 2 parties in particular where we used a joint effort to make them a huge success one being the wedding of Prince Charles and Princess Diana, the other was the Jubilee of Our Queen. We had tables down the centre of the Drive and everyone contributed something. Two wonderful days with many happy memories. I still think Christmas Eve was the most beautiful time of all. Most of the children went home for Christmas but the few that had to stay in the Home had a really good time. On Christmas Eve we all collected round the office doorway to sing Carols. On these occassions we were joined by choirs from the Police or Fire Brigade. While we sang, bells would start ringing and Father Christmas came through the gates on a decorated float. He had a sack of toys for each home. The toys had been donated by firms and well wishers. After we finished singing carols we had

70. The Guinea Pigs arrive at Elmdene to live with the other pets. Photograph by Helen Wood nee Plumley.

to go back to our Homes and Father Christmas came round each Home with a sack of toys. Then we had to sing him a song before we got the toys. I don't think we ever finished a song before collapsing with laughter.

These are treasured memories to me and I hope they are to many of the children who stayed for some of their childhood years at The Shenley Fields Cottage Homes.

Mrs Janet Reeves nee Smith
Home 9
Approx 1955

When I was 10 years old I was taken into 'The Tree's' to my dear Auntie Bowes, who loved and took over the roll of being Mom to me. She is also my sixteen year old's God Mother. Without the love and care of house mothers like her, many children like myself would have suffered. I can't sing the praises enough of people like this who did far more for us children than duty and salary paid for. When I was at Shenley the superintendants were Mr and Mrs Griffin. I was never so loved, fed and looked after so well as when I lived in 'The Tree's'. I even named my own house 'The Tree's' because of the happiness I found there. Those days were so important to me. When we were poorly, we were cared for in Sick Bay. I remember Saturday morning and our pocket money. I remember Dad Bowes, now passed away, stoking the boilers up very early in the morning, before he went

152

out to do his daily job. We had new clothes, shoes and lovely food. Marmite and curry are two things I had never tasted before but they are my favourite now.

We had a great bonfire night and until the very year Auntie Bowes left, my husband and I used to take our three daughters to sit under the Christmas Tree in the dining room. Oh the magic of Christmas in those homes, all the wonderful gifts that Cadbury's, Leyland and other big firms like that sent for us children. If only those people who donated all those gifts knew the pleasure they gave. I will never forget those Christmas's. The work the staff put in to making everthing so good for us was amazing. Even the cleaning ladies were dedicated to us. I would like to know what is going to happen to the youngsters of today who haven't got the benifits Shenley gave me.

I went to Shenley Fields Homes a few weeks before they closed 'The Tree's' down. As I drove along the 'Drive' for the last time I cried. I still think the staff that looked after us children, deserve more recognition for the wonderful job that they did. I still know a lot of people who were in the homes at the same time as me.

What about sports day. Try as I might I could never win a prize. I used to help the two sewing ladies in the sewing room over the reception office.

I spent some time in Erdington Cottage Homes as did my brother and sister. My poor brother has a different story to tell about the House-mother he had.

If I could nominate anyone for an award of some kind it would be my Auntie Bowes.

John and Brothers
1921 – 1924
Home 9

John and his brothers were brought into care when they were evicted from their home. They went into Summerhill Home first. All of them had seen hard times before coming into care. When John was 4 years old there was a flu epidemic. The whole family went down with it. They could not afford to have the doctor in. Mother did other peoples washing to get money to buy oranges and cough mixture. She never had any herself though she was also very ill.

A coach took him from Summerhill, during the night, to Shenley Fields Homes. When he got up next morning he found his 3 brothers were in the same Home. The Home was number 9. The home was run by Mr and Mrs Squires. Mr Squires other duties apart from working in the Home was mainly to work in the office and stores. John remembers many details of Shenley Fields Drive.

The house mother at number 6 was Miss Harris and number 10 was Miss Weygood. The boys homes were from number 6 to number 11. The girls homes were out of bounds to the boys.

There were swimming baths on the drive which were local to the homes. We used them every week. Non swimmers were taught to swim with the aid of a sling which was suspended to a central rail over the baths and a pulley with a rope to the side of the baths which was held and pulled along by the teacher who at my time was Mrs Salisbury. On attaining one length of the baths without help she awarded us one penny from her own pocket. Boys used to be awarded a certificate for swimming 10 lengths of the baths. My brother won one of the certificates.

I played the cornet in the 1st Band. There was a second band for learners who were moved to the 1st Band when qualified. The band master was Mr Grainger. We used to go to bookings on outside engagements. We would march to Lodge Hill Cemetary on November 11th Armistis Day and sound The Last Post alongside the Army and Navy Bands. The only long trousers were worn by the band boys. They had a silver stripe down each leg. The tunic had silver braiding and buttons, worn with a pill box hat strapped under the chin page boy style. I have to say we looked very smart. The bandmaster Mr Grainger also wore full uniform when we went out on engagements such as the Birmingham Flower Show at Handsworth Park, and other fetes and gala's. Sometimes we would march through the streets to rally the crowds to the shows playing tunes like Colonel Bogey or Marching Through Georgia. The people were amazed by what they heard. I think by the sound, they expected the Coldstream Guards to march by. We also played at the Town Hall. The big drummer had to have an assistant in front to take some of the weight of the full sized drum when we were on the march.

We went to Llandudno for a weeks holiday. We slept on the floor at a school, with one blanket over and one under us. Our clothes were folded up each night to form a pillow. We thought it was great fun. Our pocket money was about 1½d each day. This was earned by the band playing on the promenade.

There was no electricity at the homes. We had a gas stove in the scullery and a cast iron range with coal fire in the kitchen which always had a large pot and kettle on the hob filled with water ready for the washing up. We only had cold water to wash ourselves in. The homes had no heating other than a coal fire in the day room which was used for meals and general get togethers in the evenings. Only home 9 had 2 staff, the others were run by one mother only.

The infirmary was used as a hospital. One of the nurses was Miss Hall. I spent several weeks there with a scalded foot.

We had no visits or celebrations during my stay. There was a tendency to do our own thing such as organize plays, mainly Shakespeare, including making our own scenery with sheets of brown paper fastened to a few lathes and add pieces of wood. The scenery was painted and laid out by my brother Alan who attained a place at the Moseley School of Arts and Crafts.

Christmas was just another day. We made paper chains and hung them across the day room. We would sing carols amongst ourselves. We even hung our stockings up on Christmas Eve just for the devil of it. They were exactly the same when we woke up next day. Obviously food was very scarce and the house mothers dished it out as fair as possible. A typical days food would be, Breakfast; Cocoa, a boy would put 3 cups of cocoa from a sack with ½ a cup of sugar in a large bucket and fill it with hot water from a large iron kettle on the gas stove. It was served without milk. We used to scrape the cocoa off the bottom of the cup where it settled like sand. The house mother sliced the bread, then the children whose duty it was would melt a tray of fat on the stove and dip the bread in it. I think the fat used was suet. It used to set solid on the bread. Dinner was prepared by the house mother whilst we were at school. Two children would peel the potatoes before they went to school. They were peeled outside in a bucket of cold water on a box, even in winter. The meal would be mashed potatoes, a small portion of meat and greens followed by something like a dish of sago pudding made with skimmed milk. Tea would be 2 slices of bread with jam taken from a large stone jar or a sandwich of dripping. This was served at about 5 oclock. There was nothing more for that day and you went to bed at 8 oclock. Sundays was something special as at tea time we had a cup of tea instead of the usual cocoa, with a small rock cake and two slices of bread and jam. When you think that most of us children there had known what real starvation was, we were grateful for regular meals which to us was luxury beyond imagination. The small rock cakes was the only treasure we could use to trade with. Sometimes we would forfiet it to another boy for some sort of favour received during the week.

Good behaviour and discipline was the order of the day. We attended Church in the Assembly Hall every Sunday. Mr Cohen played the organ which worked on bellows. A boy would be appointed to pump the bellows as required at the back of the organ. Sometimes he would be a bit late starting and nothing came out of the organ for the first few notes, much to the amusement of the boys. The boy would hear about it at the end of the service and perhaps loose the job. There was plenty more boys wanting the job. There were choir boys complete with surplices and white collars led down the aisle to the altar on Sundays. After the service Mr Cohen would call out and introduce new boys. He used to say "I know why you are here. It doesn't make you anymore different to more fortunate children. Think of yourselves as public school boys. I am sure we shall try to teach you to be gentlemen during your stay". I would say he had a lot of success in most cases. He reminded us that gentlemen were not produced by wealth and anyone could be a gentleman if they wished. There was no play allowed on Sundays. Any other day we could do more or less what we wanted. Football between Home 9 and 10 was a regular game.

The surrounding fields and countryside was beautiful. There was a donkey in one field called the Sockwell Field. I don't know why it was called that but we used to have great fun with the donkey. There were little pools with newts, frogs and tiddlers. We kept some in a pool we had made outside the home.

Four boys from Home 9 attended grammar school. Alan my eldest brother was one of them. I remember at the time he had a drawing hung in the Birmingham Art Gallery. Underneath the picture it read, drawn by a 16 year old student at Moseley School of Arts and Crafts. The other 3 boys from Home 9 went to such places as George Dixons and King Edwards Grammar School. The boys that went out to school were allowed 10d per week for travelling expenses but they used to use it for other purposes to purchase small items of interest. This meant they used to run to school however far this was and were often late getting home in the evening. This was something the house mothers could not understand. The money saved was also used to purchase some wire and headphones for the home made wireless. It was no time before we made our own wireless all on our own initiative. Two handles off some broken tea cups served as insulators for the ariel wire which we fixed along side the day room. We took it in turn listening with the headphones often finding a good spot on the crystal with the cats whisker. The first sound I heard was a voice calling 'This is Birmingham 5 IT calling'. It was so exciting to use this new invention, it could have been the first adventure into outer space.

Some days would be long and boring but this was only in the winter period. There were the plays to be rehearsed by the older boys. At the time Home 9 had the most advanced boys amongst us. We had the Grammar School boys, most of the football team and band boys. We stood out above the rest, at least we thought so. There was a time when some boys were taken to see a pantomime. They were unable to take all of us and as these treats were few and far between, the excitement was terrific. We did lots of things between ourselves to keep busy. Our clothes would be mainly jerseys and short trousers. We had overcoats with capes Sherlock Holmes style. Two pair of lace up boots were also provided. Every week Mr Smith the shoe repairer would get us to line up outside with our spare pair of boots and inspect them to see if they need repairing. In the homes we all had our duties to do each day. Jobs were allocated to each boy on a monthly basis according to age and ability. The hall kitchen and bathroom had to be scrubbed each day. All the wash basins were cleaned, taps were polished and all the brass door knobs were polished. The shoes in the bootroom also had to be polished. The tables in the day room were layed and cleared by the boys. Everyone made their own beds. All jobs were done every day before school. We would get up at 6am. Some boys would do jobs in the kitchen helping to prepare vegetables for the mid-day meal. Band practice was at 7.30 a.m.. Once a week the dormitaries were polished with Ronuk polish applied to a tool called a bumper. This was a heavy block on a stail which was pushed along the floor. Sometimes a boy would sit on it to give it added weight. Bed sheets and clothes were changed and we would help to sort the laundry every week. Some of the washing we did ourselves. We washed and darned our own stockings sitting in a circle with wool and darning needles every Friday.

We had to take a bath every Friday evening before retiring. To get hot water for the bath we used to light a fire under the boiler which was in an out building across the yard next to the outside toilet. There were no indoor toilets. We also had a wringer in the wash house or brew house as it was sometimes called. Two boys would turn the handles while another boy fed the stockings through the rollers. The only way we could get the water into the two baths was to get one boy to stand on the surround at the top of the boiler and dip a bucket in the boiler and then pass it down to another boy who would carry it across the yard and repeat till both baths were filled. This was repeated till all the boys had taken a bath. The house mother would check our toe nails and cut as necessary. We felt the job of getting the hot water was a bit risky but we had to help out as it would not be possible for the house mother to manage without the help of the boys. We were what you would call child adults at ten years of age. We did not feel hard done by and did our chores without fuss. I think we felt capable and grown up.

There were three bedrooms in home 9. The oldest boys slept in the small room. The other two rooms were divided amongst the rest of us. We each had our own bed. There were no lights in the bedrooms. The one light on the landing used to give a certain amount of light in the bedrooms. The house mother and her husband slept in a separate private room across the landing. As we had no curtains to the windows we got enough light from the night sky to move about the bedrooms. It was sad that one boy in our room could not help wetting the bed each night. He had to remove the mattress and sleep on the spring covered with one blanket. If we found it necessary to use the toilet during the night it meant going down the stairs which were made of concrete and letting ourselves out to cross the yard to the outside toilets. It could be pretty scaring on a very dark night all by yourself. At six o'clock each morning there was a call made from the room across the landing. We all got dressed and made our beds and went downstairs to start the day which was mainly a repeat of the previous day. It was strange but we never called the woman mother or her husband father. We always called them Mr and Mrs. I think we knew we only had one real mother and father.

There was a time on Saturday afternoons, when we all played outside till tea time, one or two of us would get the girl at the lodge by the main gates to let us out, at great risk to herself, as she was just one of us. We would then run all the way to Harborne or sometimes to Northfield cinema's. We would see films like Tom Mix or Gene Autry, providing we could muster the 2d admission fee which was not very often. We would return by tea time and no one was any the wiser. There was a bus to Harborne but we hadn't got the fare and the entrance money. This meant we had to run there and back. The bus was a small single decker with solid tyres. There was only a driver, he gave out the tickets also. You can imagine what it felt like when a small coach arrived at the homes sometimes during school hours to collect the band boys who had an outside engagement. It meant we had to go to school in our uniform to be ready to go, much to the envy of the other boys. The school was for boys and girls. It had some heating provided by a small boiler. We found the teachers rather nice and understanding but very strict. It would not pay you to step out of line. A threat to send you to the headmaster who had a nasty looking cane was more than enough. He would use it if he thought fit.

There were lots of things too numerous to mention during the journey through the homes. The shoe repairer who came from the outside was Mr Smith. The others who came in daily and worked there there was Mr Brownlow the tailor, Mr Newman the gardener, Mr Humphries the carpenter and Mr Meredith the engineer who lived in the little cottage on the drive.

Lots of boys joined the Navy. They used to come back to see the boys in the homes. It made the boys very envious to see their smart uniforms. One boy came back on an old belt driven motor bike. He was a very bombastic and boastful boy. He came into the day room to tell tales of what he had done. He used to brag about lighting his cigarettes with a £5 note. The boys all believed him though none of them had ever seen a £5 note and the boy telling the tale hadn't got 2 × ½d to rub together.

I well remember the time Wembley was first built. Boys from the home was invited to London. They came back with souvenirs including monster pens and pencils. I felt Home 9 was the favoured home.

How we came to be at the homes was due to being thrown into the street by the bailiff. Times were hard and my mother had seven mouths to feed. Sometimes it meant eat or pay the rent. It finally caught up with her and the result was we ate instead of paying the rent. The only place you could turn to in those days was a place called The Parish who would give you a loaf of bread and a tin of black treacle, but only about once a month.

The journey from there was pretty traumatic. Our ages then ranged from 3 months to about 12 years. As we were only children, (I was just 7 years old), we didn't understand the real meaning of it all, but I must say it must have been terrible for our mother standing there with all of us on the pavement with our few belongings. The cold night air was drawing on and we had nowhere to go to sleep. It was late afternoon when I came home from school and saw what had happened. We had no time to do anything that day. I remember as the darkness fell, an old age pensioner let me sleep on the floor in the bedroom alongside himself and his wife. They were very dear people. I suppose what he did was a little in return for the help I gave them. I used to fetch them a farthings worth of milk from the corner shop as they were not able to get about very well. Mother was lost to us when we went into care. We were allowed visits 3 times a year. She did not forget us though and eventually we went home to a council house in Perry Common. Father worked on a building site.

I went back to Shenley Fields Drive about 3 years ago. One Sunday morning while out getting my paper, I walked on up the hill trying to get my bearings. I remembered the tall fir tree's down the side of the road. When I went through the gates I saw the Lodge and then Home 9. In my mind I could hear the band and the boys talking. It was like opening a tomb. I remembered the way we caught bees and put them in a hole in the ground covered with a piece of glass. We thought we had built a beehive. I walked along the drive as far as the nursery. I felt very emotional as it had been 65 years since I last walked that drive. It was a very strange feeling and I felt upset for days after.

Mr Kenneth Roberts nee Dunn
Home 8
1938 – 1948

As far as I know I remember being in care at the age of 3 years, sitting on a potty and crying.

I was in one of the lower numbered houses because I was too young to go into a higher home. Perhaps I was in care also because I had no relatives as I understand it.

Looking back at my 11 years at Shenley Fields Homes (interrupted by 3 years evacuation to Mountain Ash, South Wales — war years) I can only say that, never have I found such fun, comradeship, love and respect for one another as I did then — and I am sure I will never again.

My heart is full of kind and wonderous memories of those beautiful tree laden Homes in my younger days. I thank God I had those experiences, for it has held me in good stead for my present life.

The Housemothers and staff were unforgettable, the other children were all my brothers and sisters. I have them all in my heart forever. Nothing can wipe that experiences away.

If we were good children we would all go to the cinema down Barnes Hill, on a Saturday afternoon and see films about cowboys and indians (Roy Rogers and Gene Autry etc). If we played up we didn't go, also we had to go without our boiled eggs on a Sunday morning until we behaved. Communal baths and playing fields and drinking milk was the

71. The entertainment for our reunions was provided by Mr Leo Hardy and Mrs Lesley Lawrie. This photograph was taken by Mr Ken Roberts nee Dunn.

norm. Then going to outside school at Ilmington Road, dressed in our peaked caps marked S.F., blue blazers and grey short trousers.

Recently in December 1988 I had the urge to go back to Shenley Fields Homes to take some photographs and see my "old home". I was shocked to see such devastation and isolation of my previous home. But you know even in all this destruction, walking along "The Drive" tears came to my eyes at the memories of it all and truthfully I could hear and sense us all laughing and playing again. The air had definitely not changed and I felt I was back home again.

My driving job takes me twice weekly past Shenley Fields and my head always turns to look and always a tear comes to my eyes as I thank God I was part of that emotional and wonderous experience of my life.

Perhaps one day we will all meet again — I do so hope God will let it happen.

Mr Lawrence Rudd
During 1930s
Hospital and Home 9

How I came to be at Shenley Fields Cottage Homes.

Born 1926 the youngest of 4, two sisters and one brother. We were taken to Western Road Workhouse in 1927. From there we went to Marston Green Homes. I suffered from scabies, impetigo, boils, sores, malnutrition, chicken pox, measles, pneumonia, and whooping cough (not necessarily in that order). We were noted as being the worst cases of child neglect ever seen.

Marston Green Homes was a frightful place and ill treatment was the order of the day. I tried to kill myself by holding my breath. I was covered in sores and couldn't sleep because of the excruciating pains and would cry until exhausted. On several occasions my hands would swell up with the scabies and chilblains until I couldn't bear to let them be dressed. Shoes far too small, were made to fit by forcing my swollen feet into them. Ringworm caused my hair to fall out, my teeth to loosen. A Mr Reynolds was a regular visitor to Marston Green Homes. He was the dentist and would I believe get 2/6 for every tooth extracted. I recall his staggering gait most vividly (he was drunk). Having been ordered to sit in the chair I was then told to open my mouth. A needle was then thrust into my back gums. I screamed in agony and was promptly hit by the nurse. I was held down while two back teeth were yanked out. I passed out. When I came to I heard the sister berating the dentist and showing him several rubber topped bottles. It transpired that in his drunken stupor he had injected distilled water into my gums instead of anaesthetic. And so it went on and on and I slowly became inured to any form of ill treatment. Eventually I was sent to Erdington Cottage Homes. Unable to speak, because by now I was so shocked and in poor health that I couldn't or wouldn't bother to communicate. Erdington was no better and I became withdrawn. I used to wet the bed and my punishment was to stand in the yard most of the night naked except for the wet sheet draped over my head. It never cured me! I was bullied and robbed of my food by the senior boys. When I complained they sought revenge by spitting or putting soil on my dinner. The House-master would hit me.

159

I recall a most sadistic woman at Erdington, a Miss Barnes. She took enormous pleasure in forcing me to chew carbolic soap. Why this reprehensible creature inflicted misery after misery on me, I shall never understand. One day in the garden I found a rusty nail. She apparently saw me pick it up and demanded that I hand it to her, which I promptly did. She then got hold of my hand and stabbed the nail several times into the knuckles until blood gushed out of the injuries. Fortunately someone was witnessing all this. It was the Matron and Superintendant who just happened by. I related the best way I could about the freezing cold baths, the urine soaked sheets, the carbolic soap, the Epsom Salts, the bullying, the beatings etc, etc. I was immediately moved into the infirmary and found respite from it all or nearly all. I was locked up all day in a tiny two-bed side ward. As the infirmary was barely occupied I was almost a recluse and saw no one except at meal times. I asked for company, for kind words, for someone to talk too me instead of at me. I yearned to know what happiness was. I cried out of sheer depression and dejectedness. I began to rebel, to refuse food. I refused most adamantly to obey any further orders. I smashed windows. I threw chairs. I had reached the end of my tether and now people began to be afraid of me. The shoe was firmly on the other foot.

I was moved into Home 9 and was immediately picked on by the bully of that home. I pulverised him and belted the Housemaster too. I then sorted out several other tearaways and knocked them out cold. At last no more ill treatment, no more bullying and so I settled down — or so I thought. One day I was hustled away to Summerfield Remand Homes and it was there that a decision was made to send me to Canada, if my parents could be found to sanction this. I went before a committee and later found myself being driven in a car to yet another home — Shenley Fields Cottage Homes.

Memories of Shenley Fields Cottage Homes come flooding back. I have recall of Matron Miss Parry Jones, of the two nurses also named Jones and of Mr Grainger, the bandmaster, of Mr and Mrs Sturge and dog Judy, of Sister Wheeler and of Mick the groundsman. Of trips to Prestatyn and Sutton Park and Cannon Hill. The Superintendants name escapes me. I was first in the infirmary then moved to Home 9.

Dame Elizabeth Cadbury gave me a box of chocolates and a bible; she had, she informed me, a Lawrence in her family too (my name is Lawrence). Matron had budgies and I was forever at her home. She had a kind soft spot for me and called me "my lovely Lawrence". Sister Wheeler used to take me to town and lodge me in Steelhouse Lane Police Station while she attended the General Hospital (she had sugar diabetes). We would go to Lewis's to see the animals in the roof garden. Once a week I would be taken to Dr Burns Clinic held in a house somewhere off Islington Row, Five ways. I was also a regular visitor to Margaret Street Education Dept.

Yes I have very special memories of Shenley Fields Cottage Homes. I recall seeing a plane crash in the area, of picking armsful of bluebells, of Princethorpe Road School, Ilmington Road School, Weoley Castle Ruins, of sports days, of Christmas, of playing the cornet, the Clarinette and the euphonium. The death of my paralysed pal John Smith, a boy named Danks, a boy named Coles, of being taunted because I spoke to birds, squirrels and rabbits and trees and flowers. I fell rapturously in love with daffodils that grew at the back of the Infirmary. I could recite Wordsworth's Ode to the Daffodils (more remarkable because I was unable to speak to people without experiencing great difficulty). I had an awful speech impediment, hence my regular visits to the Dr Burns Clinic and Margaret Street. Birds and cats, dogs and foxes, squirrels and owls became my companions. I knew of Schubert, Brahms, Beethoven, Von Suppe, Mendelssohn, Bach etc etc before I could read and write or talk. I hummed arias from Puccini, Verdi and other composers of opera and yet I heard the music on Sister Wheelers battery and accumulator wireless but once. In my childlike innocence I didn't consider this extraordinary but apparently those in the infirmary did. I did have a poltergeist and although I couldn't see it I was very aware of its existence and it would play tricks on me at night such as tying my clothes in tight knots and tying my shoes together, pulling the bed into the middle of the room, taking off the counterpane and putting it nicely folded in my locker, covering my bed with flowers etc. It dawned on me why I was put in a room on my own, these antics kept the other boys awake in the ward. I remember the prayers we had to say before and after meals. I remember a rag doll (Sunny Jim) this came from a cereal called " Force ". We always had Force for breakfast. I have still got that rag doll.

I recall being dosed with Malt and Cod Liver Oil, Iron Medicine and Liquorice Powder and Methylated Spirits and powder for chilblains. If my memory serves me well I think I was in Shenley in 1935 or 1937. I know that it was some milestone or something because of a visit by the Lord Mayor and Dame Cadbury. We all had a long tin box of chocolates and I seem to recall red white and blue hats and feathers etc, possibly for King George's Jubilee. Shenley was so like Erdington Cottage Homes in that we had foster mothers and fathers but Shenley differed from Erdington enormously. Shenley I loved, Erdington I hated. I can recall the name of Miss Warburton. She was my house-mother in Home 3. Mr and Mrs Sturge I think were in Home 9. Mr Grainger the bandmaster had a B.S.A. motor bike with side car. He smoked quite a lot but could play the cornet. We had band practice and I recall wearing a blue, silver trimmed uniform with a round pill box style page boy hat. The doctor who regularly visited, wore plus-fours and drove an open car with a spare wheel on the mudguards and a battery on the running board. I recall a Mr Matthews (grey haired red complexion) who played cricket in the homes. He had something to do with the gardens. Sister Wheeler was a thin lady with very white hands. Strict and victorian she wore her hair plaited and in buns.

As one entered Shenley the office was on the right hand side and in the front office was a platform weighing machine and a safe and a big book press. Gass mantles, a rocking horse, a spinning wheel, a dentists chair, all of these I recall being in the infirmary. Walks to Harborne on Saturdays to the pictures, 2d pocket money, coronation cake on Sundays, a sign saying Shenley Fields Homes 100 yds on left, charabanc trips to Sutton Park. Mr Hasson (vicar) taking us to see Choo-Chinn-Chow at some hall. A coach trip to The Prince of Wales Theatre. Twice a week journeys to town to Sheep Street for speech therepy. Memories of Shenley I have hundreds and all happy ones (why did I ever grow up they were the best days of my 62 years).

The band room was up a flight of stairs and I think it was originally a store-house. It had rafters and plain brick walls. Mick the groundsman often gave me a ride on a big dray horse as it towed a grass cutter or grass roller over the playing fields. At Christmas time we used to gather acorns, paint them red, pass a wire through the base and tie them to the Christmas Tree's. On Christmas Day we all awakened to find a full stocking of sweets, apples, oranges etc at the foot of the bed.

I suffered very badly with chilblains and had to have my feet and hands massaged 3 times a day with methylated spirits after which they would be dusted with white powder. I seem to remember that the two nurses both named Jones, always had a cigarette burning, they called them 'gaspers'. They often gave me the cigarette cards that were in each packet. I remember having quite a collection. Sister Wheeler had an alarm clock. It had "Mickey Mouse" on the face and its arms were the fingers of the clock. She bought me a Mickey Mouse toy on one of her visits to town to the hospital and Lewis's.

Though she was kind I was in awe of her. She never smiled and looked very stern and very white. Of course she was ill most of the time, a fact unknown to me until much later. She knew me as a baby in Marston Green, another fact unknown to me at that time.

From Shenley I was boarded out to a man and his wife and their son. The son, a boy of my age (about 10 years of age) showed his resentment at my being the focal centre of attraction and disliked taking a back seat. He set out to undermine the relationship with lies and fairy stories. I was later accused of stealing from his mother's purse and the theft of other monies. I was in ignorance of his machinations until one day he tried to stab me. We fought and he got cut with the knife that he had tried to use on me. All hell was let loose and the mother and father set about me. I defended myself and naturally fought back. The police were called and I was taken back to Summerhill Homes branded quite wrongly as a thief and a maniac. It later transpired that the boy admitted stealing etc but it was too late for me. The dye was cast and I was sent away condemned as being mentally deficient and sub normal. Because of this boy I was to spend 5 long weary dreary years amongst feeble minded subnormal boys, girls, men and women. I eventually escaped during an air raid and to cut a long story short, walked all the way to London where I got a job at number 3 Somerleighton Road, Brixton.

I meant to re-visit Shenley but never carried out my intentions. This poem descibes my feelings when contemplating a visit to Shenley.

The Light Of Other Days by Thomas Moore.

> Thus in the stilly night,
> Ere slumbers chain has bound me,
> Sad memory brings the light,
> Of other days around me.

Thats why I never did go back.

Florence Russell nee Jones
Home 1
1907 – 1913

Florence went into care in Shenley Fields Cottage Homes with her sisters Minnie, Elsie and Lil when their mother died after an accident. She went into Home 1. The Housemother was Miss Battersby. When Miss Battersby left Miss Roberts took over and then Miss Gibbs. Florence's sister Lil went into the Probation Home and Minnie and Elsie went into Home 1. Florence was not very happy with Miss Gibbs, she was not a very nice person and once humiliated her over marking the sheets when she started her periods. Miss Gibbs also pulled her hair out. Florence is very proud that she was the girl given the job of sewing a letter L in cross stitch on the sheets for the lodge, where the Superintendant lived. She was very good at sewing and competed against all the schools in a sewing competition. She made a pair of cooking sleeves and won a box of paints. The little infants school was the first school she want to but later went to the "big" school on

72. Home 1 on Shenley Drive was where Florence Russell nee Jones spent much of her childhood. It was the first home past the office and at one time was used by girls only. This photo was taken in 1989 by Jill Plumley.

the other side of the drive. One of the teachers she remembers well was Mr Freeth who was known as Froggy after he took a live frog to school in his pocket. It jumped out during the lesson and caused uproar in the class. She was very fond of Miss Pugh and enjoyed school. All the family were quite clever. They were also quite well to do and owned land at Alcester which was put in trust for the girls but they never received it and she still does not know what happened to it.

There was a uniform worn by every child in the Homes. In the winter months the girls wore felt hats and warm coats. In the summer they had straw boaters and cotton dresses. The girls' clothes were made by Miss Hacket but each girl knitted their own stockings. Every one was taught to knit and sew. Florence makes beautiful table mats and chair backs which she makes with hairpins. In the second year the girls were taught how to do patchwork.

Florence suffered very much with chest trouble and spent many weeks in the infirmary which was situated at the far end of the drive overlooking the fields. She also spent some time in Selly Oak Hospital and her father used to visit her in there when he was released from prison. Mr Cohen used to write letters to their father in Maidstone jail for them. He was in jail for 8 years. When father wrote back to the girls Mr Cohen took them up to the Lodge to read the letters to them so the other children did not know about him being in prison. Before he went into prison father was a coach man to a famous doctor on the Bristol Road.

Florence was quite happy in the Cottage Homes. She remembers the church at the school but the children often went to church in Northfield. They used to walk there in long lines. They went on many walks to Bartley Green, Northfield and surrounding areas. The homes were surrounded by farms and farm land and was very pretty district. One walk she remembers was to the Lickey's and Frankley Beeches. Many children from the Homes walked to Northfield to see the circus. Her friend Ida Overton and brother worked at one of the local farms with her sister. Minnie went to work at Lady Beecham's as a laundry maid. She had all the sisters' pocket moneys.

One of the leisure activities at Shenley Homes was swimming in the Homes swimming baths. There was an annual swimming gala and Florence won a certificate.

There were also many less pleasant tasks to be fulfilled such as cleaning out the toilet bucket with paraffin. Vinegar and turps was used to wash and delouse the heads. On Fridays all the sheets were washed during the dinner hour. Florence always sat at the end of the long dining table. There were 24 children in Home 1 and one housemother. Everyone had to work and had their set of chores to do.

Florence left care in 1913 and went to Liverpool to work where she continued to do her sewing and eventually became head of sewing. When she left care she found out she was a year older than she had always thought.

I found Florence to be a very pleasant lady with a very happy face. She has bought her own home and is very proud of this. She has one daughter who lives in South Africa. Her grand daughter and grandson have visited her. Though she is house-bound now she still enjoys life and has a wonderful smile and really enjoys company. Her memory is very good and I found her story of her life in care at Shenley Fields Cottage Homes very interesting.

Mr Stanley Smith
Home 8
During 1930's

I went into Home 8 in Shenley Fields Cottage Homes. Our Foster Mother was Miss Sparks and her deputy was Miss Snape.

I was in the Homes brass band. Mr Grainger was the band master. He was a very strict man and taught me to play the Bass Horn.

Mr Blakey was the Superintendant and Miss Parry-Jones was the Matron. Other people I remember are Mr Dunn the Sports Master and Mr Newman the Gardener. Miss Longman was the Foster Mother from Home 2.

We had holidays while we were in care. One of the places I went to was Westward Ho.

There was a tailor who made our clothes and a cobbler who made our shoes. Everyone looked the same.

I was also in the Choir. We had church services in The Assembly Hall and the vicar played the organ. We also used the hall for scout meetings. Plays were performed on the stage.

We did not celebrate birthdays but Christmas was better. We had presents and went to pantomimes.

The discipline was very strict and I ran away once. My aunt lived down the Bristol

73. The church in the Assembly Hall. These holes in the wall once held some beautiful stained glass windows. The church had a choir and an organ. This picture shows all that remained of the church in 1989 after mindless vandals had set fire to the building.

Road and I ran away to her. I was soon brought back.

When I left the Homes I went to a Hostel for boys at Vauxhall. It was even stricter there. You could not go out at all. We joined the ARP to get out at night and used the chance to meet the girls.

One girl walked me back to the end of the road. The officer of the Home saw me and slapped my face in front of the girl. I was confined to the unit for 2 weeks.

Mr Douglas Smith (deceased)
1921 – 1933

I was brought up in care in Shenley Fields Cottage Homes. I well remember Mr and Mrs Cohen who used to be Master and Matron of the Homes during the 1920s.

Although I was brought up at the Cottage Homes between the ages of 3 – 15 years, I never remember seeing my father or mother and I always classed myself as an orphan. I can always look back at those days at Shenley Cottage Homes and say how proud I was of all those people who gave me such love and care by setting me up in this world today.

Those were certainly the days which one can never forget.

74. The Chalice Cup and plate once used in the little church on Shenley Fields Drive are now in use once again at St Gabrials Church in Shenley Lane. Photographed by Mrs Jean Coulter with kind permission of Reverend Michael Castle.

IN GRATEFUL
AND LOVING MEMORY
OF THE
SHENLEY CHILDREN
WHO DIED THROUGH
ENEMY ACTION

75. There was a memorial stone situated outside the school erected in memory of the children of Shenley who died during the two world wars. No one can tell me what has happened to the cross but the plaque that was attached to it is now in St Gabrials Church. Photographed by Mrs Jean Coulter with permission from Rev. Michael Castle.

The above letter was sent to me by Douglas in October 1989. I hoped to go out to see him about his years at Shenley Fields. I am very happy to say that Douglas was able to attend our Shenley Reunion on December 10th 1989. He met many old friends and made quite a few more. Sadly Douglas went into hospital the next week and passed away soon after. I regret I was not able to arrange a meeting with him to record his memories of his years at Shenley Fields Cottage Homes. He was really excited about this book being written and I hope that his family enjoy reading it in his memory.

God Bless, Douglas.

Mr William Sproson
1923 – 1933
Home 8

I was born on 26th January 1917 in the Jewellery quarter of Birmingham in Pope Street. I was one of five children, one girl and four boys. As you may know times were hard and in February 1923 our mother died and then the family were separated. The eldest being sixteen was already living with my grandmother so brother and sister were put in The Middlemore Homes in St Lukes Road off Bristol Street and my younger brother and I were put in Summer Hill, then after a few weeks my brother and sister were sent to Canada and my brother and I were sent to Shenley Fields Homes. Myself being six and my brother 2½ years old. We were put into Home 11 which was the probation home and then moved to Home 8. The Housemother I remember was a Miss Gibbs who was very strict. I remember I soon got used to a different way of life. We were well fed and well clothed.

I soon got used to living with other boys and as a child soon forgot my family. We were all referred to not by name but by numbers, me being number 23 and my brother number 14.

There were 4 homes for boys and 5 for girls and the only time we were all together would be when we were at school and during church services. We each had our jobs to do such as washing and scrubbing floors, dusting, sweeping and preparing food. At church, the Superintendant Mr H Cohen would play the organ. The service would be taken by the Minister from Northfield Church Reverand Haysam and every other week it would be the minister from St Michaels in Bartley Green. I can remember the Assembly Hall having the stained glass windows in the Chancell and The Bishop of Birmingham Dr Barnes consecrating it. I was a choir boy then and I still sing in a choir today. I am a member of the Canoldir Male Choir. We are singing at the opening of the International Convention Centre on June 14th. The Queen and Duke of Edinburgh will be opening it.

The times we used to look forward to were when the holidays came round in August. The boys would have ten days in Llandudno and the girls would have the next ten days. I can see the horses prancing up ready to bolt when they heard the music of our band leading us from the station with our Bandmaster Mr Grainger. There was nearly all horses then and very little motor traffic.

Then it was back to school. Mr Locke was the Headmaster. He wrote a book about the history of Kings Norton and Northfield Wards. I well remember when I was in his class, he took 7 & 8, he told us how that big stone came to be resting on the side of the road near

167

the church in Northfield. He told us it was pushed there in the ice age. His deputy Mr Dunn and his family went to Salt Lake City.

After leaving school I worked for Mr Newman and during the twelve months I was under his authority, I had an accident and I carry the scar today. I was playing with a tin can in the coal yard up by the work shops. I was between the gate when Tommy Treadwell kicked the can and it rolled round the gate. When I returned Tommy was throwing a piece of coal at the trees behind me and hit me in the eye. I finished in the Birmingham Eye Hospital. The eye isn't any use today, so that will always remind me of Shenley Fields Homes.

I can also remember stupidly running away from the Homes one summers day. I walked up to Northfield. I spent most of the time looking in shops and some time in Victoria Park. Hasn't Northfield changed. The little shops have been taken over by supermarkets and you can't see the park from the Bristol Road now. When evening began to fall I began to think where was I going to sleep. Then I walked to Selly Oak and saw the Police Station. I thought I had had enough so inside I went. I remember the policeman at his desk looking down on me. I would be about 12 or 13 years old and about 4 ft 6 ins tall. He asked me if I had eaten since I had been out all day. I said I hadn't and he gave me three thick pieces of bread dipped in margarine that had melted till it ran like water, and a mug of tea. Later on Mr Wilkinson arrived in his car and took me back.

All was not bad, we had more good times than bad. Mr Cohen was very strict but fair also his wife was a lovely person.

76. The girls are dressed for a dancing display. Photo loaned by Mrs Stallard Boulter.

Mrs Vera Stallard Boulter
Dancing Teacher

I was responsible for the dancing classes held in the Assembly Hall on Thursday evenings and also the outdoor games on a Saturday morning. I also taught at The Limes Remand Home, Erdington Cottage Homes and Middlemore Homes. With the dancing classes on a Thursday evening I taught Scottish, Irish and National Dancing. At one stage I held a competition and awarded a medal to the girls who passed the grade, but they all worked so hard that I just could not leave anyone out so Gough's Medal Factory made me about 30 medals that time. They were presented by a councillor. It ruined my pocket for a week or two but I did not mind. The look on the girls' faces gave me my reward. After a while I let the boys join in for the last half hour with ballroom dancing. I still remember the first class they were allowed to join in. They all turned up dressed in their Sunday best. They were a grand lot.

Netball went down well on Saturday morning. Our first match I arranged was with a Private School in Handsworth.

One Saturday I organised a marble match with all the children. For weeks I had been collecting marbles. That was really enjoyed by all children and they went home with pockets full of marbles.

My time at Shenley was mostly enjoyable and I used to look forward to going there. Mr and Mrs Griffin were very good and gave me the freedom to do whatever was of interest to the children and I had very good support from House Mothers and Mrs Tolley in Sick Bay.

Shenley has gone but no one can take away our memories.

Mr David Steane
Rosemead
1948 – 1958

I went into Shenley Fields Homes when I was 4 years old. I was brought up in the house called Rosemead. Mr and Mrs O'Donnell were the house parents. They were a lovely couple and brought us up as a large family. I am still in touch with Mrs O'Donnell but sadly Mr O'Donnell has passed away. I have always tried to live to the high standards they set. There was a very close family feeling and I was extremely happy there. There were many homes on the Drive and many other buildings such as swimming baths, school, assembly hall, offices, a hospital/sick bay, stores, big greenhouses, sheds and a sports pavillion on the field. The gardens were very well kept by a head gardener and his helpers. At the end of the drive near the hospital were the playing fields where we had sports days every year. I was good at sports and enjoyed football, cricket and running. I won the Shaftmoor Sports Cup in 1958 and still have it to this day.

Every year we went on holiday. We went to several places such as Shanklin on the Isle of Wight, Prestatyn in North Wales and Cromer in Norfolk.

I went to school outside of the drive. First I went to Jervoise Road Infants and Junior School and then I went to Ilmington Secondary Modern Boys School.

I remember celebrating the Queen's coronation while I was in the homes. Every

77. A display of country dancing in the Assembly Hall. Photo loaned by Mrs Stallard-Boulter.

78. The netball team and mascot. Photo loaned by Mrs Stallard -Boulter.

Christmas was made extra special by the Selly Oak Hospital Nurses carol singing. It was really nice. We went to lots of parties and pantomimes at The Alexander Theatre and the Hippodrome. The Shaftmoor Pub fostered us and we had treat days out with them.

During the year life was kept as 'ordinary' as possible. We all had our little jobs to do around the home. I enjoyed gardening and woodwork which has helped me in later years. We had physical training, films and plays in the assembly hall which helped pass many a winter evening. Occasionally we would have a visit from the Lord Mayor.

Our food came from a central store on the drive but later on it was delivered from Wrensons Stores on the Weoley Castle Square.

Besides Mr and Mrs O'Donnell I remember many of the staff from Shenley. Mr and Mrs Bowes, Mr and Mrs Cloudesley, Miss Black, Gwen Hall, Mr Colins the gardener, Mr Appleby who was a teacher and carpenter and Mr and Mrs Spencer who were houseparents.

I had a very happy and secure childhood with wonderful houseparents and many friends. I did not meet my sister until I was about 12 years old as she had been brought up at Wassel Grove and Hawthorne House Childrens Homes and only about 10 years ago I found out I had another sister who had been adopted.

Shenley Fields Childrens Homes will always be very special to me.

Mrs Lesley Steward nee Cloudsley
1955 – 1962
Child of Officer in Charge
The Trees

I can remember first arriving at Shenley just a few weeks before my 5th birthday. We had had a terribly long journey from Bristol in our little old Ford on a typical January day — cold and snowy. It all seemed so enormous, large gates and a long drive and huge houses, to say nothing of the big boys we were about to meet and I was going to share my life with for the next 7 years. There was just my older sister and myself amongst all these huge lads.

From my point of view, we seemed to settle in incredibly quickly, there was no looking back for me to our past life. I loved it from the word go. We were part of a big family and being the youngest I was totally spoiled by all around. On reflection, the boys were incredibly patient with me. I had tremendous fun, always being heaved around on somebody's shoulders.

Our small family had its own sitting room and of course my sister and I shared a bedroom. I can always remember the boys being invited in to the sitting room to watch television. This was the first television they had seen and previously they had never been allowed in the "staff" quarters. But from the outset we were one big family and my sister and I shared meals and leisure time, just the same as everyone else.

As I became older and more independent I was allowed more freedom to roam around the Shenley grounds. Making my own friends amongst the other "kids". It was a marvellous way of life for any child, all that open space, including sporting facilities. We spent a lot of time on the athletics track, training and also practising the long jump. I particularly remember the old bus, which was parked in the playground, which sent

79. Coronation Day 1953. Photo loaned by Mrs O'Donnell.

everyone's imagination running with new ideas — even if it were only to jump off its roof. The other meeting place was "the love tree". Everyone seemed to meet up here at sometime during the weekends or school holidays. We climbed up it, we carved on it, we chatted in it.

The other small thing that sticks in my mind, was " the hole in the hedge". This was the short cut at the back of Rydale. This was really "out of bounds", but everyone used it.

I think I began my first romances at Shenley, if you can call it that. We were really like brother and sister, as we all lived together. But I can clearly remember being "in love" with a couple of the boys, and carving the same in the "love tree".

The time I spent at Shenley, from the age of 5 to 12, had a big impact on my life. It gave me a lot of strong opinions that I have kept with me always, I also hope that it has given

80. Some of the initials that grew with the 'Love Tree'. Photographed in 1989 by Jill Plumley.

me compassion. I will never forget those days and I treasure all those happy moments. Shenley was unique, it was a big happy family with freedom and yet a security within its grounds.

My father and mother Frank and Nellie Cloudsley are now deceased but my sister Christine who is now called Bateman and myself hold very precious memories of our childhood spent at Shenley Fields Cottage Homes.

Mrs Eileen Sweenie nee Wood
Home 4
1925 – 1932

I was put into the Shenley Fields Homes with my sister and brother after our father died and mother abandoned us. My sister and I went into Home 4 and our brother went into one of the boy's homes. We were not allowed to go to his home or contact him. The only time we saw him was in school and church. Our mother never bothered to keep in touch at all. The housemother in our home was Miss Gent and the assistant housemother was Miss Johnson. Miss Gent was very strict but not cruel. We respected her and never cheeked her. The assistant housemother, Miss Johnson was very nice but very religious. We all had to say our prayers every morning before breakfast and just before going to bed. I remember Miss Gent getting very angry with one of the older girls. I had very curly hair and this older girl was jealous of it and plastered it with soap to make it straight.

My sister had a good education in Shenley and was taught to type. When she left care she went to work at the Childrens Department in Margaret Street as a typist. I was not so bright but I did excel at swimming and won many of the swimming races. I still enjoy swimming now and regularly go to Cocksmoors Wood Leisure Centre. Miss Bottomly taught me to swim. They were good to us in the homes. We all had our own jobs to do. I had the chamber pots to empty every morning. I also had to clean the knives in the wash house. One day a boy came into the wash house. We heard Miss Johnson coming so I hid the boy in the boiler till she had gone.

I remember the infirmary. I had my tonsils took out while I was in there. We all slept in beds on an open veranda. I saw the foxes in the fields from my bed.

We were bathed 2 at a time and the water had to be used several times before it was changed. This was because it had to be warmed up outside in the brewhouse and brought in by the bucket full. It wasn't very nice if you knew someone had wet in the water. We all slept in two dormitories. There were no lights in the rooms just the light from the landing light or the light from outside. We never had curtains up to the windows. The stairs were made of stone as were all the floors. There were no carpets or floor covering and the floors had to be scrubbed by us children. The food wasn't bad. We had porridge and toast every morning and usually a stew made of mutton for lunch. We always had a mug of warm cocoa before going to bed. Every day we had to have a spoonful of Cod Liver Oil. We all had a bottle with our name on it. The spoon was made of crock. I still take Cod Liver Oil now.

We went on holiday to Llandudno in Wales. We slept in a school hall. Our clothes were put into a pillow case. This became our pillow at night. The boys played in the band on the pier and we had to go around with boxes to collect pocket money.

I remember a girl called Lily Alcock. She had a very bad stutter. One day they took her away to Monyhall Colony to live. I felt very sorry for her and often think about her. This was quite a common thing to happen.

I felt very shut away in the Homes. We never went outside the gates even for a walk apart from when we went to Llandudno on holiday. Some children went out with their housemothers but I didn't go.

I was quite happy in the Homes. I remember having a celluloid doll and they gave me a box with a piece of string attached to pull it around by. This was my dolls pram. I had a penny pocket money each week. Our clothes were nice though we were all dressed the same. We were kept spotlessly clean.

When I was 14 years old the Childrens Department sent for me and I had to go to Margaret Street. On the way there I was stopped by a woman who said "I am your mother". I said "I haven't got a mother". I really thought mother was dead because she had never been in touch with us. When I got to the Childrens Department in Margaret Street they asked me if I wanted to go back to my mother. I said "As far as I know I haven't got a mother". My sister Dorothy said the same thing. We grew up believing she was dead as she had never been in touch with us.

When I came out of the homes I went to a couple in Kingstanding but the man kept putting his arms around me. When they came from the Department to see me I told them about him and they moved me from there. They moved me to live with Mrs Lloyd in Woodthorpe Road.

I married and had five daughters though one of my daughters died 5 years ago. I adopted a boy. He was the son of a woman who had been brought up in the Shenley Homes. I have 13 grand children. I didn't finish working till last year at the age of 71.

174

Mrs Ellen Teague nee Probert
Home 3
Mr Frederick Probert
Home 10
1926 – 1930

In 1926 my young brother and myself were taken into care as our mother had died from TB. Our father died in 1928. Our ages then were 6 years and 10 years respectively. Our first 2 weeks in care we spent at Summerfield Homes. We were then transferred to Shenley Fields Cottage Homes where we remained for the next 3½ years until we were placed in foster homes. We finally went to live with our eldest sister who had married. We lived with her until I got married and my brother entered the Army.

Being taken into care was a welcome relief as we lived in poverty and was underfed and very neglected.

We both only have happy memories of our time in the Cottage Homes and like Frank Matthews remember going on holidays. My brother also played in the homes band and I was one of the girls who shook the collecting tins, collecting coins from the public for spending money. Our time at Shenley was the best thing that could have happened to us. Their training and discipline has stood us in good stead. We had a high standard of cleanliness. Good manners and respect for others was instilled in us. All this has stayed with us. I am now 71 and my brother is 67. We have no regrets about being in Shenley only happy memories. We were well looked after. Every child had their own bottle of Cod Liver Oil with our name on it, which we lined up to take every morning. There was a hospital on the drive. My brother went into the hospital with ringworm and I had my tonsils removed in there. We went to the homes school. Before going to school we all had jobs to do such as getting the vegetables ready for the cook, cleaning the dormatories and cleaning shoes. We had to get up at 6am every morning. We had swimming baths on the drive where I learned to swim. We were taken to Harborne Baths to do 12 lengths of the baths for our certificate. My brother was in the band and he played the clarinet. We went to Llandudno for our holidays. The band came with us and played on the sea front. We took the collection tin around to the people who were listening. They put coppers in the tin which was later shared out for our pocket money. We slept on the floor of the local school. All our clothes were very nice. All the girls had pretty cotton print dresses and the boys wore uniforms of tunic and breeches. We went to the Homes own school. When we came home from school we had to go to the main gate and collect all the bread. Christmas was especially nice. We had presents etc. We didn't get anything for birthdays though because we had no parents to send us cards. All the girls had to do the sewing and darning including the boys socks. Boys were taught gardening and grew all the vegetables. We had a lovely orchard and we used to pick all the fruit for the homes. My brother was one of the boys caught scrumping in the orchard and remembers having twelve strokes on his backside. He agrees with me when we say we knew what discipline was and it didn't do us any harm to be corrected in this way. When my brother had to do Army Service during the war it was no hardship for him.

We have happy childhood memories that have stayed with us through life thanks to Shenley Fields Cottage Homes.

Anonymous
Home 5
1926/32

I was in Home 5 at Shenley Fields between 1926 and 1932. I was 1 year old when I arrived and 7 when I left. My earliest memory was of my 4th birthday when my mother sent me a birthday card which was a glossy post card with a figure 4 on. I remember days in the infant school where we were allowed to sleep for part of the afternoon and being sent round to the juniors classrooms to show off my spelling to the older children. I remember cleaning the shoes of everyone in Home 5 occasionally, also evenings by gas light playing with lead soldiers, armies of them which belonged to the Home. Homes 1 to 5 were girls homes where boys stayed until the age of seven. I left in February 1932 just before I was seven. I remember the swimming pool and being hauled its length on a pulley system. I remember blacking up for a part in Hiawatha one Christmas. The church doubled as a theatre. I vividly recall Saturday afternoon walks to Bartley Green to spend our pocket money. It was only one penny but would buy 4 bullseyes or 2 gob stoppers. I recall playing with whips and tops-tipcat, hoops and Jackstones (5 stones) also scout days, egg and spoon races, three legged races and wheelbarrow races on the terraced playing fields. There was a motor cycle dirt track beyond the bottom field, about where Long Nuke Road is now. Also an airship crash landed on the other side of Shenley Lane about where Shenley Green shops are now. I enjoyed a day out to Evesham and a steamer on the Avon to Pershore in 1930. In 1931 we went by coach to Southsea where we stayed a fortnight using a school hall as a base. We filled our pillow cases with our clothes at night to save taking pillows and slept on the floor. It was there I saw my first movie. It was Laurel and Hardy in All at Sea. I suffered from chillblains in winter and spent some time in the little hospital in the grounds. As a form of convalescence I was moved to Home 11 for a day or two. It was there I recall my first sensation of love when the Housemother kissed me goodnight and waved to me as I climbed the stairs. I appreciated the care and kindness received there.

Mr Derek Tudor nee Adams
Ferndale Home 5
1947 – 1958

I went into Shenley Homes when I was a very young boy. At first I went to Erdington Homes with my brother Peter. We were taken out of Erdington Homes by our father in 1947 and then put into Shenley Cottage Homes. My brother Peter went into Home 7 and I went into Home 5 Ferndale. We were both very upset about this but eventually settled down. I went in the Homes nursery school at first then I went to Jervoise Road School and later Ilmington Road Secondary Modern Boys School.

Mr and Mrs Moore were our Houseparents in Ferndale. Other Houseparents I remember were Mr and Mrs Collins and Mr and Mrs Judson. Some of the staff were Auntie Joyce West and Auntie Mrs Jones.

There was a swimming baths on the Drive but it was closed down which was a pity but there were lots of other sports and activities. I was in the Homes football team and

81. Mrs Lois Wilkes (pictured seated on right) walked from Woodgate Lane to Shenley Homes every day to help look after the children and do the washing. This photograph was loaned by her nephew Mr Perry.

82. The inside of one of the homes dining rooms. This photograph was loaned by Mr Perry. Does anyone know which home it was?

remember us winning the cup one year. I won 5 medals and 3 cups for football athletics and cricket but regrettably I have mislaid them over the years as I travelled about quite a lot before I met my wife.

I was in the Boys Brigade and before I left the Homes I started to learn to play the bugle. I also started to do carpentry in the workshops but never made a trade of it. I remember going on holidays to Exeter, Exmouth, Rhyl and LLandudno. They were great fun. There were about 11 homes, reception offices, Church/Assembly Hall and workshops on the Shenley Fields Drive. On the playing fields there was a large wooden pavillion. One of the homes was a sick bay. It was called Pinewood. You went there if you had infectious deceases such as Chicken Pox etc.

The Assembly Hall was a duel purpose building. It was a church on wet Sundays (on dry Sundays we went to St Gabriells on Shenley Lane) and during the week we had film shows and dancing there. We used to call it the Sembow (short for Assembly Hall).

Christmas was a special time. We had lots of presents and cards. I particularly remember the carol singing. We had a party on our birthday.

My impression of the Homes when I was there is of a very happy place to live. We didn't want for anything and generally the staff were very kind to us.

One of my happiest memories of the Homes was being allowed to go to the Square Club for dancing and gymnastics, but I have many memories all happy ones of the Homes, riding the bikes and having athletic competitions against Erdington Homes every June etc.

Mr Peter Tudor nee Adams
Home 7 Lilac View
1947 – 1953

My brother Derek and I are now called Tudor which was our mothers maiden name. When we were in the Homes we were known as Derek and Peter Adams.

We first went into Erdington Childrens Homes in 1946. Derek was 3 years old and I was 5½ years old. Our father took us out of these homes in 1947 and told me to find the way to mother from the centre of Birmingham. God was on our side. Derek and I arrived at mothers clutching each others hand absolutely petrified. I still don't know how we managed it. I thought my father was a disgusting man after that. I still feel that way. He's departed from us now and I now have pity for his memory. A cousin took Derek and I to Shenley Fields Cottage Homes. I was devastated and felt humiliated and sad that Derek was taken from me to go to Home 1. I soon settled in and learnt to fight.

I ran away 3 times. Last time I did, being artistically inclined, I scratched a picture on a Rolls Royce car and got the worst beating up I have ever experienced, by its owner and got another beating off 'Brassneck'. I hated him.

In 1949/50 Mr and Mrs Smith and daughter Sandra came. Mr Smith was very fair minded and nice. Mrs Smith was a spiteful unhappy person. Their daughter Sandra became my best female friend. My best mates in Home 7 were Richard Foster, Micheal Murphy and Albert Swaffer. I got beat up by Alberts 14 year old sister when I was 11 years old.

Mrs Parry-Jones the Matron was a lovely gentle person. She made me undergo a written course on Character and Conduct. I enjoyed the course and passed it easily because I enjoyed writing anyway. The Superintendant was a very cruel vicious man, and one of my happiest memories of the Homes was the day he left.

There was an Assembly Hall on the Drive. This was where you had to await visits from parents or relatives. It was a very sad occasion when they didn't turn up. This building has special memories for me: — I broke every window in it together with a small friend called Donny Dee. I don't know why. As a result I was stopped 2 weeks pocket money which was 4d in all.

Life in the Homes made me very angry when faced with certain situations. It gave me fight in my soul. Discipline was very rigid but benificial when all around you were seemingly worse off.

Clothing was always spotless.

Christmas's were quite poorly spent. One Christmas I received ½ box of chocolates (Mrs Smith had helped herself to the rest) and a penny whistle. I was very very grateful for the whistle. A kind old lady used to bring us all one or two each. I shall never forget her.

I was also fostered out once or twice for a fortnight at a time. The last foster parents a Mr and Mrs Tony and Jean Hurley were wonderful people.

At 13 years of age, mother got me from the Homes to go to Wales. I wanted to go back to Derek.

83. The wedding of Shelagh Waldron with the children from Jasmine Home, including little Steven Walker. Photo loaned by Shelagh Waldron.

Mrs Shelagh Waldron
Secretary to the Superintendant
1964 – 73

I started work at Shenley on 9th August 1964. That was the beginning of the best years of my working life. I was secretary to the Superintendant and Matron who were at that time Mr and Mrs Griffin. I soon got to know all of the 165 children who were at Shenley at that time. There was one little boy who I was particularly fond of called Steven Walker. At that time he was about 6 years old, and lived in Jasmine House. I suppose you would call him a mischievious child but he had the face of an angel. One particular incident springs to mind about Steven that I will never forget. The Midland Red Bus Company had donated an old red bus to the Homes for the children to play on. It was the pride and joy of a lot of people round there, until one day someone set fire to all of the tyres on this bus. A lot of rumours were flying around about who had done it but it turned out to be this little Steven Walker aged 6 years old. Mr Griffin got me to ring down to Jasmine to ask the housemother to bring Steven up to his office. We all new what it was for except Steven. As soon as they arrived in the office Steven realised what it was for. He rushed up to me and put his arms round my neck and wouldn't let me go. By this time Mr Griffin was getting rather impatient and stormed off up the corridor. He told me to put him down and dragged Steven off up the corridor screaming his head off and had to punish him by giving him the cane. I think it hurt Mr Griffin much more than it hurt Steven. It was a long time before Steven would even talk to me again but I think he did learn his lesson and it was soon all forgotten.

Christmasses at Shenley were particularly memorable. I think it was the first Christmas I was there, I went round all the shops to ask for all their spare cotton wool or anything they had used for window decorating and displays. I used this to make 3 or 4 life sized snowmen. I put one in the front hall, one at the Tree's and one at Pinewood. It took me ages and ages to make them but I loved it.

In the summer time the different houses would go away on holiday. It was with great excitement when we stood in the front office and watched all the coaches come and take them off. There was always mad panics at the end with Greenways and Betty Brookes, she was always late and had to rush down the drive dragging her kids behind her to get on to the coach. I remember in October 1965 we had a days outing to Blackpool. It was a staff only outing and we had a fantastic time. Mind you Mr Griffin never forgot it was supposed to be a working day for me and before I left on the coach he had me down in his office dictating a letter which I had to type before we went. I can't see many people standing for that now. There was quite a mixture of staff including care assistants cooks domestics and a seamstress that filled that coach and we all had a wonderful time.

In 1966 I had to leave when I got married and went to live in Bromsgrove. As fate had it my marriage broke up and in 1969 I found myself back in Shenley, and was there until 1973 when we all had to disband and the houses had to run individually. Mr and Mrs Griffin were transferred to Snow Hill House which was the headquarters of Birmingham Social Services, I had to go with them.

Such a lot happened between 1964 and 1973. Another memorable thing that happened was when I set the ball rolling by asking who would be interested in going abroad on a holiday to Majorca.

Much to my surprise I had quite a response but I had to restrict it to 21. I had never been abroad before and the organization of it all was tremendous at that time and I wasn't sure how on earth I was going to cope. I also restricted it to females. So we had a mixed bag of staff including, cooks, domestics, seamstresses, care assistants, officers in charge, deputies and we had a wonderful, wonderful time. We set off from the drive on 18th November 1971. We had a coach that took us to the airport to board our plane. It was all very new to us as a lot of people like me had never been abroad and were very excited leaving their husbands and families behind for the first time. They really took advantage of their new found freedom. I think in all we had about 6 hours sleep in all of the 4 days holiday. We were out at every possible time doing the nightclubs and seeing the sights. We were dancing and drinking till all hours. I was one of the youngest in the group at that time. I went around with Sally who was Kath Clarke's daughter; Kath was the cook to Mr and Mrs Griffin. We decided to go out on our own one evening and met up with two guys in this nightclub. We were sat talking and having a drink when all of a sudden I looked over Sally's shoulder and could see 'The Mob' from Shenley coming in, they had come to find us. We felt like naughty little school girls but we took it in good part and had a real good laugh about it. We tried all the cheap wine going at the different bars and clubs and I remember one night Barbara Head and I were dancing on the dance floor. There were hundreds of people there and we could hardly dance at all. Barbara suddenly wanted to go to the toilet, and we had been drinking quite a lot, and we couldn't make our way out as we couldn't get through the crowd. We were laughing that much that Barbara did have a bit of an accident. I was trying to rub it into the wooden floor with my feet. This of course made us laugh all the more. We arrived back at Elmdon Airport on the Sunday evening very tired. I remember on the Monday back at work I was physically sick through tiredness but I wouldn't have missed it for anything. Everyone said how they had enjoyed themselves and said what a great success it was. Since then of course I have been half-way round the world and back but my first trip abroad was that trip to Majorca and it was quite an experience believe you me.

I loved all the staff at Shenley but I think the one I had the greatest respect for was Aunty Bowes. She certainly showed me a thing or two. She was such a caring person and I used to love going over to the Tree's when they were having a case conference, to take the minutes down. Thats when I learned about all the girls she had there. There was one girl, a beautiful looking girl. It turned out she had been brought into care because she had been sexually abused by her father. She had become very withdrawn and wouldn't talk much about it. She was there for some time and then she left and had to come back again. Her story was quite sad because I did hear she later took her own life after spending a spell in Rubery Mental Hospital. It was very tragic.

Going back to the year I was married. I had a wonderful send off. Each home brought me a lovely wedding present and we had a little bit of a party. The girls knew what was happening and they all wanted to be Bridesmaids. Of course I couldn't possibly do that, but I do remember on the day, Mrs Shervington fron Jasmine, dressed all her little girls up in party dresses and the boys wore their best clothes and I had my photo taken with them. I think the memories of Shenley will stay with me forever.

Mr "Tom" Henry William Walton
Mr "Curly" Albert Walton
Home 9
1953 – 1959

Tom and Curly Walton used to live in Selly Oak by the Oak Cinema. They remember the cinema having coke boilers. Their father used to throw them over the wall with a leather bag to get the coke for their own fire.

They came into care just after the Coronation. They went into Home 9 under the care of Mr and Mrs Mallett. The Malletts were very strict and had no affection for the children in their care. Mr Mallett had a whip with boot laces on the end. He used to stand children on the landing and use the whip on them. When the Malletts left Mr and Mrs Cloudesley took over the running of The Tree's. They had 2 daughters Lesley and Christine. There were a lot of changes made and they treated the boys in care like sons. They rarely used the slipper. The worse thing they did was send them to bed early. We were like a real family. The Tree's were a group to be reckoned with. They won all the trophies for sport. If anyone hurt a boy from the Tree's they had the whole group to deal with.

When we first went to Shenley Fields Cottage Homes no one was allowed out of the Drive. After school we stayed on the Homes campus. It was about 2 years later we started to be allowed out. We went to Weoley Castle Picture House. We also had a lot of friends outside of the Drive and we were allowed to bring them back to the Home. Many of the boys in our home went to the Stonehouse Gang and Weoley Castle Club. In 1958 the Tree's won the Stonehouse Gang in the Cup Final, which was a great shock to the Stonehouse Gang. They thought they were unbeatable. Much of our leisure was spent putting bikes together and riding round the estate. We were always on bikes. We had many scrapes and accidents. One was quite serious. A canary flew over the fence. Curly climbed the railings after the bird. Tom was holding the fence. Tom let the fence go and Curly fell. He fell on the railings and was punctured by a spike. The staff had the tops of the railings bent over to avoid it happening again. The canary escaped.

The Tree's was one of the first homes to have a television. We saw the cup final between Birmingham City and Manchester City when Bert Troutman broke his neck during the match.

We used to make dens in the garden out of rubbish, also we went camping in the fields at the back of The Tree's. The gardens were lovely and there were allotments at the side of the house where lovely mushrooms grew. A single deck Midland Red bus was parked on the field for the children to play in. We had great fun in that.

Many of the Homes were sponsored by firms such as Birds Custard, H.P. Sauce, Selly Oak Picture House, The Greyhound Racing Track and Birmingham University. They all put on parties for us at Christmas and gave presents. Bonfire night was especially good. We had huge bonfires on the field.

Our clothes came from the clothing store which was in a building at the end of the Drive up a lot of metal steps. All the boys wore short grey trousers and long grey socks. We hated wearing short trousers for school and so we hid our long trousers in the deep grass at the back of the house and changed into them before school then changing back into short trousers to come home.

The grocery stores were by the office. We used to take the grocery around to the homes. Our weekly sweet ration was 4 Blue Bird toffee's. Stoking the boilers was another of our jobs. The boilers were very large. We had many jobs to do in and around the Home but we learnt a lot.

We had church every Sunday morning at St Gabriels. I (Curly) got out of going to church by helping Mrs Cloudesley cook the sunday lunch. I enjoyed cooking. Mrs Cloudesley had many of her own belongings at the home including a pressure cooker. I also got up at 5.30 every morning to put the porrage on to cook. I took the Cloudesleys a cup of tea in bed before going off on my paper round.

Holidays were spent at Gosport near Portsmouth. We also went to Exmouth. One holiday was a disaster because every-one went out stealing. We got out of the bedroom window at 3 a.m. in the morning. The stolen goods were buried in the garden before we got back into the bedroom.

One of our treats was a trip to Bingley Hall to see the circus. We remember the mice running round our feet.

I (Tom) looked forward to Friday nights. We had a disco in the Assembly Hall. It was great fun.

If any of us became ill we had to go to sick bay which was Pinewood. All medicals were held there also.

When Tom came out of care he went to stay with Mr and Mrs Dixon who lived at Perry Common. They were lovely people. Curly went to his sister Connie. They have many bad memories of their life before being put into care but many many more happy memories of life in care at Shenley Fields Cottage Homes.

Mr Thomas Watkins
1912 – 1926
Home 8

I went into the Shenley Fields Cottage Homes at the age of 2 years and went into Home 8. I went to school at the Homes. The headmaster was Mr Locke and Mr Dunn was the teacher. Our Housemother was Miss Gibbs. Other people who worked at the Cottage Homes were Mr Newman, Head Gardener; Mr Brownlow, Tailor; Mr Smith, Boot Repairer; Mr Appleby, Carpenter; Mr Meredith, Engineer; Miss Field and Miss Buffon were Housemothers.

We had our own swimming baths where many children learnt to swim. There was an annual sports day. I entered many of the sporting events but did not win any trophies. Mr Grainger formed a Brass Band with the Shenley Boys. I was taught to play the drums. We went on holiday to Llandudno. I went 3 times. The band used to play on the pier and money was collected in little tins. This was used for our pocket money for the holiday.

Mr and Mrs Cohen the Superintendant and Matron arranged the children's holidays, ordered our food and arranged many other activities including the sports events etc;

The Homes were very large with 2 large dormitories for us boys to sleep in. The toilets were outside. Electricity was installed after I arrived. We had 2 staff Miss Gibbs and Miss Latham.

At the bottom end of the drive was a small hospital. Fortunately I did not need to use it. We used to have church services in the school rooms until the Assembly Hall was built in

1923. Sometimes we went to Old Harborne Church. The Rev. Assen from Northfield Parish Church held our church services. The Assembly Hall was used as a Church at one end and the other end had a stage for putting on concerts etc.

Christmas was made special with a small party an apple, orange and a few nuts. Nothing very exciting.

My general impression was I suppose, as times were, it was O.K. but times were very hard. We had to work very hard for what we had in return which was 3d a week pocket money. If we misbehaved we lost it.

As far as I know I went into the Homes at the age of two and left when I was 16 years old when I went to Vauxhall Boys Home. When I got my first shoe repair job my wage was 10/- a week. When I earned £1 per week I had to fend for myself outside the hostel. My digs were 18/- weekly so I was left with 2/- pocket money.

I was in Shenley for a long time but sadly I have no happy memories.

Mr John Wedge
Home 8
1912 – 1922

I was born in Crewe in 1906. There was a lot of poverty and hardship. Father could not get any work in Crewe so we all came to Birmingham to live. He found some work as a moulder. We all lived in a very small house in Aston Birmingham. There were six children so we were very cramped. I was six years old when father took ill and died. Mother had no insurance on him and no money to bury him so he had to have a paupers burial. We had to sleep in the same room as him for a week before he was taken away for burial in a public grave on a Sunday.

One night mother took us on a tram along to Western Road. She told us to go to the workhouse and tell them she had left us. We went into the workhouse then were transferred to Summerfield Homes. My younger brother went into a residential nursery but my sister and I moved to Shenley Fields Homes. I went into Home 8 and my sister went to one of the girls homes. I stayed there for 10 years.

Each home housed approximately 24 children. They were looked after by a Housemother. Our Housemother was Miss Smith and after she died we had Miss Gibson. They were very strict and made us work extremely hard at the house-work. One boy had cleaned the steps one day. When the housemother checked to see if the job had been done well she noticed a speck of dirt in the corner. She then kicked the bucket over and made him do it again. We never argued or cheeked the housemothers. Their word was law and we obeyed. The housemothers job was not easy. She was on duty from 6 a.m. till she went to bed at around 11 p.m. for six days each week. This made a total of 102 hours work each week. We all had to get up at 6.30 a.m. to get our jobs done before school. Three mornings each week we had to go to band practice before school started at 9 a.m.

Miss Gibson was a very religious woman. She may have been religious but she was also very strict and dictatorial. If she heard a sound in the dormitories she would fetch whoever she thought was the guilty boys and make them stand in the corner for several hours till she went to bed. Also if she came into your dormitory during the night and you had your knee's up under the blankets, she would knock them down. Every home had different punishments. I remember asking why one girl was walking round and round the playground and was told it was because she wet the bed. The meals were very basic. Every morning we had oatmeal porridge and 2 pieces of bread and treacle for breakfast. Dinner was usually meat and veg usually boiled or stewed and tea was always bread and jam. We never had even a drink from 5.30 p.m. till we got up next morning.

The school masters were very strict. Mr Freeth the Headmaster used to clout us round the head and Mr Bowers pulled our ears. Mr Cohen gave out the cane. He was the Superintendent. The caning was always witnessed by Mr Meredith the homes engineer. He was a very fine man and greatly respected. Mr Newman was the head gardener. He was a very smart man with a moustache. Mr Brown lived just down the road in California. Mr Humphrey was the carpenter and Mr Williams and his son were the painters. Mr Williams junior took two of us boys out once for tea one Christmas

I learnt to swim in a harness at the swimming baths in the Homes. Mr Blanford used to take us for swimming. He was a lovely man. He and his wife ran Home 9. They were a lovely couple who went to the Erdington Homes after Shenley. I met up with them when I went to Erdington Homes just before I was discharged.

I was allowed to speak to my sister in the homes. She was older than me. Mother had her out of care when she was old enough to work. No one ever knew our ages because mother never gave them our dates of birth.

I had to go to the infirmary once because I was very ill with the Flu. The infirmary was at the end of the drive by the fields. We had our teeth examined there every year.

One of the regular visitors to the homes was Dame Cadbury. Another regular visitor was Lady Sturge. She was the wife of Sir Joseph Sturge whose statue stands in Five Ways. Lady Sturge organised the White Ribbon Band. This was a group of people who had taken the pledge against the demon drink. She had little brooches made with white ribbons on to signify taking the pledge not to drink alcohol.

When I left care I went to live with my sister. She had us out of care because she said the homes planned to send us to Australia. She got fed up with us and sent us to our other sister. When she got fed up I went to live in the Isle of Man where mother was living. I never shed a tear all the years I was in care or even when mother died. She was not a good mother.

I had 32 jobs in my working life. When I first started work you worked where-ever there was a job and moved on when the job finished, I have worked for B.S.A., Midland Red, four garages in the Isle of Man, Shell Mex and the bedstead trade. They say a rolling stone gathers no moss but they get a wealth of experience.

Mr Alan G White
1953 – 1971
Home 10

I went into Home 10 Ryedale on Shenley Fields Drive after I had been brutally treated by my step-mother. She hit me with a dog lead, damaging my ears, legs and body. There was no love in my life and life was very hard.

I found life in Shenley very strict and also without love. It was very much like Army life. We had to work very hard doing cleaning duties etc. There were some nice times

84. The boys in The Boys Brigade. There is always one who puts his hat on the wrong way. Photo loaned by Alan White.

especially at Christmas time when we went out to lots of Pantomimes and parties. Several of the Homes were adopted by business people such as Chamber of Commerce. There were about 13 Homes altogether also a school, nursery and workshops.

There was a large hall called The Assembly Hall where we had dancing, film shows and sports plus many other uses. At one time it was also the church though when I was at Shenley I went to St Gabriels Church on Shenley Lane. The Vicar was a Mr Tyson.

Our houseparents were Mr and Mrs Griffin were the Superintendants. We had a sports day every year and I won the Shield several times. We had a holiday every year sometimes to Exmouth and Port Albert.

I got involved in the gardening while on the Drive and continued in this line when I left.

I now work for myself doing landscape gardening.

Mr Thomas Wilkins
Home 9
1928 – 1936

I was in the Shenley Fields Homes myself many years ago but unable to find out much information about the Homes. I visited the Birmingham Public Library in 1988 and they sent me information about my two brothers and my late sister. They were all admitted to the Homes in 1930. I was born in 1928 and admitted to Shenley in 1931. I was about 3 years old at the time. I was later boarded out with my brother George in 1936.

I have fond memories of the Homes. The last cottage I was in was cottage 9. The playing fields and cricket pavilion were at the back of cottage 9. I remember the swimming baths where we had swimming competitions. There was also a cottage hospital. The photograph of the gardens and the drive are just as I remember them. We all had a small piece of garden to look after. Across the road from the Shenley Homes was a farm. I remember one of the horses got stuck in the mud and they were unable to rescue the animal. It had to be destroyed, which was very sad for us.

I went on holiday to Westward Ho, I think twice. This was from Snow Hill Station. I used to go to school in the Cottage Homes School and eventually went to Ilmington Road School.

Thank God there were such places as Shenley Fields as goodness knows what would have happened to us.

Mr George Wilkins

I am writing to let you know my sister, brothers and myself were in the Shenley Fields Homes, in the 30s. My sister was in the last home on the right and the boys in the home at the top of the Drive. I used to play in the Brass Band and we had a Captain teaching us. We played at local sports grounds and fetes. We had a housemaster who took us for long walks in the lanes.

When our father came to see us we had to go to the big house by the road. We did not do too badly.

Albert Ernest Williams
1914 – 1921

My Grandfather, Albert John Williams, died aged 37 in 1914 (at 3 Oak Terrace, High Street, Harborne) leaving his wife Florence with several young children. My father (now dead) told me that she used to take in washing, but evidently she was unable to cope, so he Albert Ernest Williams (born 5 – 8 – 1907) went into Shenley Fields Cottage Homes. He may have been accompanied by his two younger brothers Thomas Arthur (born about 1910) and Albert (no details known).

My father spoke well of his time at the Shenley Cottage Homes. I seem to recall that for part of the time there he had problems with his eyes and stayed in a darkened room. Almost certainly he learned music there, for later he played in Harborne Silver Band and was an accomplished musician on several instruments in later life.

I believe that he may have left the Homes (aged 14 1921) and gone to work at the Foreward Radiator Co in New Canal Street Birmingham.

Doctor Maurice Williams.

187

85. This staff group photo was taken in the Superintendent's Garden. It was strictly out of bounds to everyone. Right up to the day the homes closed it was still called Griffins Garden after the last Matron and Superintendent to be in post. Photo loaned by Mrs Dorothy Williams.

Mrs Dorothy Williams
Melplash and Elmdene
1962 – 1983

I started work on the Shenley Fields Drive in June 1962. It was a beautiful Saturday morning and the day of the Morny Cup Contest and sports day. All the homes in Birmingham competed in the games and prizes were presented to the children for some of the lovely articles they had made during the winter evenings when they could not take part in outside activities. The whole drive was trimmed up with flags and I remember joking with Mr and Mrs Gough (whom I was going to work for as a domestic in Melplash) "I know you are short staffed but you didn't have to put the flags out to welcome me. I grew very fond of the children of Melplash, even though some of them used to hide their cigarettes and matches in my bag of dusters.

The Goughs left to take up another position in Gloucester.

After the Goughs came Mr and Mrs Mackintosh with their son and daughter Keith and Jean. Mr and Mrs Mackintosh were a very kind couple but the children of Melplash did not appreciate them and played them up. They did not stay very long and when they left we had a couple from Whitby named Mr and Mrs Wilkinson and their two daughters Sharon and Karen. They stayed about 18 months. A young couple came from Field House (a girls remand home in Clent) but they only stayed a short while before moving to London. Then Mr and Mrs Jones came to us. They had previously worked at an approved school.

188

By this time Melplash was made into an assessment centre, and we were taking in children straight from the courts on 21 day interim care orders. Some were very tough but it all seemed to stem from their backgrounds.

After the Jones's came Mr and Mrs George Neish with their son Paul. They were lovely to work for and so homely. Mrs Beryl Neish used to make cakes by profession before coming into child care. She had previously run one of the Erdington Cottage Homes before coming to Melplash. They stayed at Melplash for about 2 years before moving to a larger home at Triumph Walk in Chelmsley Wood.

When the Neish's left a very nice couple called Mr ans Mrs Kiczma came to Melplash. When I heard they also would be moving on, I decided to transfer to another home. I moved to a home at the end of the drive called Elmdene, where I was to work for Mr and Mrs Thompson who had two children John and Audrey.

I had previously been working at Elmdene 2 evenings a week while the houseparents had their night out. First it was for a Mr and Mrs Sabin and then Mr and Mrs Thompson, so I knew the children well. It was an all boys home. Alas believe it or not after 2 years, Mr and Mrs Thompson emigrated to South Africa.

The next houseparents were Jill and Roy Plumley. I had already worked with Jill for a short time at Melplash. We had a lovely group of staff at Elmdene and we all got on very well together and still kept in touch after the drive had shut down. When any of the staff at Elmdene retired we all went to the 'Night Out' a nightclub in town and had a marvellous time. I also went on holiday with the children from Elmdene to Barry Island and Pwllheli. When I was 60 years old we all went to The Albany Hotel for a celebratory meal where I was presented with a lovely wall clock and a picture of all the children who were at Elmdene. They also presented me with a cake with 60 on it. I have worked with some lovely staff whom I now count as friends and also children, who are now married with their own children. They all still call me Aunt Will.

I can remember when I first started to work at Melplash, it was opposite the office and Mrs Griffin, the Matron, used to sit at her desk with the window open and say "Good morning" to all of the children as they walked past on their way to school. On Saturday mornings the children went to the assembly hall to see a film. I used to take the children up to Mr Brookes at the stores to be measured for shoes and clothes. We had 2 handimen, Fred and Bert, who used to have a long barrow. The children used to call them Steptoe and Son and whistle the theme tune. Though we used to correct them and say it was rude, I used to have to turn away so they could not see me smile. I also remember Mr Thompson asking a boy named Christopher to push his motor bike into the shed. Instead Chris got on the bike and started it going. He could not stop it and kept going round and round the shed till one of the other boys told him how to stop it. He never did it again. I used to collect one little boy named Patrick from the nursery on the drive. He had a habit of bringing home the dinky toys and cars belonging to the nursery. When I went to collect him one afternoon I searched through his pockets as usual to find any cars and held his hands all the way home. He went upstairs to change into his play clothes and one of the other children came downstairs and said, "Aunt Will, Patrick has got a fire engine and a police car upstairs". I called Patrick downstairs and asked him where about he had them hidden when I was seaching him. He wouldn't answer and I still do not know. He would be about 30 years old now and I would love to meet him to ask him just where he had hidden the toys that day. Another incident that comes to mind involved a boy called Edward. Every now and then it was his turn to clean the shoes on a Saturday morning and he hated it. One Saturday he put the two brushes used for shoe cleaning, into the fire

86. Two boys in the Shenley Groups. Photo loaned by Mrs Dorothy Williams.

boiler and said they had gone missing, but unfortunately for Edward the boiler went out and when the housefather cleared it out the two brushes were still in there and had not burnt. Poor Edward had to do the shoe cleaning job for a month as a punishment.

When the homes on the drive began to close down I moved to a home in Millmead Road. It was called a family group home and had 12 children of mixed ages in residence. I was then working as an RCCO which was a Residential Child Care Officer. I worked 20 hours a week and did 4 sleeping in duties each month. I worked at 36 Millmead Road until I retired at the age of 65. The staff and Peggy O'Connell, the officer in charge of the home gave me a wonderful retiring party. They presented me with a beautiful clock. I had been working for Social Services for 24 years and 4 months.

Mrs Helen Lynne Wood nee Plumley
1971 – 1983
Elmdene Home 11

I was brought up in the Shenley Fields Homes from 1971 when I was 3 years old till 1983 when I was 15 years old. I was living in the Homes because my parents were House Parents of Elmdene Home 11. There were good and bad points about living in the situation my brother Steven and I lived in. We had our own bedrooms and we should have had use of our own sitting room but that didn't always work out like that. Many times I arrived home from school to find a meeting going on in our sitting room involving social workers, police and my mother who was Officer in Charge of the home. The key to my bedroom door was kept in the sitting room so this meant I could not go up to my bedroom to get changed. I used to get very angry about this especially if it happened on the nights I used to go to my ballet dancing lessons and I had to miss going because I could not get my dance gear from my room. Sometimes a member of staff would interupt the meeting for me but that depended on how important the meeting was. I have known these meetings go on till 8 or 9 oclock in the evening which meant we did not see much of mom or dad that night. We had the same meals as the children in care though if they were having something we really didn't like Mom would cook us something different. Most of the meals were very good.

Most of the rules of the Home applied to us also, such as wearing slippers indoors and getting out of our school uniform as soon as we arrived home.

The other children had a fixed rate of pocket money according to their age. We had the same rates but mom often gave us a little extra if we needed it. The other children resented this.

Our bedroom door was kept locked because some of the children were jealous of us having our own belongings and our own room and they would steal or break our things up, especially if they had been told off by mom.

All our Christmas's and Bank Holidays were spent at the home because mom always gave the staff the time off then. I didn't mind this very much because we often went out in the mini bus on day trips. Because we lived in the Homes we were also included in any treats like pantomimes etc. that the other children went on. Once we went to see Genesis in Concert at the N.E.C. That was a really thrilling day and we all had sweatshirts and hats to bring home with us. We had two holidays each year, one with the children in Elmdene and one with our parents.

Sometimes the children gave mom a hard time and when she was very tired she was grumpy with us. We found that very hard to understand but realize now how difficult her job was with 12 children to look after, I used to get angry when I wanted time on my own with mom but she could not switch off from the other children. They used to be on her mind day and night.

The department (Social Services) held a Christmas Card Competition and we were allowed to enter and go to the presentation party. There was also a big party arranged for the Queens Silver Jubilee. We had long tables put down the Drive and everywhere was decorated in Red, White and Blue. There was a sports event on the playing fields and we still have a film of the events. Another party was when Princess Diane and Prince Charles got married. Our house won the prize for being the best decorated house at one of the parties.

Sometimes the Lord Mayor visited the Homes on Shenley Drive. He often took several

87. Ferndale children and staff on holiday. Photo loaned by Mrs M Haynes.

88. Helen Wood nee Plumley at the Jubilee Party held on the drive. Photoby Jill Plumley.

children for rides in the Lord Mayors official car.

We always had to be careful what we did or said as we didn't want to show mom or dad up with bad behaviour. We did sometimes misbehave of course. The other children loved telling tales on us if we did anything wrong. I felt we were being watched all the time either by staff, social workers or other children. When we made mistakes everyone knew about it. If we had a day off school for any reason the other children wanted time off as well and became quite spiteful towards us.

We had some very young children in care for a while and I enjoyed helping mom and the staff to bath them. I also played with them in our old caravan and took them for walks. Some of the older boys helped me with my homework.

I used to get very upset when some of the children were horrible to my mom and some even hit her. It was worse when we had girls in the home as well as boys. Some of the girls were really vicious. I got on quite well with most of the boys and really enjoyed going out with them to places like Clent Hills.

We had some lovely holidays in Weymouth and Great Yarmouth. The most upsetting holiday we had was in Great Yarmouth. We went to the Model Village and mom trusted the older boys to go round unsupervised. We were very embarrassed when the police tapped us on the shoulder and told us they had our boys locked up after they found them stealing money from the wishing well. I don't think I have ever seen my mom so angry or humiliated. Some of the best holidays were in Weymouth. We used to go for midnight drives into Portland in the mini bus.

We were lucky in a lot of ways because we had our parents with us most of the time even when they were working. They could not always give us undivided attention because of the demands the job put on them, but we knew where they were and they knew where we were.

I enjoyed living in Elmdene most of the time. Having 11 brothers and about 6 aunts can be fun but not all of the time. I really enjoyed the odd days we went over to our own house for short breaks with mom and dad. I made many friends and still see some of them. We had pets including Matthew the donkey, Goldie the little Whippet, 3 guinea pigs and some tropical fish. Because both of our parents worked we had more than our fair share of personal possessions, though these can never compensate for having to share your mom and dad with dozens of others.

When the home closed in 1983 we were all very upset. I found it very hard coming home from school to an empty house. All of the children had to go to other childrens homes. Most of them were very upset. One of the boys was about to go into the regular Army so a place in a childrens home could not be offered him. Mom and dad asked us how we would feel about having John come to our own house to live with us as a member of our family. We thought it was a great idea and John was asked how he felt. He said he would like to live with us. His social worker made all the arrangements and he moved in. He is still with us now and still in the Army. We are very good friends and he is my daughter's God-Father.

Mr Edward Wright
1932/33

I was in care in Shenley Fields Cottage Homes. I was in Home 1 at first then Home 8. I went to school in the Homes school and sat by a girl called Lillian (my first love). There was a Housemother in charge of each home who we had to call Mom. I don't remember any of their names. There was a brass band run by Mr Grainger. I was not in the band but I did pump the church organ. The Superintendant's name escapes me but I remember his strong arm and I think he had a moustache.

There was an infirmary at Shenley. I was in there for 3½ months with rheumatic fever. The treatment was Asprin and a cradle. We had blankets but no sheets.

My happiest memory whilst in Shenley was my first sexy try on! We were in Home 1 playing hide and seek when purely by accident we both tried to hide behind a settee. She wore 'combinations'. I don't suppose I really knew what I was doing. I remember most, the deep hurt about the seemingly unnecessary partings. There were four of my family involved. I was about 10 or 11, there was a brother one year younger and one who was a baby and a sister who was 4. It appears that we might have been kept together as a group, hardly as a family because we weren't then. I can't even remember being left in the same house with my brother Norman. It appeared to be the ruling policy at the time. I must have been numbed by all this.

I do remember how the voices of crows grew on me. My proper home was in Balsall Heath but Shenley Fields was deep in the Birmingham countryside and there was a lot of trees around the Homes. I recall that whilst I lay in my hospital bed that was the strongest and most regular sound to reach me. No headphones or telly in those days.

I also recall finding that oasis amongst the trees which was the Masters own private garden. I think I was asked to take something into there once. I found it again when I visited recently.

Mrs Kitty Edwards nee White
1924
Home 1

I was put into the Shenley Fields Homes when I was 6 years old. I went into Home 1 and my 3 brothers went into Home 9. I remember there being about 10 Homes altogether plus a hospital, workshops and sewing rooms where our clothing was made. I went to school at the homes school. My teacher was Mrs Marshall and the Headmaster was Mr Locke. We also had our own swimming baths. The swimming teacher was Mrs Tabbener. There was plenty of activities to take part in. I took part in hockey, swimming and country dancing. Two of my brothers were in the band. One played a clarinet and the other played the drums. We also went on holiday every year to South Sea. I was confirmed at the church at the homes by Reverand R J Haysome.

We were happy enough in the homes and lived like a large family.

89 – 90. Two of the dancing shows put on in the Assembly Hall. Photos sent in by Ray Bickerstaff.

Mrs Margaret O'Neill nee Mitchell
1946 – 1948
Home 3

I was in the Shenley Fields Homes in 1946-1948 when I was age 6 to 8 years old. I was in the third house past the office on the right hand side of the drive. My name then was Margaret Mitchell. I have some happy and funny memories of the time I spent there though I must be honest some of my memories are a little cloudy now. My best friends then were Betty, Irene and Queenie King. I would love to hear from them again.

Mrs P Miley nee Hill
1946
Bythorn

I was put into the Shenley Fields Homes with my 2 sisters and 3 brothers when our mom died and dad could not look after us. We were the biggest family in the Homes so they gave us a house called Bythorn. It had been the residence of the previous matron and when she left they thought it better to let us stay there as a family rather than leave the house empty and split us up into the other homes. Our house mother's name was Mrs Bedall.

Our names were Marion, Betty, Pauline, Roy, John and David Hill.

91. Just look at those bonnets. A group of Shenley Children pictured in the late 1930's or early 40's. Photo loaned by Ray Bickerstaff.

Mrs Carol Ann Wixey nee King
1948 – 1958
Home 5 Ferndale (later changed its name to Cherry Garth)

My brother Michael and I were put into the Homes when mom and dad parted. We had lots of happy times at Shenley. Mr and Mrs Moore were our houseparents. They were lovely people and we lived as one big family. Some of the houseparents were not as nice as mom and dad Moore and you wonder how they got the job of looking after children. There was lots to do on the drive. I took part in the dancing lessons where we learnt tap and ballet. At Christmas time each house put on a small show and I took part in this. The activity I enjoyed most was sports. I won 4 cups for running, 2 medals for dancing and a medal for the outward bound course. We had lovely holidays at Prestatyn in Wales and Exmouth in Devon. One of the big celebrations I remember was the Coronation of The Queen. My happiest memories are when I ran for my Home and won a cup and having my first new coat. Sadly my brother is now dead. I often wonder where some of my old friends from Shenley are.

Miss Barbara Bickerstaff
Home 2
Suncrest

I went into Shenley Fields Homes when I was only 2. I had some very happy times there. My Housemother was Miss Longman. She was like a real mother to me. There were 24 children in our home and Miss Longman looked after us all. She did the cooking and washing and bathed every one of us.

Our house was always the best decorated house at Christmas time. The table decorations were lovely. My brother Raymond was also in the homes. He is desparately looking for another sister called Audrey. She was adopted and we do not know where she is now. We both have one burning ambition to meet Audrey again one day. Raymond did some voluntary work at Shenley right up till it closed down.

I stayed in the homes till I was 16 years old. I cryed when I had to leave Miss Longman. She was like a mother to me and the best I could wish for. She still remembers my birthday and sends both birthday and Christmas cards every year.

Mrs Dorothy Tilly
Elmdene
1960s

I have happy memories of Shenley. I worked in Elmdene with Mr and Mrs Bowes as the Houseparents. They were a lovely couple. I always recall the table on Sundays being laid for lunch for the children. Believe me it was laid lovely with a large joint. Also the children were clothed well and loved. We had many laughs and heartaches. I often think of Auntie Bowes as we called her. I also worked for the Platts.

I don't know what some of the kiddies would have done without the love and care of Shenley Fields Homes.

Mrs Barbara Tongue 1945 approx

I did not live in the Homes. My friend was Diane Smith nee Parry. She was the daughter of Mr and Mrs Parry who ran Home 9. Many of the boys from Home 9 were also my friends in Jervoise Road Junior School. One vivid memory I have of The Homes happened 47 years ago. I was 12 years of age and Diana and I used to stand outside the gates waiting for two youths to walk their dog along Woodcock Lane. That makes me sound rather cheeky at a very tender age, doesn't it? . I have been happily married to one of them now for 37 years.

Mrs Edna Homer 1945 approx

I am writing after reading the most interesting article about Shenley Fields Homes, in the Evening Mail, where you asked for people to write to you with any memories of the Homes.

I still have lovely memories of 46 years ago. I was about 13 years old, I used to go to Ilmington Road School, Weoley Castle, and every week we used to love going to the Homes. One week we used to have to clean, dust and polish a room and other times we had to lay the tables and help cut little jam sandwiches and pieces of cake and make the drinks ready for the children's tea.

If we were well behaved at school we were chosen to do this. Every week I used to look forward to it. It may not seem much to you or anyone else but to me it is one of my lovely memories of those days. I can remember it as if it was only yesterday. I have cut out the lovely photograph of the Homes that was printed in the paper and I have put it in my scrap book. Any day if I feel a bit down, I can look back on lovely memories.

Mr Barry Franklin 1950 approx

My happier times at Shenley Fields Cottage Homes was on Sports Day. We competed against Erdington Cottage Homes and in 1950 we won them. I remember a holiday we had in 1951. I was happier then but I am not happy now. The homes have been pulled down and a Rest Home stands on the site.

The Christmas parties at the Homes were wonderful and the film shows in the hall. I have been unemployed since 1969 following a hit and run accident, so my memories of Shenley are all I have left.

Mrs Mary Meehan nee Johnson
1934 – 1937

I am writing to say how nice it was to read in The Evening Mail about the Shenley Fields Homes. I was there myself from 1934 to 1937. I was 7 years old when I went in and 10 when I came out. They were the happiest days of my life. The house-mother was very kind to all of us.

Mrs G Walker
1919 – 1933
Home 4

Shenley Fields Homes were large with about 12 homes, a school, a church, a hospital and the swimming baths. Mr and Mrs Cohen were the Superintendant and Matron. Our Housemother was Miss Gent and Miss Field was the Housemother in Home 3 next door. We went on holiday to Llandudno and Wallasey.

I am sorry to say my years spent at Shenley were the most most miserable days of my life and I still think of them with horror.

Mrs Renee Hirst nee Bloor
1933 – 1939
Hospital and Nursery

I started work in the little hospital at Shenley Fields when I was quite a young lady of 18 years. I worked there for only a short while before being asked if I would like to work in the nursery with the very young children.

I worked with Miss Uletta Angwin. I must say I really enjoyed working at Shenley Fields and have some very happy memories of my time there. I left when war broke out and the little children were evacuated out to Wales. I was getting married at the time and it was a policy that married women could not work in the homes. I still have a very treasured present that was given to me by the staff on the occasion of my 21st birthday. It is a book called People of Importance by J. H. Dowd. It contains the most wonderful pencil sketches of little children. I have stuck many of the lovely photographs of some of the Shenley toddlers on to its blank pages.

92–93 and 94. Mrs Hirst nee Bloor with her colleagues from Shenley. The uniforms had been borrowed from the boys in the Shenley Band.

95–108. These photos show many of the toddlers who used the Shenley Nursery They have been loaned to me by Mrs Renee Hirst who keeps them all safely in a wonderful book called People of Importance by J. H. Dowd.

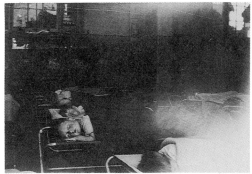

201

Mrs Kath Spencer
1966 – 1982
Rydale — Greenways — Cherry Garth

I worked at the Ryedale home for two years. Mr and Mrs Stephenson were the houseparents. Mr Stephenson was a lovely man but Mrs Stephenson was very sharp tongued and strict. The one thing that really upset me was the favouritism showed to one of the little boys in care at Ryedale. He was one of the youngest boys in the home but was allowed to stay up latest and was given sweets and fruit which were denied to the other children. He was a very naughty child with frequent temper tantrams. One of my jobs was to stoke the boiler in the kitchen but I sometimes forget it and it went out.

Next door to Ryedale was a smaller home called Bythorn. Mrs Bowprey was the housemother there with about 6 children. The only help she had was from a lady named Mrs Allen. When Mrs Bowprey retired she moved to a small flat in Shenley Lane. When I left Ryedale in 1968 I went to work at Greenways with Mrs Norma Bickley. She had just changed Greenways into a nursery unit. I loved working in this home and stayed until it closed in 1980. I then moved to Cherry Garth. This was an older age group of children. I was not happy there, and left two years later. Years ago my mother used to have a girl from Shenley at our house every weekend. The girls name was Phylis.

Mrs Dorothy Hill nee Hart
1928 – 1937
Home 2

My sister Daisy and I were both in care in the Shenley Fields Cottage Homes. We were in Home 2 which was the second home on the right hand side. The boys homes were on the left hand side of the drive. When I was quite young I went to the homes school but I later went to Ilmington Road Girls school. Some of the children went to Jervoise Road School. We had our own swimming baths. Miss Tabbener was the swimming teacher, I did not win any of the swimming awards, or any of the sports awards. There were about 12 homes and a hospital where I was once a patient. I remember a large hall that was used for Christmas parties. My happiest memories are of Christmas parties and visiting days when my older sister and her husband came to see us. We were well looked after in the homes but it wasn't like having you own parents.

Lily Irene Harris nee James
1932 – 1940's

I was born on 2nd February 1932. My mother died a few days after my birth and I was taken to Shenley Fields Homes where I lived until the war broke out. I was evacuated sometime in the 1940's though I don't remember exactly which year and I came back to Shenley Fields Homes on 30th June 1944.

SHENLEY FIELDS CHILDRENS HOMES

June 1966

Can you fill in the missing names of the Shenley Staff?

Back row L to R	Middle row L to R	Front row L to R.
1. Mr Frank Collins	1. Mr Rewhorn	1.
2. Mr B. Brookes	2. Mrs Rewhorn	2.
3. Mrs Bickley	3. Mrs G Allen	3. Mrs Pemberton
4.	4.	4.
5.	5. Mrs Ella Nutting	5.
6. Gwen Muldoon	6.	6. Mr Stephenson.
7. Lianna Brown	7. Mrs B Brookes	7. Mrs Stephenson.
8. Mrs Shirvington	8.	8.
9.	9. Lena Taylor	9.
10. Mrs Ball	10. Mrs Moore	10. Mrs Neale
11. Mrs Baker	11. Floss Cartridge	11. Mr Griffin.
12. Mrs Head	12. Marge Haynes	12. Mrs Griffin.
13. Mrs Hancox	13. Dorothy Williams	13. Mr Head.
14. Mrs Daniels	14. May Mahoney	14. Mrs Toy.
15.	15. Mrs Wilkinson	15. Alma Niblett
16. Fred ?	16. Edna ?	16. Shelagh Waldron.
17. Bert Pyatt	17.	17. Mrs Bowprey.
	18. Pat Whitmore	18. Mrs Hickson
	19.	19. Mrs Sabin.
	20. Mrs Jones	20. Mrs Wardell
	21. Mr Jones	21. Mrs Joyce Foy
		22.
		23. Mrs Edie Downes.

109. The last day of work at Shenley for the Elderly Specialist Team, (the A team). From left to right; Zoe Goodwin, Pat Schofield, Margaret Stewart, Maggie Krupinski, Lionel (dad) Springer, Jill Plumley, Liz Young, Gill Adams, Ray Bickerstaff and Team Manager Leo Hardy (note who gets the cup of tea).

110−113. Within a few days of us leaving this is what happened to the building Two very young boys from the neighbourhood set fire to the home and very nearly got burnt themselves.

114. The Assembly Hall just before it was demolished.

115. Some of the Trophies. In the centre is the Shaftmoor Cup. This is the cup presented to the Home which won most of the sports events. The two smaller cup are table tennis cups presented to the boys from Elmdene by The Birmingham Junior Chambers of Commerce. The table cloth they are standing on was made Miss Field Housemother of Home 3 in 1923. It was given to me by Mrs May Pearson.

116. Looking out on to Woodcock Lane from the new Shenley Fields Drive. This is where the big black gates were once locked to the outside world. Photographed in 1992 by Mrs Jean Coulter.

117—119. Some of the buildings on the new Shenley Fields Drive. Photo's by Mrs Jean Coulter June 1992.

SHENLEY FIELDS COTTAGE HOMES

The great object of the Guardians is to provide for the children entrusted to their guardianship a "Home," where they may receive parental care, a sound education, and industrial training to enable them upon leaving the Home to earn an honest livelihood.

The Foster Parents and Children are to rise not later than 6 a.m. in the Summer and 7 a.m. in the Winter.

Breakfast	- - -	at 8 a.m.
Dinner	- - -	at 12.15 p.m.
Supper	- - -	at 6 p.m.

No child is to be out of bed after 9 o'clock p.m.

Fathers and Mothers. You will have charge of the Home in which you reside, and for all domestic purposes of the children in the Home. It is your duty to be to these children as their Father and Mother, to care for them and train them rightly.

Whilst you are allowed a large amount of liberty in the management of your house, yet the Superintendent is primarily responsible for the management of the "Homes," and any instructions from him must be implicitly obeyed.

3

Employment of Children. The Superintendent shall (subject to the approval of the Guardians) determine the occupation or employment of the children. Certain children will be selected, from time to time, as House-children (Boys' Homes two each morning and afternoon, and Girls' Homes three each morning and afternoon), who will assist in the house-work and attend School or the Workshops alternately as directed. As many as necessary, however, will be at home all day on Mondays to assist in the washing, etc., which is to be done, as far as possible, in good time on Monday morning.

Age of House-boys Boys are not, as a rule, to be kept as House-boys after they are 12 years of age, but are to be put to learn a trade as directed by the Superintendent.

Service. Girls before being sent to service will be employed at the Lodge, where they will receive their final training before being sent out.

Household work. It is the duty of the Mothers to personally assist in the washing, scrubbing, cooking, and all other household work, as well as to instruct the children in the same.

Making and Repairing of Clothing. You will see that the children's clothes are kept in proper repair. All the underclothing is to be made as well as repaired by the Mothers in the Homes, the girls assisting in the Girls' Homes. When repairs are needed to boots and shoes or to boys' suits, the articles are to be sent in a cleanly state to the Office at the appointed time. Every article should be marked with the number of your Home so as to avoid mistakes. All the children should be taught, as far as possible, to mend their own clothes and to knit and darn their own stockings. All clothing when made must be sent to the Stores, at the appointed time, and will be booked out as required for use.

Report of Articles made, etc. A report will be made by the Superintendent to the Guardians of the articles of clothing made in each Home, and also of the crockery, &c., broken, and other matters in regard to each Home.

Books, etc., for Children. All books and printed papers introduced into the Homes, otherwise than by the Committee, shall be submitted to them for approval.

Prayers and Grace. Grace is to be said before and after meals, and you will read prayers with the children before breakfast and after supper each day.

2

Admission of Children to Homes. On the admission of a child to your Home, you are to see that it is properly bathed and clothed, and report at once to the Superintendent if any marks or eruptions are found on the body of the child, or any other particulars in regard to the condition of the child. You are also to report same in your fortnightly report book.

Clothing of Children admitted. The clothes in which the child is admitted are to be at once returned to the Home from which the child is admitted, or to the Office as the case may be.

Discharge of Children. Upon receiving notice from the Superintendent to prepare a child for discharge, you are to at once bath and get ready the child, and take it to the Office when required.

Discipline. The heads of the Homes are responsible for the discipline of their Home, and the trade instructors for the conduct of the children while at work.

Punishment. You are not to inflict corporal punishment on the children, or deprive them of their food, but trust to a kindly control and treatment of them, rather than to any system of severity; but if any serious case of misconduct occurs, it should be reported to the Superintendent, who will give such instructions as he may deem advisable.

Cleanliness. Before being sent to work or school, every child in your Home is to be present in the day room, and inspected by you as to cleanliness of person and clothing, boots cleaned, hair and clothes brushed, &c.

Cleaning, etc, of School. The Boys' Homes will take it in turn, a week at a time, or as otherwise directed by the Superintendent, to properly clean and arrange the Schools daily, and the Fathers must regularly, night and morning, inspect the work to see that their boys have done their work properly, and they will not only be held responsible for the cleanliness of the Schools but for the lighting and extinguishing of the lamps and fires, safely locking up, and any damage done during the time of cleaning.

Bathing. Once a week, at least, all the children are to have a warm bath and be thoroughly washed, the girls and infants in the presence of the Mothers, and the older boys in the presence of the Fathers. The water in the bath must be first tested by means of a thermometer, and must in no case exceed 95 degrees.

4

Report Book. You will fill in your Report Books, with all the required information, regularly every fortnight, and report any special circumstances, if any, that require notice. The book is to be sent to the Office every other Tuesday morning, at nine o'clock, to be examined by the Superintendent and seen by the Committee when they meet.

Absence. You are not to be absent from the premises without the leave of the Superintendent. A book is kept at the Lodge in which the names of all persons entering or leaving the Homes will be entered, also the times of going out and coming in. This applies to visitors as well. Officers wishing to be out after 10 p.m. must obtain special leave.

Friends and Relations of Children. No relatives or friends of the children are to be allowed to visit the children without permission of the Superintendent. Special days are set apart for this purpose, and then it is only permitted in the schoolroom. The Fathers and Mothers are not to hold any communication whatever with the relatives or friends of the children.

Orders. All orders are given through the Superintendent's office, and are not to be received from any other source.

Applications, etc., respecting Children. You must at once communicate any application made to you respecting any of the children to the Superintendent.

Divine Service. All the children are to be present at Divine Service, which is held in the Schoolroom each Sunday. The Guardians, also, wish the Foster Parents to attend as regularly as possible.

Meals. The Foster Parents are distinctly to understand that they are to take their meals regularly with the children in the Day Room.

Washable Dresses, etc. The Foster Mothers and Nurse will be supplied with the material for washable dresses, and the Mothers must wear them regularly during the morning, and all day, when any case of an infectious nature has occurred in the Home, as long as the Medical Officer deems it advisable, and the Nurse regularly when on duty. The Nurse also is expected to wear the usual Nurse's cap.

Walks, etc. You are expected to take the children walks, weather permitting, as often as convenient, without interfering with the work of the Home, etc., but they must not be left or kept standing. If you wish, at any time to take them a distance that will necessitate their being away from home at the appointed time for a meal, you must have the consent of the Superintendent, and state where you wish to go.

5

Officers are strictly prohibited from smoking during shop hours, or carrying a lighted pipe into the shops, etc. *Smoking.*

Any case of sickness is to be at once reported to the Superintendent. *Sickness*

Officers wishing to have a friend to stay for the night must obtain the sanction of the Superintendent; and all Officers wishing to have friends to stay with them for a longer period than one night, must make application to the Superintendent, who shall lay the same before the Committee, and first obtain consent thereto. *Visitors to Officers.*

Floors and Windows are to be thoroughly cleaned every Saturday morning. *Cleaning of Workshops.*

CLOTHING.

Each Suit to consist of

BOYS.		GIRLS.	
Jackets	2	Frocks	2
Vests	2	Upper Petticoats	2
Pair Trousers	2	Under ditto	2
Day Shirts	2	Shifts	3
Pair Boots	1	Pair Boots	1
Pair Socks or Stockings	2	Pair Slippers	1
Caps	2	Pair Stockings	2
Handkerchiefs	4	Bonnets or Hats	2
Neckerchiefs	2	Handkerchiefs...	4
Pair Braces	1	Scarf or Crossover	1
Collars	3	Cape or Jacket	1
Night Shirts	2	Pinafores	4
Pair Slippers	1	Night Gowns	2
Flannel Vests (if required)	2	Drawers	2
		Flannel Vests	2
Total Articles	28	Total Articles	31

In addition to the above, 12 Working Aprons are supplied to each Home, 6 Working Frocks, 12 Bathing Costumes, 6 Bathing Cloaks, to each Girls' Home, and 6 Scrubbing Trousers, 6 Over Capes, 12 Bathing Drawers to each Boys' Home. Working Aprons are also supplied to the Workshops.

MAXIMUM TABLE FOR STORES.

The Fathers or Mothers are to make out their List of Articles of Food required for the week for their Home every Tuesday Evening, and send it to the Superintendent not later than *8 a.m.* on the Wednesday Morning.

The quantities in such List *must not be more* than are given in the Tables below, for the number of Children actually in the Home at that time, and *as much less as you require*, having due regard to the *avoidance of waste.* This scale represents the maximum allowance, but does not entitle the Superintendent to issue or any Officer to demand the quantities set forth unless required for actual consumption.

A good housekeeper will as far as possible always have a *small* store of Provisions in the House to meet *any extra requirement* which may arise.

Officers Rations are provided for their own consumption on the premises only.

Number of Children.	ARTICLES OF FOOD.																			
	Bread. lbs.	Flour. oz.	Raw Meat. lbs.	Suet. oz.	New Milk. pints.	Peas or Lentils. oz.	P'tatoes & other Vgtbls. lbs.	Butter. oz.	Lard. oz.	Cheese. oz.	Oatm'l. lbs.	Rice, Sago, or Tapioca oz.	Sugar. lbs.	Leaf Sugar lbs.	Tea or Coffee lb.	Cocoa. oz.	Treacle. oz.	Cur'nts, Raisins, or S'ltanas oz.	lbs. Bacon	No. Eggs
1	7	6	1	1	7	1	3½	1	1	2	¼	2	½	...	...	3	2	2	...	...
2	14	12	2	2	14	2	7	2	2	4	½	4	1	...	...	6	4	4	...	...
3	21	18	3	3	21	3	10½	3	3	6	¾	6	1½	...	...	9	6	6	...	...
4	28	24	4	4	28	4	14	4	4	8	1	8	2	...	...	12	8	8	...	...
5	35	30	5	5	35	5	17½	5	5	10	1¼	10	2½	...	...	15	10	10	...	...
6	42	36	6	6	42	6	21	6	6	12	1½	12	3	...	...	18	12	12	...	...
7	49	42	7	7	49	7	24½	7	7	14	1¾	14	3½	...	...	21	14	14	...	...
8	56	48	8	8	56	8	28	8	8	16	2	16	4	...	...	24	16	16	...	...
9	63	54	9	9	63	9	31½	9	9	18	2¼	18	4½	...	...	27	18	18	...	...
10	70	60	10	10	70	10	35	10	10	20	2½	20	5	...	...	30	20	20	...	...
11	77	66	11	11	77	11	38½	11	11	22	2¾	22	5½	...	...	33	22	22	...	...
12	84	72	12	12	84	12	42	12	12	24	3	24	6	...	...	36	24	24	...	...
13	91	78	13	13	91	13	45½	13	13	26	3¼	26	6½	...	...	39	26	26	...	...
14	98	84	14	14	98	14	49	14	14	28	3½	28	7	...	...	42	28	28	...	...
15	105	90	15	15	105	15	52½	15	15	30	3¾	30	7½	...	...	45	30	30	...	...
16	112	96	16	16	112	16	56	16	16	32	4	32	8	...	...	48	32	32	...	...
17	119	102	17	17	119	17	59½	17	17	34	4¼	34	8½	...	...	51	34	34	...	...
18	126	108	18	18	126	18	63	18	18	36	4½	36	9	...	...	54	36	36	...	...
19	133	114	19	19	133	19	66½	19	19	38	4¾	38	9½	...	...	57	38	38	..	...
20	140	120	20	20	140	20	70	20	20	40	5	40	10	...	...	60	40	40	...	...
Rations of Father	8	16	6	4	7	...	7	8	4	16	...	16	½	¾	½	...	...	8	1	3
Rations of Mother	8	16	5	4	7	...	7	8	4	12	...	16	½	¾	½	...	...	8	1	3

NOTE.—Annual allowances in lieu of ale to Male Officers £4 10s., and to Female Officers £3 10s.

City of Birmingham Education Committee.

The following notes have been drawn up in the hope that they will be of use to parents in the choice of suitable food for children of different ages.

P. D. INNES,
Chief Education Officer. 1919 - 1946

HINTS ON FOOD.

GENERAL RULES.

1. **Arrange for three meals a day, at fixed hours.** This is enough for healthy people, because the stomach, like the rest of the body requires rest. If meals are taken at irregular times, and extra food is eaten between meals, the stomach has no time for rest. Children under ten should not have supper, and should be in bed before eight o'clock.
2. **Food is more easily digested** if it is broken up by thorough chewing, and does more good if eaten slowly.
3. **Drink plenty of water,** especially between meals, as this is necessary to supply the needs of the body.
4. **The Foods which contain** all the things necessary for a proper diet, are :—
   Butter, carrots, dripping, eggs, fish (especially herrings), fresh fruit, green vegetables, milk, and tomatoes.
   Avoid too much pastry, tinned food, pork and pork pies, vinegar and pickles, shell fish, ices, and unripe or over-ripe fruit.
5. **The child should have a hot Breakfast** in the winter, having bread with dripping or bacon, and porridge or cocoa with milk.
   Dinner should be the child's principal meal, even if two courses are not possible, it should be easy to vary the one course given, and the dinner should not be the same for two days running, and such things as the following may be given :—
   Bread and dripping, bread and cheese, baked potatoes and grated cheese, lentil soup with boiled carrots, etc.
   For tea the child should have a mug of milk with bread and jam, or bread and golden syrup.

RULES FOR FEEDING CHILDREN.

Every child can be trained to eat wholesome food. Until the child is five years old, clean milk should be the principal food, and for the first six months the child should have nothing but milk and orange juice. If possible, from one to five years, allow one pint of milk per child per day.

P55896—B29 (a)

All children require **good plain food,** well and simply cooked, and varied as much as possible. For example :—

Eggs, boiled, poached or fried.
Soups, made from bones, meat pieces, vegetables, split peas, haricot beans, lentils, etc., with the addition of rice, barley or sago, to thicken the first three kinds.
Fish, steamed or baked. Steamers may be obtained cheaply and easily.
Meat, such as beef, mutton, tripe, cow-heel, liver, rabbit, should be baked or stewed, the gravy being given to the younger children.
Potatoes, to get the best value from potatoes, they should be baked, roast, or steamed in their jackets.
Green Vegetables, of all kinds, fresh or cooked in boiling salted water. No soda should be used. Lettuces and young cabbage should be shredded and eaten raw.
Milk Puddings, well baked or boiled. (Rice, Sago, Semolina, Tapioca)
Suet Puddings, well steamed or baked.
Stewed Fruit.
Fresh Ripe Fruit.
Cheese may be used instead of meat, especially in the summer.

RULES FOR FEEDING ELDER CHILDREN.

1. Growing boys and girls need as much food as adults. If poor foodstuffs are used while a child is growing, the growth of the body may not go on well, and poor health may result.
2. Give plenty of protein food (meat, fish, cheese, eggs, peas, beans, milk), to all growing children.
3. Fats are a very necessary part of daily food. More fats are needed during cold weather. Butter, margarine which has been "vitaminised," cream, good beef and mutton dripping are better fats than ordinary margarine. Vitaminised margarine is equal in value to fresh butter, and is much cheaper. A teaspoonful of cod liver oil is a useful addition for all children during the cold weather of the winter.
4. Avoid giving rich or heavy foods at night just before going to bed, for example, pork pies, fish and chips, sausage rolls, steak and onions, etc.
5. Efficient daily action of the bowels is a most important rule of life, and can be helped by taking daily some fresh uncooked green vetetables, such as lettuce and watercress, and fresh clean fruit. A cup of hot water first thing in the morning is very useful.
6. Children should be encouraged to wash out the mouth and to brush their teeth after their last meal in the evening. If this is not done until they go to bed, they are often so sleepy that they forget. It is chiefly during the night that the small pieces of food between the teeth decay, and so lead to decay of the teeth.

The Chief Question in the choice of food is how to get the best value for the money spent. The list of dishes given below should be of value in choosing a suitable and inexpensive diet. It is a mistake to think that children require much meat, and meat is expensive.

POTATO SOUP.

1lb. potatoes, 1 onion, 1 oz. dripping, 1 tablespoonful flour, ½ pint milk, 1 pint water, pepper, salt.

Peel and slice the potatoes, melt the dripping in the pan, and shake the potato slices in the dripping until they have absorbed it, add the onion, cut into fine rings, then add the water, bring to boiling, then simmer gently for 1 hour. Mix the flour to a paste with the milk, and add this mixture to the soup, after mashing any pieces of potatoes not quite mashed by cooking, with a fork. Boil the soup well for another five minutes, then flavour it well with salt and pepper. This is enough for 4 people and will cost 5d.

SAVOURY ROLL.

6 oz. flour, 3 oz. shredded suet, 3 oz. minced meat or bacon, pepper and salt, a little gravy.

Mix the flour with the suet and ½ teaspoonful salt and ½ teaspoonful baking powder, then add enough water to make the mixture to a thick dough, roll out to about half an inch thick, finely mince or chop the meat or bacon, spread this over the dough after the mince has been moistened with a little gravy, roll up the dough, wetting the edges so that they will hold together, place the roll in a greased stone jam jar, and steam for 2 hours. Enough for 4 people, cost 8d.

HOT POT.

1 lb. beef pieces, 1 lb. potatoes, 3 onions, a little dripping, 2 teaspoonfuls flour, pepper and salt, 1 pint water.

Cut the meat into small pieces and roll them in the flour, peel the potatoes and onions and slice them finely. Arrange the meat, potatoes and onions in layers in a pie-dish or casserole, sprinkling pepper and salt to taste, and finishing with a layer of potato slices, half fill the dish with water, gravy, or stock, put some small pieces of dripping over the top layer of potatoes, and bake gently for 1½ to 2 hours, keep the dish covered for the first hour of cooking. Enough for 4 people, cost 1/-

CORNISH PASTIES.

6 oz. flour, 1½ oz. suet, 1½ oz. lard, pinch of salt, 3 oz. meat, 3 potatoes, 3 onions.

Make pastry with the flour, suet, lard and salt, and mix to a dough with water, roll it out thinly, cut into small pieces, and in the middle of each have a spoonful of a mixture made by cutting the meat into small pieces, and mix that with the onions and potatoes, also cut up small, damp the edges of the pastry and fold together with the meat mixture inside. The pasties should look like little pillows. Bake in a moderately hot oven for ½ hour. Cost 10½d.

RICE AND CHEESE

3 oz. rice, 1½ oz. grated cheese, 1 dessertsp. flour, ½ pint milk, seasoning, ½ oz. butter.

Boil the rice and flour slowly in ½ pint milk until it is soft, it will take about 20 minutes, add butter, and cheese, and salt and pepper to taste. Serve hot. Cost 4½d.

BAKED POTATOES WITH GRATED CHEESE.

Bake some large potatoes in their jackets until they are soft, then cut them in half and mash up the potato with enough butter and grated cheese to make the potato really soft and tasty, put the potato mixture back in the skins, heat up, and serve really hot.

STEAMED FRUIT PUDDING.

1½ lb. fresh fruit, ½ lb. flour, 3 oz. suet, ½ teaspoonful baking powder, 6 oz. sugar, a pinch of salt, water.

Make a dough by mixing the flour, suet, baking powder and salt with just enough water to make it bind without being too sticky. Line a greased pudding basin with this pastry when it has been rolled out thinly, and keep back enough to cover the pudding when the fruit is in. Prepare the fruit and put it into the lined basin with the sugar and a little water, cover with the extra piece of pastry, damping the edges so that the lid will hold to the basin lining, cover the basin with a piece of greased paper, and steam for 2 hours. Cost, made with apples, 11d.

BAKED APPLES.

Prick some apples all over with a fork, put them on a greased tin, and bake until they are soft. Serve with sugar, and if possible, custard.

STEWED FRESH FRUIT.

To every pound of fruit allow 1 pint water and ½ lb. brown sugar. Boil the water and sugar for 10 minutes. Prepare the fruit, put it into the syrup, and cook slowly until it is tender.

IDENTIFICATION PLAN OF DRIVE

1. The Lodge. 1, Shenley Fields Drive. Later called Shangri-La. Home of the Superintendent and family. Later Home Help Office.
2. The Stores. 2 Shenley Fields Drive. Later called The Office, The sewing ladies made girls clothing upstairs. Later Centre 12 Offices.
3. Home 1, 3 Shenley Fields Drive. Later called Merriland later office for Elderly Services Team.
4. Home 2, Rose Cottage. Later 4 Shenley Fields Drive. Later called Suncrest, later South District Home Finding Team.
5. Home 3. Later 5 Shenley Fields Drive — Rosemead.
6. Home 4. Later 6 Shenley Fields Drive — Jasmine.
7. Home 5. Later 7 Shenley Fields Drive — Ferndale later Cherry Garth later transfered to Moseley Road.
8. The Workshops. 8 Shenley Fields Drive.
9. The Hospital. 9 Shenley Fields Drive, Later calleed Sick Bay later called Pinewood. Became home for Mentally and Physically Disabled Children.
10. Home 6. Later 10 Shenley Fields Drive — Greenways. Later used by Elmdene when they began to take in girls
11. The School 11 Shenley Fields Drive. Became Shenley Fields Nursery.
12. Home 7. Later 12 Shenley Fields Drive — Lilac View.
13. Home 8. Later 13 Shenley Fields Drive — Melplash. Later moved to Moseley.
14. Home 9. Later 14 Shenley Fields Drive — The Trees, Assessment Centre.
15. Home 10. Later 15 Shenley Fields Drive — Ryedale Boys Unit.
16. Matrons House 16 Shenley Fields Drive — Bythorn — later used as small childrens home, later as accommodation for Mr and Mrs Bowes later as minimal care unit for girls from The Trees.
17. Home 11. The Probation Home. Later 17 Shenley Fields Drive — Elmdene Boys Unit later moved into Greenways and took in girls and boys.
18. The Assembly Hall. Dual purpose building. Church, stage, indoor sports and dance floor.
19. The Swimming Baths.
20. The Sports Pavillion.
21. The Superintendents Lawn — Griffins Garden.
22. The Engineers Cottage. Now a privately owned residence.
23. The Infants School. A wooden building later demolished.
24. The Boiler House.
25. The Engine House.
26. The Water Tower.
27. The Orchard. Where the 'Love Tree' grows.
28. The Sports Field. Also used by Ilmington Road School.
29. Matthews Paddock.
30. One of several Air Raid Shelters on the drive.
31. The Memorial Cross.
32. Entrance to the Drive. Once had big black gates but they had to be removed because they were to narrow for a fire engine to drive through.

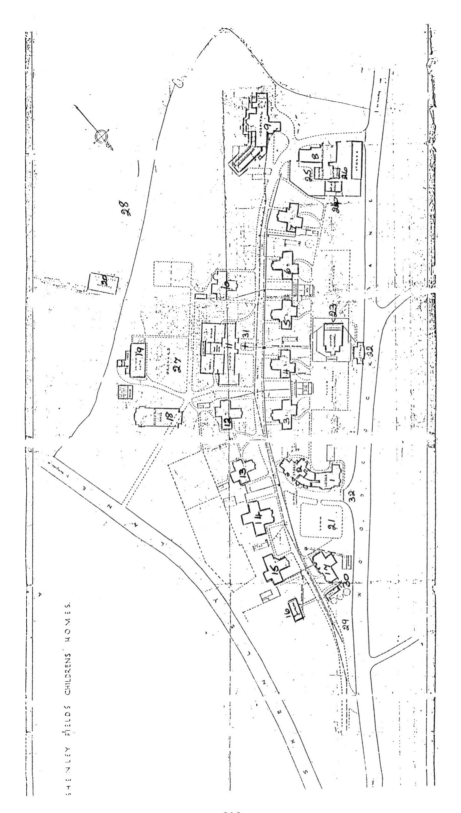

SHENLEY FIELDS CHILDRENS HOMES.

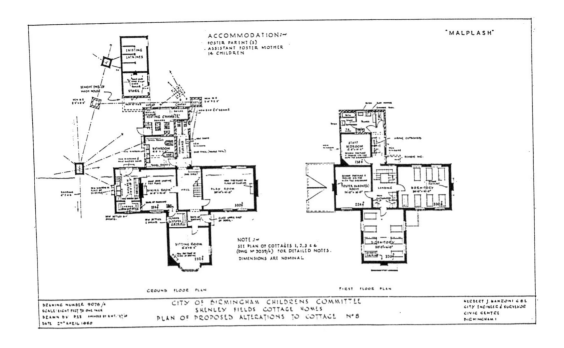

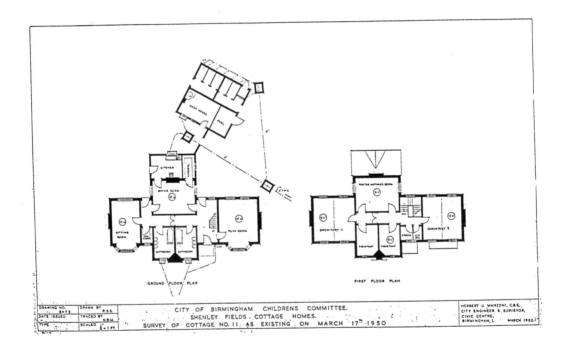

214

CONCLUSION

From the information given to me and from the many enquiries that I have received, it has become very clear that not enough information was given to the child when they left care. Many children have never known their parents christian names, mothers maiden name, fathers occupation, their place of birth and parents place of birth. Some didn't even know until years later that they had brothers and sisters though they had been living at the Shenley Homes at the same time as they were. They found this more difficult to cope with than the years spent in care.

Some of this information has been discovered through the efforts of their own children who became curious about their heritage.

Medical background was another area that the children were given no information on. Girls especially, found it humiliating when they became pregnant and they could not answer a lot of the medical questions they were asked. The boys said they felt the same when applying to go in the forces.

One ex Shenley girl vowed that when she had her own babies she would make sure every detail of information is written down in a book. This she has done and her daughter said it was and still is very useful especially when she herself had a child.

Being able to talk to your spouse and children about your parents and your brothers and sisters does seem perfectly normal but for children in care this was not always possible as the information contained on the childs file was limited. A family fact file on every child would have been benificial and possibly would still be of enormous interest to children and grandchildren.

A lot of information is gathered about the child when they are admitted to care or fostered but is this information given to the child when they leave care or does it get filed away and only produced if and when the child requests or needs the information. This lack of family and personal information can be quite a stigma to a person who has been through the care system.

The very strict discipline of the homes was the one thing that helped a lot of the people cope with whatever life threw at them when they left care. Though it seemed very harsh at the time it helped them gain an inner control. It was this inner control which gave them strength to carry on through really tough times. "It gave us respect for ourselves as well as for others" is what many of the older Shenley people said. The majority of the older Shenley people were very proud of the fact that they were 'Brought up strict', they said it showed they cared what was going to happen to us when we left their care and not only while we were in care. One old lady said "I know they cared for us in material things but I would have loved a hug".

I feel very privileged to have shared some precious memories with so many people. It has given me a great deal of pleasure to hear of the families and friends that have been reunited through this book of memories. I hope the book continues to stimulate people to take the plunge and contact friends from the past and share even more memories of The Shenley Fields Cottage Homes.

120. Some of the many people who came to our first reunion in 1989. This photograph was taken by a Birmingham Evening Mail reporter and was featured in the evening paper.

Recollections

Mrs Christine Bateman nee Cloudesley.
Mrs Joan Blackwell nee Price.
Mr Frederick Bright (deceased).
Mrs E. M. Burrows nee Norris.
Mrs Doris Bushell nee Oakley.
Mr Denys Cohen.
Mr Harold Cohen.
Mr and Mrs Cooper.
Ms Connie Cooper.
Mr G. C.
Mr H Cockayne.
Mr Horace Davis (deceased).
Mrs Joan Fletcher nee Kimberley (deceased).
Mr John Dossett-Davies.
Mrs Patricia Eaton nee Telling.
Mrs Marjorie Englefield nee Toy.
Ms Patricia Faulkner.
Mrs Joan Firth nee Catchpole.
Mr Eric Fisher.
Mr and Mrs Gough.
Mr George Edward Green.
Mr and Mrs Griffin.
Mrs Rose Guest nee Skollin.
Mr Raymond James Guy.
Mr Brian J Harvey.
Mr Barrie Peter Hawker.
Mrs Evelyn Haynes nee Stanley.
Mrs Violet Hawkins nee Wiltshire.
Mr Peter Henrick.
Mrs Frances Hornby nee Bowes.
Mrs J Jones nee Cooper.
Mr George Judson.
Mrs Ivy Kelly nee Bagley.
Mrs Wyn Kelly nee Ford.
Mrs Betty Keys nee Turner.
Mr Edward Kilroy.
Mr Derek Lee.
Mrs Lucy Lee nee Shackle.
Mr Ernest Little.
Mrs Long nee Hughes.
Ms Longman B. E. M.
Mr Anthony Lovatt.
Mrs Jean Marston nee Drover.
Mr Frank Matthews.
Mrs Barbara Maullin nee Green.
Mrs Irene McFadyen nee Woodfield.

Mr James Mclean.
Mr Robert McDermott nee Oakley.
Mr John Mead (deceased)
Mr Frederick Meredith.
Mrs Moore.
Mrs Alma Niblett.
Mrs Sheila North nee Birkenhead.
Ms Christine Noxon.
Mrs Marjorie Nutt nee Staveley.
Mrs Irene O'Donnell.
Mrs Doris Oxley nee Perks.
Mrs Laura Palmer nee Sayce.
Mrs Parry (deceased)
Mrs Asbury nee Parry.
Mrs Margaret Payne nee Barker.
Mr Harold Barker.
Mrs May Pearson nee Griffin.
Ms Jackie Pearshouse.
Mrs Elaine Platt nee Higgins.
Mrs Jill Plumley.
Mrs Janet Reeves nee Smith.
Mr John and brothers.
Mr Kenneth Roberts.
Mr Lawrence Rudd.
Mrs Florence Russell nee Jones.
Mr Stanley Smith.
Mr Douglas Smith (deceased).
Mr William Sproson.
Mrs Vera Stallard -Boulter.
Mr David Steane.
Mrs Lesley Steward nee Cloudesley.
Mrs Eileen Sweenie nee Wood.
Mrs Ellen Teague nee Probert.
Anonymous Home 5.
Mr Derek Tudor nee Adams.
Mr Peter Tudor nee Adams.
Mrs Shelagh Waldron.
Mr "Tom" Henry William Walton.
Mr "Curly" Albert Walton.
Mr Thomas Watkins (deceased).
Mr John Wedge.
Mr Alan White.
Mr Thomas Wilkins.
Mr George Wilkins.
Mr Albert Ernest Williams.
Mrs Dorothy Williams.

Mrs Helen Lynne Wood nee Plumley.
Mr Edward Wright.
Mrs Kitty Edwards nee White.
Mrs Margaret O'Neill nee Mitchell.
Mrs P Miley nee Hill.
Mrs Carol Ann Wixey nee King.
Ms Barbara Bickerstaff.
Mrs Dorothy Tilly.
Mrs Barbara Tongue.
Mrs Edna Homer.
Mr Barry Franklin.
Mrs Mary Meehan nee Johnson.
Mrs G Walker.
Mrs Renee Hirst nee Bloor.
Mrs Kath Spencer.
Mrs Dorothy Hill nee Hart.
Mrs Lily Irene Harris nee James.